ROBERT COLES

The

CALL

of

SERVICE

A Witness

to Idealism

HOUGHTON MIFFLIN COMPANY

Boston New York

1993

For information about permission to reproduce selections from this book,
write to Permissions, Houghton Mifflin Company, 215 Park Avenue South,
New York, New York 10003.

Library of Congress Cataloging-in-Publication Data
Coles, Robert.
The call of service : a witness to idealism / Robert Coles.
p.   cm.
Includes bibliographical references.
ISBN 0-395-63647-7
1. Social service — United States.   2. Volunteer workers in social service —
United States.   3. Voluntarism — United States.   4. Vocation.   I. Title.
HV91.C62   1993 · 93-2317
361.973 — dc20   CIP

Printed in the United States of America
AGM 10 9 8 7 6 5 4 3 2 1

To the memory of Dorothy Day

· CONTENTS ·

CONTENTS

William Carlos Williams:
The Knack of Survival in America

The Mind's Fate:
Ways of Seeing Psychiatry
and Psychoanalysis

Eskimos, Chicanos, Indians
(Volume IV of Children of Crisis)

Privileged Ones:
The Well-off and the Rich in America
(Volume V of Children of Crisis)

A Festering Sweetness
(poems)

The Last and First Eskimos
(with Alex Harris)

Women of Crisis, I:
Lives of Struggle and Hope
(with Jane Coles)

Walker Percy:
An American Search

Flannery O'Connor's South

Women of Crisis, II:
Lives of Work and Dreams
(with Jane Coles)

Dorothea Lange

The Doctor Stories of
William Carlos Williams
(editor)

Agee
(with Ross Spears)

The Moral Life of Children

The Political Life of Children

Simone Weil:
A Modern Pilgrimage

Dorothy Day:
A Radical Devotion

In the Streets
(with Helen Levitt)

Times of Surrender:
Selected Essays

Harvard Diary:
Reflections on the Sacred and the Secular

That Red Wheelbarrow:
Selected Literary Essays

The Child in Our Times:
Studies in the Development of Resiliency
(edited with Timothy Dugan)

Anna Freud:
The Dream of Psychoanalysis

Rumors of Separate Worlds
(poems)

The Spiritual Life of Children

The Call of Stories:
Teaching and the Moral Imagination

Their Eyes Meeting the World:
The Drawings and Paintings of Children
(with Margaret Sartor)

The Call of Service:
A Witness to Idealism

For Children

Dead End School

The Grass Pipe

Saving Face

Riding Free

Headsparks

· INTRODUCTION ·

N EARLY MEMORY of mine has my mother smiling as she
thanked the postman for her monthly copy of *The Catholic
Worker*, the newspaper Dorothy Day founded in the 1930s.
I knew as a child of six or seven that the heart of the Catholic
Worker movement had to do with the volunteerism of its members, who were willing to work in soup kitchens so that the poor
could eat; willing to put themselves in the shoes of others and try
to respond to their needs by serving them food, gathering clothing,
providing shelter, and paying attention to their medical, psychological, and spiritual distress as well as to the kind that is social,
economic, and racial in nature. Often I'd hear my mother read an
editorial or a featured essay or one of Dorothy Day's reflective
columns to my father, who was far less in awe of the religious
tradition that informed *The Catholic Worker*. Their discussions still
live in my mind, as does my mother's eagerness to extend herself
on behalf of others in a quiet, unassuming, generous manner.

For my dad, such efforts were admirable, yet he considered
them in all likelihood doomed to futility. He was a skeptical scientist and not unduly impressed with human nature as he had witnessed it during a lifetime that covered 90 percent of the twentieth

century. Even as my mom loved Franklin D. Roosevelt and Harry Truman, and sent checks to the Catholic Worker and other organizations working with the poor, my dad admired Wendell Wilkie and, later, Robert Taft. He had little use for bureaucrats or their pronouncements, so heavily saturated with the language of social science. He worried about the moral life of the poor (as well as of the well-to-do and the rich), whereas my mother worried about injustice, discrimination, and poverty. He stressed *will* as the all-important virtue, along with honesty and self-respect. He also wondered whether federal laws meant to help people might "weaken their spirit" and "turn them into a class of dependents." How well I remember that last assertion — spoken as the nation debated a federal housing program for urban neighborhoods. Today a number of thoughtful liberals would understand what my father was trying to say, even if they disagreed with him. Back in the 1940s and 1950s, he was, for one of my polite college roommates, "a Tory." (Since my dad was born and grew up in England, he was not as troubled by such a designation as I was!)

Yet when Dad retired as an engineer, he, too, gave himself wholeheartedly to people who were far less comfortable than he. For twenty years, from his middle sixties until his middle eighties, my father worked with poor, elderly men and women in Boston. He learned to become an advocate for those who were confined to hospital beds or nursing homes; he learned to argue with bureaucrats who worked in city, state, and federal agencies; he learned also to spend time with individuals who often were hard to understand — victims of strokes, of Alzheimer's disease, of Parkinson's disease. Once, when he came home tired, frustrated, and downcast after a long day of such effort, my mother asked him whether he ought to continue doing work that so clearly was wearing him down. He said yes, he certainly did wish to "keep at it." She pointed out, not for the first time, that he might do so at a slower pace. After all, the hours were his to choose: he was an unpaid volunteer.

He would have no part of a slowdown. He was feeling fit in general, even if exhausted at times by the demands he encountered in his daily efforts. My mother did not take him on directly. In fact, she nodded her agreement and said the obvious — that he was most certainly "dedicated" to his newfound work. Dad did not disagree, but he wondered aloud whether "work" was the right word to use, even though he had many times mentioned the work he felt he must do. The two of them struggled with language, tried to figure out how best to describe the nature and satisfactions of that kind of daily activity. My mother favored words such as "idealism," "goodness of heart," "charitable souls." My father avoided those terms, which he had been keenly suspicious of when my mother used them over the years to describe the virtues of, say, Dorothy Day or Jane Addams or Cesar Chavez or Martin Luther King, Jr.

How *did* he regard his newfound commitment, his late-in-life vocation? He was unwilling, it seemed, to settle for explicitly political or religious or psychological language to answer that question. My mother pressed him on this, and in a long discussion failed to obtain an unequivocal explanation of his concerted, even fervent, activity. "Your father was practical and modest to the very end of our talk," I recall my mother saying. A week after I'd spoken to her about this, I visited my parents, and my father and I took our customary walk, a habit going back to my early childhood. I told him of my mother's account of their extended discussion. I will never forget my father's terse comment, at once a summary and a moment of moral introspection. "Your mother was trying to figure out why I do what I do. I told her not to bother! I told her I like talking with the people I meet!"

He went no further, though I tried to get him to do so. He tended to be shy and reticent, anyway, in contrast to my mom's open manner and inclination to have heart-to-heart exchanges with friends and family members. With her husband, these talks took the form of statements by her, even exclamations or confessions, answered by a nod, a smile, a frown, or sometimes a laconic, pointed assent or dissent — maybe five or ten words — from him. His comment to me, in contrast, was practically an outpouring! Not that my father wouldn't go on at great length on certain subjects. He would virtually lecture us — my brother, Bill, my mom, and me — on English history (he was born and grew up in Yorkshire), and he imparted a great deal of information on the direction of modern science. He read and reread novels with great enthusiasm, especially those of the nineteenth-century English masters — Dickens, Hardy, Eliot, James — and he could be quite forthcoming about his views of their significance. Yet when I followed my mother's lead and asked him about his quite evidently passionate devotion to people far less lucky in life than he had been and who were essentially strangers to him, his reticence was even more unyielding. At last he was sufficiently alert to my intent (and perhaps annoyed by it, though he'd never acknowledge that) to hoist what I felt to be a red flag of warning — or was it a white flag of surrender? He said, finally, "I don't think it matters why we do something — but it does matter a lot that what we try to do is right and good!"

I was not totally surprised by his statement. The phrase "right and good" was vintage Dad — a bit of nineteenth-century rhetoric he had thrown my way many times as he urged me to try to do better at home, in the neighborhood, at school. Now he was less interested in asserting inspirational uplift than in being rid of psychological analysis, for which he had no great enthusiasm. Indeed he held to a bemused disinterest in contemporary psychology and psychiatry, and what he deemed the futile and strained pretensions of the social sciences.

I immediately took issue (maybe I took the matter personally and so took offense). It was important, I argued, that we understand the reasons people find for the actions they initiate. He wanted to know why! I wasn't sure how to answer. I had for so long simply assumed that *causes* were of significance. Had I not learned so initially from him, a man schooled in physics, chemistry, biology, and mathematics? I muttered something about reason, about reasons: a muted plea for inquiry as a valuable moral and intellectual principle — something not to be confused with the kind of psychological inquiry that becomes a social fad, a cultural obsession or, worst of all, a religious or ideological displacement. Dad had no interest in long-winded discourse — not then, not ever. Yet again I heard him speak very much to his point. "We've got to keep ourselves busy with the worthwhile, or we'll end up with you folks!"

I thought that remark was unfair to those who see psychiatrists and unfair to those of us who are psychiatrists and, not least, unfair to his own purposes and convictions, elusive as they were proving to be. I rose to the occasion as I had not in a long time with him. I talked and talked, as if to make up for his parsimony with words. I was especially upset at the self-derogation implicit in his comment. He wasn't just keeping himself "busy," I insisted. His life's values were at work as he went about his demanding, self-imposed obligations. At least they ought to be acknowledged in general, even if they were to be disregarded in their complex and maybe murky particularity.

When I was through, my dad was at pains to quiet me down in his usual laconic fashion. "All right," he said, and then paused, making me think I had heard his last word on the subject — a mixture of impatience, even irritation, and resignation. But then he added, "I frankly doubt I could continue [volunteer activity] if I looked too hard within." I noted that last word — an almost nineteenth-century way of signifying psychological exploration of oneself. In his own way, he was saying so very much about his mind, his way of thinking, of being. I no longer could regard him as someone who fled from self-recognition or, more broadly, denied the rest of us the authority to do so. Rather, he was telling me that what he did in the way of service to others came to, finally, a matter of unspoken faith. This was not a faith in the imperatives of a transcendent code but, ironically (for all his lack of interest in psychiatry), a faith in the essentially benign workings of the mind, in its capacity to turn to good account all sorts of wayward or turbulent or egoistic impulses.

In a sense he was implying that I could pursue the matter any way I might wish — but I should know that others have *their* own wishes. If I was to understand what drove my father's earnest counseling of the many age-mates he was seeing, I had better learn to be a more subtle and indirect investigator. All this was given as a father's utterly tactful, even confessional, sidelong advice. I have to admit that I wasn't all that quick, back then, even to recognize the message extended to me. Only later, as I remembered and talked out our exchange with my mother and with my wife, Jane, did I begin to fathom what motivated my father — a certain stoic idealism, put to work unstintingly and with scant resort to self-scrutiny.

I often hearken back to such family occasions because I believe that they inform much of what came later in my life. I have felt a tug between wanting to document deeds — to note their quite explicit nature and worth — and desiring to learn the origins of our actions and their connections to our worries, fears, and aspirations.

Not that these two different objectives are necessarily at odds. Sometimes the difference can be a matter of attitude or tone: how do we describe what we have seen and heard, how do we look, in my father's word, "within" others and ourselves — what kind of light do we choose to shine? I think my elderly father was making a gentle but urgent plea for care and caution as we try to look at the world and at ourselves — to use a filtered light, a lonely, small flashlight, with restraint, rather than searchlights burning relentlessly in every direction.

Once, as I talked with the sociologist David Riesman about what I was trying to learn from speaking with students involved in a community action program, his cautionary reminder evoked memories of my father's concerns. "Sometimes it's best to decide early on what you're *not* going to find out — at least right away and with great zeal!" He was letting me know that an observer can easily cross a certain line and become more than an irritant — can become an intruder who generates perplexity, if not outrage, even as he claims the dispassionate, even-handed mantle of the student, the social scientist, the psychological or sociological investigator.

I mention such vexing questions right off, as I introduce this book's subject matter, because from my early years as one of a group of high school volunteers in a hospital (we carried trays, pushed people in wheelchairs) to my recent stint as a part-time elementary schoolteacher in a ghetto school, I have wondered what to make of what I have seen and heard, and what to make of those of us who put ourselves in situations where we straddle our "regular" world and a world we "visit." (I use those words because so often I have heard them used.)

Sometimes I have been asked about these issues by a child who has quite pointedly challenged all sorts of assumptions and conventions, as a nine-year-old girl, Ruth Ann, did in one of my fourth-grade English composition classes at the Martin Luther King School in Cambridge during the spring of 1988. She said to me, "We were wondering why you come over here to us. We thought, he must be busy with his regular life, so why does he take time out to come visit here, when he could be someplace else that's more important — that's what we asked."

I quickly tried to dispel her doubts with a well-intentioned, earnest affirmation of good intent. But Ruth Ann did not seem entirely convinced. "Well, it's nice that you're here, but where did you get the idea, that's what we wondered. Did you hear something bad about us?" I recognized the dangerous social and emotional and racial crosscurrents swirling around me as I prepared to answer a question disarmingly simple yet laden with complex undertones. Before I could speak, she continued, "A lot of people say they want to come here and help us. My momma [she worked in a Head Start program] says she's tired of the 'orientations' she has to give to all these folks: they come to you and they're ready to do what you ask, but it's a 'trip,' she says, Momma — they'll go back and stick their chests out and say, 'Hey, look at me and what I do!' So we're being a lot of help to them — it goes that way, too, you see."

I did see, and I indicated so with a nod, an exchange of looks I still remember: her eyes were aimed right at mine, with a moment's detour directed at my shoes, my pants, my shirt. I was sure that she was being sardonic, a brutally candid observer taking in a stranger's all too relaxed, casual self-presentation. I constructed in my mind a devastating critique of myself and my kind — confirming her uncompromising appraisal of me as yet another slummer, eager to wet his feet in a fashionably different terrain, all the more to inflate his sense of himself and the view others had of him. But Ruth Ann had another train of thought to pursue, I learned. She said, "It's nice that some of you folks come here to volunteer, and we'll try to tell you everything we know."

I was once more stopped in my tracks. Exactly what did she have in mind? How should I ask that question? She saw me mutely struggling, saw me uncross my legs and cross them again, saw me open my mouth and say nothing. She changed the subject, told me she liked my shoes and asked me where I got them. I was puzzled by her shift of direction, but I knew to be forthcoming: "There are lots of stores in the Square that sell loafers." She replied, boldly and directly, "Why do a lot of you folks always talk about 'the Square,' as though there is only one square?"

Again I felt myself being examined rather toughly, even scornfully, given a searching once-over. I was about ready to tell her I had to leave and go back to "the Square." She sensed we were at an impasse that could be broken only by her. This she did in a startling about-face (or so I interpreted her remarks then). She told me she knew I had to leave, but she wanted to tell me something: "If you folks need any help, we could come and help, you know."

I saw on her face, at last, what I judged to be a thin smile — but a friendly one, I began to feel. I wondered, though, whether I wasn't trying too hard for a sentimental reconciliation. Of course that smile should be thin — a child's shrewd sense of irony, of detached curiosity, directed at a stranger who didn't know how strange he was felt to be by a child more familiar with his ways, his assumptions, than he had any way to comprehend. As such a line of reasoning raced, unexamined, through my stymied head, she took the lead in ending things between us, at least for that day: "I know you've got to go. See you on Friday!"

I was in no mood to say anything but yes, and then good-bye. I wanted out. I wanted time to stop and think, to separate my own preconceptions and nervous attributions from what she had actually intended to let me know. Her intent was admittedly not something I could figure out on my own, and I was having trouble even beginning to understand my own preconceptions, never mind the ambiguities and obscurities that beclouded our communication. As I left the room with her, we went in opposite directions, and she shouted, "It's beautiful out there! Enjoy it!"

For me, that moment brought to life both the trials and the opportunities that arise when volunteers, people doing "service," encounter those to whom they are offering "help." I would never really know what was going through Ruth Ann's mind — and maybe, as my father would say, I would get to know too much about what was in my own. She and I had struggled to know each other and had only partially succeeded — not a rare description, of course, for any human encounter. She was at once grateful and doubtful, standoffish and engaging, wryly distant and quite openly responsive, attentive to a would-be teacher's eager, apprehensive intentions.

As I walked back to the Square, I thought of my mother and father and of the different ways they would have reacted to her — and the different reactions each of them might have elicited from her. I also thought that someday I would try to confront for myself, and for people like me, the implied challenges I thought this girl was posing for me.

My parents, in their own fashion, had challenged me to think hard about what one is doing as one renders service to others. For my mother, service was a religious obligation, part of the Catholic Worker tradition she so admired.[1] For decades she gave her time to clinics visited by the poor, to soup kitchens, to working with children suffering from cancer. For my father, service meant direct action and clear, unsentimental thinking, a comradeship with others. We are all fellow human beings, his attitude said, so "let's get on with it" — a phrase he used again and again. For Ruth Ann, service meant, I think, not only certain educational and human favors but also the chance to learn not only *from* others but *about* them. Who are these people, and what are they doing here, and why do they keep returning? Of course, these three views of service, two belonging to participants in extending it, one belonging to someone meant to be a recipient of it, hardly exhaust the various possibilities or paradigms. Many kinds of service are offered, and the attitudes that inform such activity are varied, as are the ways the "beneficiaries" respond to what is put before them in a clinic, classroom, retirement home, prison, nursery, or playground.

My conversation with Ruth Ann occurred after I had spent many years trying to work my way through the potential impasses she had put on the table for contemplation in her own polite and forthright way. After high school, I tutored children while at college; I lived in a Catholic Worker hospitality house and worked in its soup kitchen while in medical school; and I gave time to a state-run children's psychiatric hospital while taking my training in pediatrics and child psychiatry at university-connected hospitals. I joined the civil rights movement in the South for five years, working with children caught up in the school desegregation struggle, and later, in the North, I got to know boys and girls similarly challenged in schools being "integrated" in response to *de facto*, as opposed to *de jure*, segregation. During the late 1960s and all through the 1970s, I spent much time with a group of young people known as the Appalachian Volunteers, who were very much like their age-mates at the Student Non-Violent Coordinating Committee. SNCC was in the vanguard of the sit-in movement and was the major force behind the Mississippi Summer Project of 1964, which marked a turning point in the South's resistance to voting rights for blacks.[2]

In 1978 I returned to Cambridge after years of doing research in New Mexico, Arizona, Alaska, and the Rio Grande Valley of Texas.[3] During that time I met many VISTA volunteers who were assisting Spanish-speaking families or Native American people or Eskimos, even as I was trying to learn how children of these traditions come to terms with their situations. I worked in two south Texas clinics where the children of migrants received the pediatric care they so urgently needed. I also worked in a clinic devoted to the medical problems of Pueblo families, and, in Alaska, in a similar clinic for Eskimos. In each place I worked, VISTA volunteers and college students taking time off from school were a notable presence. So were older people, some in their fifties or sixties, who were eager to give of themselves for a few weeks or months.

I had more than enough to do, meeting with children, learning from them about their lives and about what they intended to do when they became adults. Yet I often heard questions not unlike Ruth Ann's, as I realize in retrospect. A Pueblo boy once asked me, referring to two VISTA workers he had come to know, "I was wondering why they came here. The teacher said to help, but they argue with her [about educational, philosophical, and political questions]. My dad said the VISTA people want to change the world, and the teachers just want to teach, so there's a difference. But both VISTAs say they want to be teachers when they're older, so they could end up the same" — meaning the same as the Bureau of Indian Affairs teachers this boy had come to know well and did not especially like.

In his own unpretentious way the boy was raising the biggest of issues — what happens down the road to young idealism and activism as it contends with advancing age and with a society's notions of what is appropriate when? Back then I had little time to ponder this question. But later (in the late 1970s and early 1980s), when I returned to Harvard and was teaching medical students and undergraduates, I had plenty of occasion to wonder, with my students, how particular youths connect with the work of and commitment to service, and what it is that sustains them or, indeed, works to undermine their passion for such activity.

When I worked during the summers in Africa and Latin America, trying to understand how children learn their political convictions and attitudes, many times those young men and women, teaching the same children I was getting to know, made clear their own educational struggles.[4] One day I was sitting outside a rural school near León, Nicaragua, talking to a Georgetown University student who was working with a Jesuit-sponsored project that built and staffed schools in Third World countries. He said, "I've got four more months here, and when I leave, that's when I'll be starting to figure out what this has all meant! Probably for the rest of my life I'll be influenced by what happened to me here — I now think differently. I agree, it all could begin to wear off later. But I doubt it. Some of these kids have taught me a million times more than I've taught them. But maybe it will happen — maybe I'll just start in with the rat race again, and my memory will take the rear seat while my greed grabs the wheel and steps on the gas."

I realized, as I listened to this young man reflect upon the events of that summer and wonder what would happen during the years ahead, that his experiences were as morally persuasive as those of the civil rights activists I'd come to know in the South almost two decades earlier. Moreover, the children he was teaching and I was interviewing made clear to me how important he was in their lives. He shared with them openly the moral ambiguities that pressed upon him as he contemplated his future. And they had plenty to say to him in response: these empathic boys and girls were quite willing and able to step into his shoes, to try to imagine what they might do, given his choices. One afternoon I listened to those children and their teacher discuss their nation's civil war. As I heard them worry about people who had lost family members and heard them try to connect the teachings of Jesus to the proclaimed pieties of a revolution (and to those of the Catholic church), I began to realize that the volunteer teacher was truly one with his students, even though at moments they placed him on a pedestal.

In New Haven a few months later, as *my* teacher, Anna Freud, read the transcript of that class discussion, in which both the volunteer teacher and I took part, she lifted her head, smiled, and remarked, "You are all together in this — in the way you talk. I know you are doing a study called 'the moral life of children' — but I wonder if you aren't considering moral questions yourself, with the help of those children! And your friend, the volunteer, the young teacher, he's trying to decide how he should live his life — and that's another study that's going on!"

Obtusely, I resisted her wry, gentle comment; she had to become more didactic and explain to me that the observer, while observing others, was struggling with his own dilemmas, as was the volunteer teacher. She was suggesting that a research project on the moral life of children was also about the moral life of volunteers, and perhaps also about "the moral life of someone who does this kind of research." When she used that last phrase, I was quick to ask for an explanation. She said, "All of you were wholeheartedly into that class — you and the young teacher and the children. You are observing, but you are part of what you observe. The young teacher is teaching, but the class is a laboratory, and he is learning from it. I agree, that always holds [I had suggested this]; or rather, it always can hold. But under some circumstances the bonds between the teacher and the student are stronger — and, as you know, some research is more personal than other kinds!"

As I listened to her, I was reminded of the many people I'd met, young and older, who had given their time as volunteers to the children I was getting to know. Once more my mind drifted back to my parents' commitments to service, and to the agreements they forged on the nature of their work as well as the disagreements, some of them quite serious and severe, with which they had to contend. Once more I thought back to my own efforts, sometimes halfhearted and faltering, to live up to the rather insistent and exacting moral standards my mother and father tried to uphold in their daily lives.

A few years later, when my parents were in their eighties, they both died. In *The Call of Stories* I was moved to write about an important aspect of their lives: the novels and short stories and poems they read by themselves and to each other and carried with them, in heart, mind, and soul, as treasured companions. They urged my brother and me to read these books when we were going to school and shared them with us as we became grown up. Those novelists and poets and essayists were especially helpful as my parents stopped and took stock of their lives. My father was forever learning from his beloved George Eliot, or from Charles Dickens or Thomas Hardy, and my mother kept her copies of Tolstoy close to her until the last day she lived; his novels and stories were a mainstay, she often declared, of her moral life. Like Dorothy Day, she summoned the masters of fiction to help her understand or search for meaning and purpose.

For me, *The Call of Stories* was a way of affirming the moral energy I had seen at work in my parents and in some of their heroes, my heroes. I had tried to connect with this moral energy myself, and I had asked my students to connect with it. This book is, in a sense, a companion to that one; together they convey two summonses my mother and father eagerly heard and repeatedly took very seriously. In the tradition of Emerson, Thoreau, Tolstoy, William Carlos Williams, and William James — each of whom tried to connect moral ideas to the lived life — my parents realized the link between stories and service. They knew that stories are a means of glimpsing and comprehending the world; they knew that service is a means of putting to use what has been learned, for in the daily events designated as service, all sorts of stories are encountered and experienced.

"There is a call to us, a call of service — that we join with others to try to make things better in this world," Dorothy Day said at one of the Catholic Worker Friday-night "clarification of thought" meetings in February 1955. She was at the height of her powers then — active in a million projects, it seemed to those of us who were trying to keep up with her. The "call of service" to which she referred has been heard by so many of us — but with different messages, at different pitches and frequencies, and with different outcomes.

I am writing this book to explore the "service" we offer to others and, not incidentally, to ourselves. I am hoping to document the subjectivity, the phenomenology of service: the many ways such activity is rendered; the many rationales, impulses, and values served in the implementation of a particular effort; the achievements that take place, along with the missteps and failures; the personal opportunities and hazards; and the consequences — how this kind of work fits into a life. I am hoping as well to discuss the connections between community service and intellectual reflection — how a story or poem can prompt a special kind of clarifying wonder for someone who has made himself or herself available in some form of service. Not least, drawing on my own profession's struggle to understand human behavior and on many helpful discussions with Erik H. Erikson and Anna Freud, I will take yet one more look at idealism or altruism through the lens of psychoanalysis in order to understand the complexity of the "good" side of our nature — the sources of our ethical life and its vicissitudes, victories, and defeats.

I have spent most of my life within sight of service being lived out. As a child, when I heard my parents read to one another from *Middlemarch* or *Little Dorrit* or *Anna Karenina*, I also heard them discuss their "projects": my mother's Catholic Worker activism, my dad's far more conventional Community Chest activities. When I was a teenager, the last thing I wanted to do was read the novels my parents espoused so vigorously. I was equally uninterested in their "good works" — the phrase a friend of mine used with barely concealed scorn. I was with him all the way — put off by, fed up with, a certain pietistic side of my mother, made all the more intolerable, I felt, by her insistence on putting her body as well as her voice on the line. I welcomed my father's more relaxed, even hedonistic view of life — and his sometimes profound doubtfulness, if not pessimism, about human beings and their prospects and purposes. Yet he too would yield to the pieties he heard from his wife and from Dickens, Hardy, and Eliot — and then take that next step toward community service himself.

What I wanted to do, in high school and in college, was have a good time with my friends, go to the movies, search out jazz bars (an early and long-time interest). I also did a lot of running — as a sport, not for exercise. Sometimes, as I kept my body moving as fast as possible, I wondered whether I could end up someplace new and different — far from the home I knew and, of course, loved as well as wanted to escape from: a place where Benny Goodman and Ella Fitzgerald and Count Basie and Glenn Miller were triumphant, and where Lady Day (Billie Holiday) rather than Dorothy Day ruled the day; a place where I could listen to jazz or big band concerts and read Zane Grey westerns, the newspaper sports pages, the travel adventures of Richard Halliburton, or the visions of the world provided by *National Geographic*, the promises of a better life offered in *Popular Mechanics*.

But at other times I felt the tug of my parents' involvements. When I halfheartedly signed up for a volunteer tutoring program in college, I learned rather a lot about my own ignorance. In medical school I was always on the verge of dropping out because I felt utterly inadequate to the lock-step requirements of memorization that characterized the first two years of that course of study. I went to visit Dorothy Day's community on the Lower East Side of Manhattan more as a refuge from my own life than in response to what she and her coworkers were doing. I worked in that community (and for a time lived there), but with an abiding sense of inadequacy, and at times under a shadow of self-accusation: as a hypocrite who loved a good time I had no right to be there.

Eventually I learned that I had plenty of company. In response to my self-dramatizing confession of hypocrisy one day, Dorothy Day offered a memorable reply: "If we were going to forbid hypocrites to work here with us, there'd be no one to do the work, and no one to do the forbidding! Each day we try to do the best we can — for all our faults and imperfections." After a second or two of silence, her softly spoken afterthought knocked me flat on my face: "Pride has us think ourselves to be especially wicked sometimes, when really we're just trying to get from one day to the other, and of course we do stumble every now and then."

Her thin smile greeted me after she'd spoken — and I was furious. Enough of these people, always ready to be understanding and charitable in their view of others! I told Dorothy I had to meet someone, and I didn't go back for a month. When I did return, I fumed and dragged my feet; I collected observed moments of the smugness, officiousness, self-righteousness, and self-deception of others — as if to prove her right. Finally I left the Worker; the reality of clinical work — at last! — on hospital wards gave me a new life. I was practically a doctor now, with important things to learn and do. Talk about self-importance and self-deception!

Years later, when I went back to the Worker to be a part of it and to visit with Dorothy Day again, I had begun to see how complicated this notion of service is, how it is a function not only of what we do but of who we are (which, of course, gives shape to what we do). My father might have argued otherwise, stressing the primacy of the deed; but the doer of the deed wears a face, has a touch, and speaks in a particular way. Only later in life did I realize how truly self-effacing and modest Dad was. He was a lovely and loving man, hugely kind and generous, and those qualities, along with his humility, were masked by a tough, sardonic presentation of self, one all too successful at times, I fear, in warding off a proper recognition from others of his essential nature, and of what he was doing and what he was giving of himself.

As the reader will see, I am drawing upon a life's observations and experiences; upon interviews with and reflections by people who have been my teachers; and upon thirty years of "field work" as a teacher and as a volunteer. This book, not accidentally, comes after my research work with children has come to a close and after publication of its companion volume, *The Call of Stories*. I believe I am drawing on my own efforts as a son, as a husband and father, as a citizen, to figure out what my various responsibilities are and in what proportions. I will try to discuss these struggles not abstractly but in connection with a host of lives that I've been privileged to witness in their unfolding.

Over the years I have accumulated many debts. I have been given so much, and shown so much, by so many individuals. My parents still hover over, even haunt, this subject matter, as the reader has already noticed. For many years, while doing this work, I have heard my mother's and my father's voices — and I still do. I still hear them literally, too. I have a tape of a radio interview done with my father, discussing his extraordinary work with ailing and poor elderly people, and I have a tape of a talk my mother gave to a charitable group devoted to the needs of children.

I have already mentioned the enormous help given me by (the example of) Dorothy Day — and in a different way, Anna Freud and Erik H. Erikson: long talks, plenty of stories to tell and be told. I have discussed Miss Freud's views on altruism in a biography I did of her, and in my biographies of Dorothy Day and Simone Weil[5] — but here she appears in connection with the volunteers whose lives, I think it fair to say, both challenged and educated us as she and I thought about them together. I doubt I could have written this book without Miss Freud's constant encouragement and steadfast intellectual interest, even at times excitement. There were moments in that Yale dormitory, or at Hampstead, England, when I felt her shed many decades of life; once again she was the young idealist who wrote so knowingly and shrewdly (and, to use a word favored by George Eliot, so ardently) of altruism in that important last chapter of *The Ego and the Mechanisms of Defense.*

I worked with Erik H. Erikson as a section teacher in his large course and as an assistant in his seminar. We had many valuable talks about "young man Luther" and his idealism and, of course, about "Gandhi's truth," which meant so much to the civil rights workers I was getting to know as he was writing that book. I still remember fondly a trip I took with the Eriksons to Mississippi in 1966 so that they might meet with some Americans who took Gandhi seriously enough to carry on the kind of nonviolent political struggle he waged for so long.[6]

Once more I must mention, with pleasure, my wife, Jane, and our sons, Bob, Danny, and Mike. They would be embarrassed if I talked about the call within them to service, but in fact, in my more morose moods, I have felt them to be engaged in a conspiracy with my parents to make me feel like a guilty do-nothing, a mere detached witness. If it has been otherwise, I must acknowledge my spells of kicking and screaming — a son following his parents, a husband following his wife, a father following his sons!

Last but not least, my heartfelt thanks to Bob Moses, for all I learned from him in the South and later; to Greg Johnson, for his work at Phillips Brooks House, a home for Harvard's volunteers; to Arnold Hiatt, who has done so very much for the idea and ideal of community service at his alma mater and elsewhere; and to my students, to the young and not so young volunteers I have met, and to those who have helped me teach my courses and have so often taught me plenty.

In connection with this manuscript, I thank Jon Karlen and Chris Hollern, good friends indeed. I am exceedingly grateful to the Lilly Endowment, for generous help one more time, and to John Sterling, a kind and thoughtful editor, who leapt to the idea of this book when I was pulling away fast.

I only hope that I have done justice to the richness, the texture, the nuances, the thickness and complexity of the lives of the many youths and men and women who, in all they have done, stand for a good deal of what is best in human beings, no matter our down side, so evident so often.

The

CALL

of

SERVICE

· ONE ·

Method

B Y NOVEMBER 1961 I had come to know for a year the four
black six-year-old girls who initiated school desegregation
in New Orleans at the behest of Federal Judge J. Skelly
Wright. I have many times described the ordeal of Ruby Bridges,
who had to fight her way through angry, threatening mobs every
day for months.[1] Federal marshals escorted her to and from the
Frantz School because the city police and the state police were
unwilling to protect her. Obscenities were her everyday fare, and
often she heard grown men and women, mothers and fathers, tell
her she was going to die one day soon. She withstood this ordeal
with remarkable resilience and even managed to find time occasionally to pray for her tormentors.

I have also described, though in less detail, the three other girls,
who went through a similarly harrowing trial at the McDonogh 19
School. One of them, Tessie, figured prominently in some of my
first writing, three decades ago, as I tried to understand her stoic
courage. Like Ruby, she was a mystery and a challenge to a young
pediatrician and child psychiatrist. I was in the midst of psychoanalytic training and was all too eagerly on the prowl for psychopathology.[2] I was especially interested in Tessie's maternal grand-

mother, Martha, a tall, handsome woman with gray hair, carefully groomed, and large, warm eyes that often settled on her grand-daughter. Tessie's eyes, in turn, sought out her grandmother's, as if she was thereby nourished and strengthened. This woman of fifty had lived a life of poverty and pain (she had fairly severe rheumatoid arthritis), but she had never lost her sense of humor, her capacity to laugh and laugh — she had a big laugh that shook her ample body and was sometimes punctuated by a clap or two of her hands and a two-word exclamation: "Lord Almighty!"

She spoke those words in church repeatedly, of course. I would sit with Martha and her daughter and son-in-law and Tessie and her sister and brothers, and when one of the Hebrew prophets — Isaiah or Jeremiah or Micah or Amos — was quoted, she would commonly add her affirmation to their pleas for justice, to their denunciations of iniquity and arrogance and self-indulgence. In conversation she seemed to be aware of the "culture of narcissism" long before it was the subject of popular analysis: "There's so much selfishness in us, and we have to fight it this whole life long." After the slightest pause, she would raise her voice, exclaiming, "Lord Almighty." On occasion in church, she raised her voice higher still — and when the words of Jesus were spoken, she really gave forth her *"Lord Almighty!"*

She was often the one who delivered Tessie to the federal marshals. They arrived in their cars promptly at eight in the morning, and as they approached her door, she would fling it open, greet the men, and greet the day: "Lord Almighty, another gift!" She was referring to the hours ahead, I soon learned — no matter the travail she knew to be in store for her granddaughter. Tessie would emerge from behind her, lunch pail in hand, and go off with those tall, white, dark-suited men, who carried revolvers underneath their jackets.

On one such morning I heard Martha use a phrase that was almost identical to the title of this book. Her amplification of that phrase has rung in my ears over the years as a rationale of sorts for a way of being, and even for the kind of research described in a chapter that takes up the somewhat pompous matter of "methodology" — how we do what we do. On that day Tessie was not so much reluctant to go to school as tired and weary. She was emerging from a bout of the flu; she had slipped and fallen while playing in a nearby back yard; and she didn't like her substitute teacher. The grandmother, privy as always to the child's worries, doubts, and difficulties, knew full well her granddaughter's state of mind that early morning. Tessie had suggested, over a breakfast that included her grandmother's homemade corn bread (celebrated by friends and relatives, many of whom received now and then what Martha always called "a little something"), that perhaps, for the first time, she would stay home from school.

As I arrived and sat down to some of that "little something" myself, Tessie once more, shyly and guardedly, suggested that she might stay home. The grandmother said yes, that would be fine if Tessie truly wasn't well. But if she was more discouraged than sick, that was quite another matter. Then came a disquisition which my old bulky tape recorder fortunately was prepared to receive.

"It's no picnic, child — I know that, Tessie — going to that school. Lord Almighty, if I could just go with you, and stop there in front of that building, and call all those people to my side, and read to them from the Bible, and tell them, remind them, that He's up there, Jesus, watching over all of us — it don't matter who you are and what your skin color is. But I stay here, and you go — and your momma and your daddy, they have to leave the house so early in the morning that it's only Saturdays and Sundays that they see you before the sun hits the middle of its traveling for the day. So I'm not the one to tell you that you should go, because here I am, and I'll be watching television and eating or cleaning things up while you're walking by those folks. But I'll tell you, you're doing them a great favor; you're doing them a service, a big service."

She stopped briefly to pick up a fly swatter and go after a bee that had noisily appeared in the kitchen. She hit it and watched it fall to the floor, then she plucked a tissue from a box on a counter, picked up the bee, still alive, and took it outside, where it flew off. I was surprised; I'd expected her to kill the bee and put its remains in a wastebasket. She resumed speaking and, again to my surprise, connected her rescue of the bee to what she had started to say.

"You see, my child, you have to help the good Lord with His world! He puts us here — and He calls us to help Him out. That bee doesn't belong here; it belongs out there. You belong in that McDonogh School, and there will be a day when everyone knows that, even those poor folks — Lord, I pray for them! — those poor, poor folks who are out there shouting their heads off at you. You're one of the Lord's people; He's put His Hand on you. He's given a call to you, a call to service — in His name! There's all those people, scared out of their minds, and by the time you're ready to leave the McDonogh School they'll be calmed down, and they won't be paying you no mind at all, child, and I'll guarantee you, that's how it will be!"

As she was speaking, Tessie finished her breakfast, marched confidently to the sink with her dishes, put them in a neat pile, and went to get her raincoat and empty lunch pail from her room — all without saying a word. She was going to school, I realized. No further words on the subject were exchanged. The grand-mother told Tessie what she was putting in the lunch pail, and Tessie expressed her thanks. In no time, it seemed, the girl was out the door and walking with the marshals, who had waited near their car.

Later that day, playing that tape, Jane and I tried to understand what had taken place. Tessie had tried to beg off just a bit — not to escape from her educational (and personal) fate, but simply out of a moment's queasiness. Her grandmother was by no means insensitive to Tessie's daily ups and downs, nor was she a stern taskmaster — indeed, Tessie's parents worried sometimes that she was spoiled a bit by her granny. Yet that morning she was obviously urging her granddaughter on, and with biblical sanction. This approach was quite familiar to Tessie — she may have even ex-pected the miniature sermon she received.

Weeks later, sitting with Tessie as she drew a picture of the McDonogh School and then one of Martha, I asked whether she had followed her grandmother's meaning. "I wasn't sure what your granny meant that morning. I wasn't sure how you should be of 'service' to those people out there on the street."

The girl had no trouble at all in seeing what was on my mind and in helping me out. She hesitated only a second, then told me, "If you just keep your eyes on what you're supposed to be doing, then you'll get there — to where you want to go. The marshals say,

'Don't look at them; just walk with your head up high, and you're looking straight ahead.' My granny says that there's God, He's looking too, and I should remember that it's a help to Him to do this, what I'm doing; and if you serve Him, then that's important. So I keep trying."

She was getting to the heart of what she had learned that mattered. For her, service meant serving, and not only on behalf of those she knew and liked or wanted to like. Service meant an alliance with the Lord Himself on behalf of people who were obviously unfriendly. Service was not an avocation or something done to fulfill a psychological need, not even an action that would earn her any great immediate or long-term reward. Service was itself a challenge — maybe a bigger one than the challenge of getting by a truculent, agitated mob twice a day.

"If I can help the good Lord and do a good job, then it'll all be okay, and I won't be wasting my time," Tessie announced once, as she tried to divert me from my interest in her responses to what she heard on the street. She had told me often how awful those men and women were and how upset she was by their stubbornly persistent attention to her. "They never seem to give up," she said one day, four months into the experience of being in the school with only two other black students, while a mob stayed outside much of the time, especially to greet her in the morning. But those segregationist voices of hateful outrage and bitterness, of deep disappointment, even of threats, were not enough to deflect her abiding concern for the voices of her parents, of the minister who visited her home once a week, and, not least, of her grandmother. "You have to listen to the right people; otherwise you get yourself into trouble!"

I agreed, of course — and I could hear her trying to strengthen her resolve, lest she become further prey to the anxiety and apprehension with which she had to contend. But she was letting me know that without losing sight of the danger, she had turned her attention away from that trouble and toward something else. She wasn't resorting to a valiant, desperate effort at "denial" to get through a most scary time. She was fully aware of what was happening, but also fully aware of why she was going through this ordeal. Here was a major crisis in America's history of desegregation, and children had become the adversary of an entire city, it seemed.

Yet Tessie had learned to regard herself not as a victim, not as an outsider trying hard to enter a world bent on keeping her out, not as a mere six-year-old black girl from a poor family with no clout and no connections but rather as an emissary from on high, a lucky one designated to lead an important effort, a child given the errand of rendering service to a needy population. She had connected a civic moment in her life with a larger ideal, and in so doing had learned to regard herself as a servant, as a person "called to service."

The elders in her life, especially her grandmother Martha, used those words or phrases insistently as they tried hard to give her not only reassurance and affection (the "support" many of us today talk about so much), but also something else. What they were giving her was most powerfully expressed one day toward the end of that long first year of school when the mob was still holding fast to its daily vigil. Martha said, "We're the lucky ones to be called, and we've got to prove we can do what the Lord wants, that we're up to it."

A grandmother was prepared not only to say that — a rhetoric of urgent, even desperate survival — but prepared to give of herself and ask of others in the interest, finally, of something (Someone) larger than herself. No wonder, then, that at certain moments when I thought Tessie vulnerable — a passing flu, a hard lesson at school, a fight with her brother — and in need of a little extra consideration, Tessie's grandmother became sterner, more exhortative than usual. I eventually realized that what I interpreted as a somewhat strained, even overbearing declaration was for an entire family quite something else: it was a rationale for a life, a pronouncement with enormous moral and emotional significance for young and old alike.

Tessie knew that service meant offering oneself to others as an example, a teacher; one bears a message and hopes that it will, in time, be understood and accepted. When white children at last began to return to the McDonogh School — when their parents tired of seeing them get no education at all — Tessie was glad for the company (not to mention the disappearance of the mob); but she was happy for another reason, as I found out one afternoon, much to my astonishment, when she told me that she wondered what her "next thing to do" would be.

I couldn't figure out what she meant, so I asked. She said, "Those people have gone back home, and they don't mind their kids coming here to school with us anymore. So that's what we were supposed to do." She stopped abruptly, as I waited, wondering where she was headed. Rather soon, with no prodding from me, she resumed. "We were supposed to get them to stop being so angry; then they'd quiet down, and we'd have the desegregation — and now it's happening. So we did the service we were supposed to for New Orleans, and Granny says, 'Next it'll be some other thing to do,' because you always should be trying to help out God somehow."

Tessie was, in her own mind, a missionary, deputized by no less than God — a first-grader doing service on behalf of her own people but also on behalf of those who railed and ranted against her. I mention Tessie's ideas about herself, as well as the origins of those ideas in a family's life and in a people's cultural and moral life, at the start of this book because the very definition or notion of service has to do with the ethical and spiritual assumptions that inform a family's life.

As a pediatrician and child psychiatrist, I was trained to discern symptom formation, both medical and psychiatric, as I talked with Tessie and the other children in New Orleans. I was trained to take stock of a crisis in a child's life, then work with the child and his or her family and teacher to develop relationships, achieve insights, make interpretations, and establish communication. The first time I discussed this work with my New Orleans medical colleagues (at a meeting of Tulane psychiatrists) I heard a lot about the sociological and anthropological side of the research. I was warned to keep in mind cultural differences in habits, customs, and traditions.

But none of us was quite prepared for Tessie or her grandmother (or for others whose ways of seeing things were similarly challenging). Tessie and her grandmother turned many of my ideas and assumptions upside down. Where I expected trouble, they saw great opportunity; where I waited for things to break down, they anticipated a breakthrough of sorts; where I saw a child bravely shouldering the burden of a divided, troubled society, they saw a blessed chance for a child to become a teacher, a healer, an instrument, maybe, of the salvation of others.

To listen to Tessie carefully turning a word on its head, taking the notion of service so seriously that her tormentors, she hoped, would become her beneficiaries, was to engage in research, all right. A child's idiosyncratic and utterly spiritual notion of service was a key. If you want to understand me, do your research in my home with my family, she was letting me know, you had best pay the closest attention to what I say, because the meaning I give to a word such as "service" may not at all resemble your sense of that word. Many times, as I have heard men and women talk about the service they "do," the volunteer effort they are making, I think of the standard Tessie held up to herself, though it was not necessarily one that others would consider desirable or germane.

After spending time with Tessie and the other six-year-olds, I began to view the nature of my research somewhat differently. My job had always been to listen, but now I was aware that at times we can be deaf listeners, thoroughly unable to hear some remarks while all too attentive to others. We can even take what we don't want to hear — what we are unprepared to acknowledge because of our own preconceptions — and turn it into what we're expecting to hear. Tessie's talk about offering her city, her tormentors a service could be heard as evidence of denial, as a rationalization or a maneuver of a beleaguered ego trying to mobilize various mechanisms of defense. That's how I heard her, at least for a while. Tessie's account of her purposes was surely evidence of anxiety and fear concealed by high-flown pronouncements connected to religion.

In time, ironically, the influential people who vehemently opposed school desegregation came around to Tessie's point of view. She and her three fellow pioneers received the begrudging acknowledgment of the city's leaders: these little girls *had* done the city a service, its mayor finally admitted, as did some of the segregationists I was getting to know in the mob that awaited Tessie with such rancor. "Those [three] girls, they're not the real problem," I heard one of the hecklers, a parent, say in front of the McDonogh School. "They're just trying to do what they think is right, what they've been *told* is right — trying to be of help to their people. I suppose they've done something for us. We had our fight, and we've lost it, and now we've got to put it all behind and try to get an education for our kids, because if we don't, we'll be in worse shape than having a few Negroes there at school with our white children."

This mother was beginning to recast her judgment and even find evidence of assistance offered, a service done: Tessie was no longer a devil (as she had often been called) but a hapless victim, maybe, or, on a more upbeat note, someone who helped "clear the air." That was the phrase the woman used two years later, as she looked back with some awkwardness, even a growing disbelief, at what had occurred "back then," as she put it — as if the subject were ancient history.

Sometimes, unfortunately, attentive listening (so that one hears one's own constraints as well as those of the people one is studying) doesn't quite work because there seems to be no way to agree upon a conversation. I spent years talking with Tessie and other children, and gradually some of them began to wear me down, even as they had worn down the street mobs. At last I began to fathom some new definitions of words I thought I knew backward and forward (maybe words I thought I owned), such as "service" and its variations.

In 1962, however, I found myself in a situation where I was anxious to be all ears, but no one was interested in talking. I had by then expanded my study of school desegregation to include Atlanta, where a federal judge had sent ten black youths into four of the city's high schools. I came to know these youths fairly well, and I have described that work at some length.[3] One consequence of that work was that one of the high schoolers became involved with the sit-in movement and regularly went to the office in downtown Atlanta of the Student Non-Violent Coordinating Committee.[4] There he helped plan and later implement sit-ins, and there he learned how to work with his own people to persuade young blacks to become politically awakened and energized. When this

young man, Lawrence Jefferson, went to the Ebenezer Baptist
Church to hear Dr. Martin Luther King, Jr., Jane and I often went
with him. When he told me he was working at SNCC headquarters, I also wanted to accompany him — and one day I did so.

When we arrived, he went off to his regular tasks, but I was
taken to another room, where I was questioned and questioned
with considerable intensity. I well remember noticing my watch at
one point — and being noticed doing so. My questioners were
James Foreman and Stokely Carmichael, two black leaders of the
young organization, and Bob Zellner, a white Alabamian. The
three, already veterans of southern jails, sat near one another in
chairs; I sat on a sagging couch. By the time I looked at my watch
and discovered that over two hours had passed, I felt as if the couch
had collapsed altogether and I was sitting on the floor. That
thought turned out to be rather prophetic.

I was asking these young men for permission to interview various members of SNCC. I spoke of my work with children in New
Orleans and Atlanta and mentioned the Southern Regional Council, a group of black and white Southerners much interested in
working toward desegregation throughout the eleven states of the
old Confederacy. I offered to obtain letters of support from the
officers of that council and from the distinguished black psychol-
ogist Kenneth Clark, who had been quite helpful to me in my
research in New Orleans, and even from Thurgood Marshall and
Jack Greenberg, then important members of the NAACP Legal
Defense Fund, which had been arguing one desegregation case
after another through the courts. The three youths were vastly
uninterested in this mobilization of affirmative reassurance. The
more I spelled out my credentials and training, the less interested
they seemed.

What was I trying to learn? Again and again they posed that
question, and each time I tried to answer with as much intelligence, tact, and sensitivity as I could summon. I talked of the
youthful idealism I would no doubt·be witnessing and of my wish
to understand the motivations for it and the manner in which
the mind struggled with the threats and dangers and stresses and
strains that go with such an idealism. I used some psychiatric and
psychoanalytic terms, but by then I had learned to be a bit skeptical

of such language — partially because I was seeing its limitations. Psychoanalytic jargon sometimes closed off avenues of inquiry, and overwrought, self-serving, parochial shop talk put people off.

I tried to relax, share my convictions, and indicate my strong enthusiasm for what the SNCC workers were trying to do. Whereas two years earlier I was very much the eager psychiatric researcher, now I was a somewhat shaken and perplexed doctor, trying to get my bearings and learning, almost daily, it sometimes seemed, what I didn't know and hadn't even thought to want to know about. But my three hosts, or interrogators, were singularly unimpressed. Eventually they told me they had to leave — and said that they were not at all inclined to let me interview anyone at SNCC.

I can still feel the floor falling away. I sat there in silence. Part of me wanted to summon the old, familiar retaliatory reflex, to go on and on to myself about their suspiciousness, even paranoia — a peculiar naming or name-calling habit that is rather congenial to my kind. Part of me wanted to continue with my self-presentation a bit longer, to *somehow* convince these three that I was truly on the up and up. I wanted to tell them that my heart was with them and that in no way would my inquiries be disruptive or rude or unsettling. Part of me was fuming: they weren't really asking me the right questions, and they were being rude, even patronizing. I felt sad because it was very important (so every researcher feels) to know more about the lives of these young activists, about the origins of their attitudes, about the kind of work they did, about their accomplishments, and about the psychological costs.

As all of this ran through my head, I was brought up short. Almost in unison all three men stood, and I, reluctantly, stood up with them. We chatted only a minute or two as we walked out of the room. Just as we were saying good-bye, I blurted out, "I'd still like to help — any way you'd want." Silence — and then I said, "Isn't there something I can do that you need done?" More silence, and then Jim Foreman's response (one all of us would recall years later with smiles and laughter): "You can help us keep this place clean!"

Foreman was at the time the nominal head of SNCC, and the day before he had complained (I later learned) how "messy" the offices were getting. I was initially surprised by his words, but I was quick to accept the offer. Within minutes I was sweeping floors, dusting, scrubbing down the bathroom, washing dishes in the small room that served as a kitchen. In my mind, of course, I was being tested; soon they would permit me to talk with these young people, to observe and interview them rather than clean up after them. I have to confess I felt no small amount of pride at how persuasive I had been and how resourceful and flexible I'd turned out to be: the effective, persistent field worker.

Days of sweeping a suite of offices in an old, dusty downtown building turned into weeks, then months. I had an official position with SNCC: I was the janitor. I even bought us a vacuum cleaner and did such unexpected extras as cleaning the windows. Gradually I was greeted by my first name, was offered coffee or food, and was invited to evening meetings and parties. Sometimes a young man or woman asked to talk with me, and I obliged with great interest, of course.

It would have been easy, I realized after two or three weeks, to stop my janitoring work and carve out, gradually and informally, one of those "roles" that social scientists describe. Less pompously, I could join "the movement" and take care to learn all I could through casual exchanges and attendance at strategy meetings or discussions where ideas were debated. Yet as I mastered my janitorial routine, I felt increasingly secure with the position, and I reminded myself that a good half of the black parents I knew did similar work as a full-time career.

I also began to be aware of all that was happening as I did my work — the comments I heard and overheard, the thoughts that crossed my mind and, not least, the range of feelings that I experienced. Even today, when I do volunteer teaching in a school and see the janitor or see children seeing the janitor, I realize that I was not being rebuffed or shortchanged by those SNCC members. For some time I kept thinking that they were testing me, maybe cutting me down to size a little, and letting me know who was boss. In fact, they were teaching me — or, better, enabling me to learn, putting me in a situation where I had plenty to do, yet could listen to my heart's content. I was constantly learning by experience rather than through abstract discussions.

A year later, when I'd held on to the job so long that everyone (myself included) simply took for granted that I would continue, I stumbled into a memorable talk with Jim Foreman. The year was 1963, and the civil rights struggle was becoming increasingly strenuous, even fierce. It was a week after Labor Day, and the schools had just reopened. The weather was quite hot, and the fans didn't do enough to make us comfortable. I'd finished my morning chores, and Jim asked me if I wanted a cup of coffee. Sure — and soon we were talking away. At one point he changed the subject abruptly with a brief question, somewhat coldly, even provocatively asked, "So, what have you learned from all this?" A second's silence, and then, to make clear what "this" meant, "The janitorial research."

Surprised, I fell silent. We'd been exchanging small talk, and now I wondered what to do. Should I turn that question into an excuse for a bantering, self-mocking continuation of small talk? I was tempted in that direction, but a glance at Jim's face told me of his seriousness. I lowered my head and heard myself grasping for words, fumbling incoherently. Jim finally spoke for me, told me he thought I had come to like the work and not feel demeaned by it, indeed, to take a certain pleasure in it.

I concurred. By accident, at a particular moment in the life of SNCC and in the lives of its members and in my own life, all of us had acted in such a way that I was able to connect with a group of young people bent on connecting with impoverished, voteless, legally segregated blacks. In doing my everyday tasks, I was able to observe, learn, and come to some understanding of how life went for the SNCC workers and for people in the communities where they were living and "organizing."

With Tessie, I had learned very slowly what service meant for her and her grandmother. With my SNCC friends, I slowly learned to abandon my reliance on questionnaires and structured interviews and instead to *do*, to experience service, and thereby learn something about what those young people had in mind as they went about their activist lives. I learned that the "methodology" for a research project had to do with *definition*, first, and then *vantage point*, meaning the way a word such as "service" is variously interpreted and the manner in which an observer looks and listens.

*   *   *

Years later, back North after almost a decade of work in the South, I became involved with a group of teachers, black and white, who wanted to help some black families in Boston's Roxbury neighborhood. A number of parents had decided to remove their children from Roxbury's terribly overcrowded schools and send them elsewhere in hopes of securing a better education. We had many evening meetings, long discussions that reminded me at times of the soulful, passionate encounters I'd witnessed in the rural South during the early 1960s. We talked about the purposes of education and the best ways to reach and teach children.

We wondered aloud many times whether integration was desirable, whether the long bus rides the black children were taking to distant, all-white schools were worth the effort. Some of us wanted to tutor these children locally in afternoon and evening classes aimed at strengthening them medically and psychologically as well as educationally. Others saw the less crowded, better equipped schools in white neighborhoods as places where poor black children would learn not only about reading and arithmetic but about the larger white world that was so fearful and uninviting.

The buses that carried these children across the city were privately supported (a desegregation case was then being argued in federal court by black plaintiffs against the Boston School Committee). I was a volunteer teacher, but I wasn't getting very far with my evening class, a reading tutorial. The children were obviously tired and had other ideas as to how to spend their after-supper time. I was ready to disband the class, and one evening I told the children what I had in mind. They perked up, all ears to one another as comments were made and questions asked. A boy said he could see why I wanted to end the class, because it was probably interfering with my "suppertime" and, he added, my "social life." A girl pointed out that I was married. Another girl laughed and exclaimed, "So what!"

After more chatter that I found sadly pointless (if revealing about the lives of these children) a boy said, "What's the matter? We're not doing good enough for you?" A stunned silence from everyone — normally a restless, talkative crowd. I was as mute as the others. I simply had no idea what to say. A denial, perfunctory or impassioned, was not what these young people wanted or needed, I felt. I let them see me struggling amid the room's still-ness. Finally I said that I wanted our class to continue, but I frankly thought we weren't getting very far; I thought they all had better things to do in the early evening hours, and maybe I just didn't know how to be of help to them — perhaps a more skilled teacher would fill the bill.

More silence, to the point that I got nervous and was preparing to end the class, say my last good-byes, and chalk up a failure. Then one child raised a hand and asked, "Why don't you get a job in the school where we're going [to which they were bused], then we could have you and not one of those teachers we have?" Others agreed, and of course I wanted to know about "those teachers." They told me a lot about the teachers' indifference, if not outright prejudice. "You should come and see," they said, almost in unison. Aroused, curious, I said yes, I'd try to come and see. They im-mediately wanted to know when. Without hesitating, I said, "To-morrow."

And so I showed up the next morning to ride with them on the bus to a school across the city in Boston's Back Bay area. I had intended, actually, to go directly to the school on my own, but I realized I couldn't just walk into a school, find my way to their various classes, then disappear into the woodwork so that I could take in what they were experiencing. Anyway, how could I see all of them together? Not in that school, where they were dispersed in various classrooms, and not in our evening class, which did seem to be dead, though we all felt sad about that. So I got up early and drove to that bus almost as a way of saying hello and good-bye one last time. On the spur of the moment I decided to board it, sit with my young friends, and enjoy their company on the half-hour trip downtown.

That trip turned out to be the first of many.[5] I became a regular traveler, and we even got some homework done on the way. Usu-ally, though, we sat and looked out the windows and talked. I began to realize how eventful that ride was for these boys and girls, many of whom had never before ventured out of the few city blocks they called their own. I began to notice how noisy the bus was at first and how quiet it became as we approached a world of fine homes, fine stores, fine restaurants. The passengers gawked, smiled, frowned, and sometimes laughed and laughed. They mocked a good deal of what they saw, but clearly they felt in awe of some aspects of the passing scene. On the rare occasions when they caught sight of a black man or woman, they paid particular attention, then speculated on who the person was and what he or she was doing there — as one boy put it, "in Whitey's back yard."

Eventually we settled into a humdrum routine, one that began to bore us, even in the wealthier, more dramatic spots. Still, the ride almost invariably got the children talking about matters I suppose could be subsumed under the topics "race" and "class." Often a child would use a particular scene as a text of sorts, a basis for personal reflection. I started taking notes and eventually began having more formal talks with the students as we traveled (some of which I would record).[6] The boys and girls seemed to like those times and told me so; indeed, they told me a lot that I suspect I'd never have heard otherwise.

A month into our daily busing venture, Sally, a girl of ten, pointed out one store as we approached a block of elegant dress shops, antique shops, restaurants, and men's clothing stores. She asked me if I'd ever been in that store, a place that obviously catered to stylish wealthy women. No, I said. Then she smiled and asked if my wife had ever been there. No, I said. Then she asked if I'd ever been in any of the stores we had just passed. No, I said. She looked at me and declared with deadpan seriousness, "I've been there." By then I didn't know where "there" was — and I was wondering why Sally was telling me this. I had to contend with her obviously intended irony, if not provocation: she had visited a rather fancy place that I, from a world she knew to be relatively comfortable, had not visited.

Perplexed, I said nothing, until she broke the impasse with a question *I* ought to have asked: "Why do you think I went there?" I told her right away that I didn't know. She wanted to drag the matter out and maybe tease me: "To buy clothes for my momma or my sister?" I smiled. She didn't, however. She continued, "Maybe to meet a friend there?" Again I smiled, but she continued to look serious. "I could have needed something real bad for myself — that's why I could have gone."

This time I don't smile. We are sitting side by side on the first row of seats, and I look at her. She returns my look, shifts her gaze to the view outside, then comes back with a final query: "Have you ever gone into one of the stores near where we live?" She means Grove Hall, a section of Roxbury. I shake my head, feeling on the spot and wondering how to shift into another gear and get us away from where we seem to be — stalled, or even ditched.

Sally suddenly decides to help out. "I have a brother, and he worked there for a while."

"He did?"

"Yup."

"How long?"

"Until he had a fight."

"With whom?"

"This guy, he was the owner."

"What happened?"

"I don't know."

"You never were told?"

"No."

"Where's your brother now?"

"He's in the service."

"Which branch?"

"The army."

"Where is he stationed?"

"In Europe someplace."

"Where in Europe?"

"I don't know."

I wanted to go back to the subject of the store and her brother and, most important, her visits to the store. That was what she meant for us to discuss — so I reasoned as we sat there, saying not a word to each other. But a friend of hers came over and stood in the aisle talking, and the next thing I knew, we were at the school. (I would then ride back to Roxbury with the bus driver, get into my car, and retrace much of the bus's route as I headed to the school again to observe the children, then to my office in Cambridge.)

The next day, as I boarded the bus, Sally asked if she could sit next to me again. Yes, of course, I said, and we took the seats we'd had the morning before. Right away I thought of the block of stores, and so did she: "Do you remember those places — the store, from yesterday?"

"Yes, I do." I hesitated, then decided to ask her directly about her brother. "Did your brother work there long?"

"I don't know — maybe a year, maybe more. He liked the job for a while. They gave him tips sometimes."

I waited briefly, then asked, "What did he do?"

"I don't know. I think he carried things around. They called him a clerk when they were being nice. When they weren't being so nice, they called him 'boy.' He was supposed to smile, but he didn't. I think it was once, when the lady [the wife of the owner, I later found out from Sally's mother] called him 'boy, boy,' shouted at him because she needed him real bad, it was then that he blew up."

"Do you know what he said?"

"No."

"You don't have any idea?"

"I think I can guess."

I stopped short of asking her — I'm not sure why. I was doing research of the kind I had done in the South, trying to learn how black and white children came to terms with racial matters and other aspects of growing up — but now in a city far from the supposed trouble spots in Mississippi or Georgia or Alabama or Louisiana.[7] I was trying to be in touch with these children by teaching them and even by spotting medical problems, telling their parents whom to see at Children's Hospital. Still, something prompted me to hold back here — perhaps because I wanted mostly to sit back and take in that daily bus ride for another few weeks rather than get further into stories such as this one. If I really was interested in pursuing intense "interviews" with the children, those interviews ought to be conducted elsewhere, at home or in school.

But I soon decided that the methodological issue was not to the point. "Learn what you can, where you can," my old hero William Carlos Williams had told me once as I accompanied him on his medical rounds in Paterson, New Jersey.[8] He wasn't advocating greed or presumptuous intrusiveness, only a certain willingness to meet people on their own turf, especially those who had good reason to tighten up outside their own neighborhood. As the bus moved out of Roxbury and into more prosperous white territory, I looked at Sally and said, "Your brother really told them off?"

"You bet!"

"Did the police get into it?"

"Why do you say that?"

"I didn't mean to suggest — I was just asking."

"Everyone thinks we're going to do something wrong!"

"I'm sorry; I didn't mean that. I was just . . ."

"The lady and her husband, I think they said they'd call the cops."

"They didn't?"

"I don't think so."

"Your brother told someone in your family what happened?"

"Yes."

"Your mother?"

"No. My momma would have gotten too upset. She has high blood pressure. She gets terrible headaches. They say she could get sick, and she'd be paralyzed all of a sudden. They told her not to put salt on her food, and she should take pills when she gets up and during the day. So my brother told my aunt, and I heard her tell my grandma. He called them everything, and they called him everything — and he walked right out!

"I'd been there to visit him a couple of weeks before. I said hi, and he showed me around a little. They were all friendly then, so he even introduced me to her [the owner's wife]. She called me a nice girl, and she asked me if I was going to stay in school. I said sure — but I could tell she wasn't buying it. She was asking me — but she knew the answer already. I felt like telling her off! But my brother said they're not so bad — back then he did. He said there are lots worse white folks. He said they're all bad if you want to wait around long enough to hear the truth come out from their mouths!

"That lady, she kept after me: 'Now, you nice girl, tell me what you want to be when you grow up.' I didn't answer her. So she asked me again, and I was still standing there and not opening my mouth. So she waited, and then she asked me again, and I figured I'd better get her off my back, so I told her I wanted to be a brain surgeon. Boy, she looked at me, and it was as if I'd gone crazy right in front of her, and she didn't know whether to call an ambulance or what. She just stood there, staring at me, and her husband, he'd heard me, and he stared, too. Then she said, 'How cute.' That's what she said! I was going to say something, but I knew my brother would lose his job on the spot, and I'd be told to get off their property! So I didn't say a word back. But she wanted to talk, so she asked me, 'Where did you get that idea?' Before I had a chance to think of what to say, she answered herself, 'On TV, I'll bet — that's where!' She said, 'You must have seen a program . . .'

"I decided I'd take her serious, real serious. I said, 'No, ma'am.' I tried to be polite, real polite. I said, 'You see, I was in school, and they gave us this book, the teachers did. They are college guys, and they want to teach us, and they read with us, and that's where I heard of being a doctor who fixes up people who get into bad trouble.' I told her that, and she looked at me, and she said, 'My, my, little girl, you really are a serious one!' I can close my eyes, and I see her, and I hear her! Every time we drive by that place, I hear her telling me I'm 'a serious one!'

"I never said another word to her, and she never said another word to me, and it didn't take long for my brother to tell me he had a break, and we could go get a Coke, and we did, and I went home. I wasn't so little — I was almost up to her chin, and *she* was little; she was this short, fat thing. I could call her a lot of things!"

I sat there, saddened by what I'd heard, and wondered what to say that wouldn't sound gratuitous or patronizing to this girl whose seriousness and shrewdness I had just begun to comprehend. I suddenly realized that any number of children on this bus might have similar stories to tell. I'd only begun to be acquainted with them as a teacher, and none too successfully. I'd hoped to hear more about their lives, about their hopes and worries, but I hadn't figured out how to do that. And now there was this moment in a bus as we moved along noisily through the crowded streets of Boston, a city known across the land for its universities, its abolitionist leadership in the nineteenth century, its museums, its desirability as a place for young Americans to live and work.

Right then I decided to make another attempt with that class. I mentioned the idea, on the spur of the moment, to Sally: "What a lousy thing to go through. I'll bet others, plenty of others, have heard people talk like that to them. I was thinking, maybe we should try to get that class we had going, and we could do some work, and we could talk about what you say, what you do, when you run into a situation like that."

She was silent for a few seconds. When she answered, she was terse and not too encouraging: "There's nothing to say." I wasn't sure whether she meant a direct answer to my suggestion that we discuss what you say in such situations or, rather, a double-barreled refusal: no to my suggestion about the class as well. I wanted to press that suggestion again, but I also feared doing so. I had to admit that Sally was justifiably wary of all of us white folks, including the ones who considered themselves to be friends.

I took a chance and said, "Well, there's something you can say sometimes; I guess I believe that." I had more on the tip of my tongue, but I didn't want to talk too much. I wanted her to reply, but she said nothing, so I resumed, "I've been in a room, and someone has made a remark that really hurt me — an insult. I've kept quiet, but later I've been as upset as can be, and I've thought of all the things I could have said, all the ways I could have gotten even."

She immediately turned to me. "It's different with you people." She stopped abruptly, though I could tell that there was more on her mind. I was going to reply with all that was on my mind, but I thought better of it and only said, "What do you mean?"

I had hoped to persuade her to do some more talking, but she was looking sullen — as if this white guy was proving to be not only a little slow but a little innocent, to say the least. Finally, not looking at me — indeed, pointedly looking out the window — she said, "You know what I mean!"

I felt the impatience and disgust in her voice, and I realized the legitimacy of her reaction. Of course I knew what she meant. As a white man, I had all sorts of choices that she knew weren't available to her. True, the incident in that store could be examined psychiatrically. I could say that some of us have trouble giving back in kind what we get from prying, hostile people; or we're slow on the draw and think of a reply afterward, when the subject has changed and the offending person has gone; or we are plain polite, or shy, or disdainfully reluctant even to engage and thereby to give the person the satisfaction of our anger.

But Sally was letting me know that she regarded the issue we had been circling as essentially racial in nature. As she kept her gaze away from me, I wondered how to move the conversation in a different direction. Suddenly she pointed with her right forefinger, even as she avoided looking at me. (She did not try to see if I was looking where she was pointing.) I shifted my gaze, and there was that block of stores, that dress shop. I spoke without pondering: "Well, here we are again. How long will it take a lot of us to learn about other people, so we really know them?"

Now she was ready to look at me. She said just one word: "Forever." As that duration of time began to sink into my usually hopeful head, she decided to qualify it: "Maybe sooner, but it doesn't look like it'll be too soon." That was the beginning of a more relaxed and flowing conversation. I asked her if she had any idea how we all might move things along. She did not, though she did say there were moments when she thought of taking a baseball bat to the heads of people such as her brother's one-time employers. But she had come to realize, with the help of her mother, that the best revenge she could take on those two bosses, and on others like them, was to nurture and strengthen her own head rather than lash out at them. She really did hope to become a doctor, she told me, and if she did, she wanted to learn how to cure her mother. At that point, since her mother's chief symptom was severe hypertensive headaches, why not dream of being a brain surgeon who could cut out what was causing all that unremitting pain?

Weeks later we resumed our tutoring "club," as the children wanted to call our assembly of seven youngsters and an elementary school teacher who lived nearby. At our first meeting in the new series, we all understood, almost without needing to say it, how different the situation was. We were like old friends in that church basement room where we met. After all, we'd been traveling together morning after morning. We'd sat together and looked and laughed and agreed and disagreed. For my part, I'd learned what some of those children carried as memories, as instructive reminders of what happens in this world. But I'd also come to see what I often have not been able to see: the reasons others have to notice what I overlook — or, conversely, to ignore with all their might what I want to regard closely and carefully.

Sally still had grave doubts about my ability to understand her life, in spite of my efforts as a volunteer teacher and my appearance every morning, Monday through Friday, on her street corner. It was not that she was suspicious of me the child psychiatrist doing research, or of tutoring as a means of establishing contact with those I hoped to observe and interview. She drew the line, rather, with race, with skin color, and held back accordingly. She watched constantly, kept her own counsel, and every once in a while put her cards of skepticism on the table through a glance or grimace, a question or rejoinder. Also she worried whether she would ever be invulnerable to the power of store owners, even black ones: "If I went to work for people, and they weren't nice, I could be in real trouble, even if they were black, even then. There's a man, he has a variety store two blocks from where we live, and he's sure not a white guy, and he's always after us, and he calls us every name you can think of — it's that bad! 'It goes to show you,' my momma says."

I asked what we were thereby "shown." She immediately replied, "Black or white, you can turn into a really bad person — you can care for no one but yourself; you can just lord it over everyone, all because you've got the dough and the rest of the folks don't. The same goes with cops: don't think a cop's skin color will make him be fair to us — I mean, we have our cops, and they're cops is what they are, and they'll even be meaner with us, because they have a thing against their own people, that's what's happened to them. It can be real bad here in this neighborhood, with us kicking each other! If I ever leave, if we get out, I hope I'll remember, and I'll try to help out the ones who are left behind. If you're just out to boost yourself, and that's all, then you're no good. It's only right to admit that — we have our folks who aren't any better than the worst on the other side."

Sally was now a year older than when we first had ridden the bus together. She'd met some fairly decent, even appealing white children at the school she was being bused to. She had learned to be grateful to some doctors who had helped her mother's headaches by reducing her blood pressure with medication. She had seen a lot that made a difference: children who defied her notions of what they had to be because of their race, hospital workers who had a lot to offer.

By the same token, she had been able to help me with my "vision"; by her attentive seriousness and concentration, she had helped me see what I had failed to notice. Riding on that bus, in a way, drew me into a world I was all too intent on studying and trying to figure out — from a distance. Unwittingly I had been drawing conclusions based on a limited capacity to absorb and reflect upon what the children around me were seeing and saying and feeling, and I had missed a lot.

"I try to put myself in the shoes of others," William Carlos Williams said about his patients — but he immediately acknowledged the difficulty: "We're completely lost in our own world — egoists! Or maybe we're locked into ourselves, and even though we want to break out, we can't seem to do it. It takes someone else to help us, a person who breaks in or has a way of letting us out. Or we stumble into some moment, some situation, that wakes us up, gets us enough off track to open up our eyes, our ears, our musty minds!" As he talked about his struggles to take stock of people and places ("outside / outside myself / there is a world")[9] he was also describing the task of the psychiatric or sociological or anthropological observer. How do we place our mind (and heart and soul) in a position — a place both literal and symbolic — that encourages our eyes and ears to pick up what we might otherwise miss?

As we talked about this challenge, Williams could be both vague and utterly concrete. "I'll go on my rounds, and some days I'm behaving like an automaton! I know my medicine, and I'm as impatient as I can be with anyone who tries to get in my way. I'm signaling all those people I see, Watch out and stay away while I slap medical words on you and recite by rote what you should do! I'm not really looking at individuals; I'm not trying to learn from them. I'm telling them what I already know, what I pick up real fast — and boy, are they in trouble with me if they try to slow me down by saying, even in the most tactful and roundabout way, 'Hey, doc, it's *me* you're with, *here*, so work *that* into your equation!'

"On the right day, though, I'm all eyes and all ears. And I go even further — I stop myself in my tracks, and I talk to myself, and I say, Try to be a fly on the wall, or try to disappear into the crowd so you're not right smack in the middle of things, and people are responding to *you*, because when that happens it doesn't always mean they're being *themselves*, you know! I try to pull my hat down over my face, or wrap my scarf around it, or I've got nothing to hide behind but my tongue-tied mood, and that can be a good hiding place if I'm hoping to pick up on others, not do a dance for them!"

All my working life I've remembered those words, delivered in the irascible, cranky manner I'd come to know so well. I've tried to remember, as well, some of Williams's modest strategies for heightening his own awareness and his patients' responsiveness. Once, when I went with him to a tenement in Paterson to visit several poor families, I saw him at his best. He was lively, engaging, and utterly inventive in the way he presented himself to the children and their parents. He sat down on the floor and let the youngsters listen with his stethoscope and use his neurological hammer on themselves and him. He plucked out some Hershey's Kisses from his pocket and put them on the floor and waited for the children to take them — whereupon he'd ask if he might have one or two. He asked the children if they wanted to give *him* any advice, inasmuch as he was dispensing so much counsel; and he'd look askance, cupping his ears, paying regard to their language and to the small details of the apartment and what the people were wearing.

Before we entered the building, he wrote on his clipboard: "Things I noticed today that I've missed until today." I wondered what in the world he was intending to do and what point he was making. Later, after a few house calls, he snatched that clipboard from the rear seat of his car and made a list — an almost childlike way of holding himself to account. Again and again, during or after house calls, he would write down phrases his patients used. He would note what they were cooking and mention any new furniture, curtains, or glassware. He would be excited by the sight of something, cut out of a newspaper and posted on the wall or the refrigerator. He would notice playing cards left on a table or parents playing checkers while their child talked with the doctor. He would spot a phone treated as if it were an altarpiece or see that a housewife's most precious purchase was a prayer card carried home from church and kept on the kitchen counter.

Once, curious and confused, I asked him indirectly why he worked so hard to pay heed not only to others but to himself — as if any slipup was a disaster. He let me know, in good humor, that he was trying to heighten his consciousness: "I'm not whipping myself — just trying to get a little more mileage out of myself!" I suppose, to call upon the big, important words of social science research, he was attempting to achieve a research methodology, a procedure that would help him acquire reliable "data." He put it this way: "I'm trying to dive in, not dip in — and I hope I don't make too many waves, just see what there is to see and hear what there is to hear, and the more, the better."

I don't believe I could have understood Tessie and her family's capacity to live as they did, do as they did for so long, against such great odds, had I not begun to hear what *they* were saying and meaning, what *they* intended others to know about their reasons and values — as opposed to the motivations and reactions and "mechanisms of defense" *I* attributed to them. Not that there wasn't much to be learned by a psychoanalytic approach. Tessie and her companions, like human beings everywhere (including those who study or treat other human beings), most certainly did demonstrate fearfulness and anxiety; she also tried to subdue those developments by not acknowledging them, for instance, or by belittling their significance. Mostly, though, she clung hard to a way of thinking in which she was *not* a victim, *not* in need of "help" but someone picked by fate to live out the Christian tradition in her life. "I'm trying to think of the way Jesus would want me to think," she told me one evening. When I asked how she thought Jesus wanted her to think, she replied, "I guess of others, and not myself. I'm here to help the others."

A declaration of service, for sure — a summons lodged deeply in a child's consciousness. No wonder she harbored toward her outspoken critics, her tormentors, a good deal of pity; no wonder she continued to hope that they would, one day, see the light:

"There will come a morning when my job will be done." I thought she was referring to a peaceful transition to desegregation. In a way, she did have such an outcome in mind, but she also had a more radical notion of her assignment, the accomplishment of a change of heart in those she'd come to know daily on the streets.

My realization of how essential her sense of purpose was for her was an important moment of understanding for me. Until I was able to take Tessie's avowals of service seriously rather than dismiss them as rationalizations, I was not able to figure out what sustained her. Until then my research project awaited its means of implementation, its methodology, the language that would give *it* direction.

Similarly at SNCC headquarters and on that school bus in Boston, I needed to locate myself not only with respect to particular individuals but with respect to a situation given shape by particular currents. Until I listened to those civil rights workers talk about their humble origins or the restrictions and confinement they had experienced while they worked in the movement, I was not able to comprehend their passionate outcries, their fierce insistence that their cause must prevail.

Talking with people while sweeping floors and cleaning latrines or sinks enabled me to construct a frame of reference for my research project: so *this* is what bothers them so much, prompts talk and actions that I might be tempted to describe in the language of psychology as "defensive" or as a consequence of personal background (class and race exerting their influence). Now I knew that theirs was an outcry that wouldn't be stifled — a moral ideology that seemed to defy all logic, even that of psychoanalytic or political theory.

One day, as I was cleaning the office, I heard some youths describing what they had done while in an Alabama prison. They had asked the sheriff imploringly if they might clean up his jail cells from top to bottom, from ceilings to lavatory bowls. The sheriff promptly called them "nuts" (so much for the psychology of masochism); his deputy called them "wise guys" and "weirdos" (so much for the politics of nonviolent protest). Neither man was deterred by the offer; they told the youths to go right ahead, which they did with great enthusiasm and energy. The boss-men were neither grateful nor impressed — a failure of a Gandhian exertion, I recall thinking. Yet the young activists *themselves* seemed grateful and impressed; they were glad to have a chance to test themselves, as they put it, inspired by a faith that would carry them through that grim and dangerous time with sense of humor intact and commitment to the cause as strong as ever.

"I almost wanted to thank that sheriff for letting us do the cleanup job," one of them said — and no one disbelieved him, not even me. "I didn't know why I was doing this until I actually *was* doing it," another said. Immersing themselves in an activity was a way (a methodological means) of learning a good deal about their reasons, assumptions, and aspirations.

As for those bus-ride conversations as we traveled across town, they, too, helped connect "research" to social and psychological realities otherwise overlooked or forgotten (by the children themselves, never mind their observer). Like the volunteer activists on freedom rides down South, those northern children on *their* rides learned something: "All it takes is a trip through that fancy place [downtown Boston] for me to know what all this commotion is about!" I asked the girl to explain herself, although by then I had an inkling of what she was getting at but wasn't sure (the risks of condescension!) that she herself did. She answered, "They've been talking [her mother and other parents] a lot about what's right and what's best for us, but it didn't matter to me, because how are you supposed to know what's different, and what should be, because all you know is what you know. You see what I mean? Then they got us this bus, and this is a *trip*. I mean, you go on the bus, and you see a lot you've never seen before; so, when they [the leaders of a group advocating school desegregation] came to church I knew what they were all talking about. I could just close my eyes and see it!"

Saying that, she shut her eyes for a second or two, not as an exercise in drama but as a way to recall the social and economic disparities that bothered her. "I'll be lonely over there; it's far away from here [in her aunt's apartment in the neighborhood where she'd spent all her life]. If I get too lonely, I'm tempted just to quit. We're supposed to be volunteers, but if you don't feel like volunteering, then you shouldn't, because it's not volunteering when you're feeling forced and you have to do it or else a lot of people will be upset with you. 'There's a lot riding on you kids,' some of those people say, but it's *us* who are *doing* it, the *riding*, so don't lecture us, because we already know — that's what I want to say back, tell them, but I don't."

Instead she shut her eyes to recall some of what she had seen, sights that became for her a sustaining vision. In the same way, for me the memory of what had passed before my eyes as we sat on that bus became a pathway, a conversational road. I will always remember a moment of methodological breakthrough, a child's drawing called "The People That Go on the Bus." The artist portrayed us all, the "driver and the doctor" and the twenty-four boys and girls. After she had finished her crayon work she explained her intent, and maybe mine as well: "Once you go on the bus, you want to stay there — keep going. You're all there together, and you don't want to walk out on the friends you've made."

I could add a lot about the solidarity we felt, morning after morning, and the connections made through various "adventures": the day the bus broke down; the day a car hit the side of the bus; the day the driver felt sick and pulled the bus over, and I called an ambulance, and we all waited for another bus; the day one girl had a birthday, and her mother sent pieces of "early morning cake," a prelude to more cake after school.

But the heart of the matter was that morning-by-morning experience of shared looking, which in turn gave a child and me talking a chance to look again and to reflect on what it meant to offer one's school life as a gift of sorts to one's people, as they struggled to enter worlds hitherto firmly closed to them. "Before I get to school, I see why I'm going there," one boy told me. Having sat beside him, I was a bit better able to grasp what he was trying to tell me and a bit better able to explore various matters with him during our time together — and so much for a bus ride (or a janitorial job) as an aspect of "method" in the life of a "research project" which some of those youths or children might want to describe as (settle for calling) a life.

This book offers many such stories and conversations and observations about those who render service and, in two interludes, about those who are served. In relating my own experiences and memories, I write as a witness trying to do justice through narration to lives I have met that have been instructive, lives that have made a difference in the lives of others, lives called to action in different ways and for various reasons and for varying lengths of time. This is research, I think it fair to say, living up to its literal meaning of an inquiry made again and again, through meetings and more meetings with those whose deeds, finally, are the subject matter of this book.

· TWO ·

Kinds of Service

D URING THE SPRING OF 1964 the leaders of SNCC were
planning their most ambitious action yet: a summer-long
attempt to enroll black voters in Mississippi, then the most
formidably segregationist of the southern states. It is hard, now, to
evoke the fear and terror that the Delta of Mississippi inspired in
civil rights activists. Indeed, I well remember their widespread
conviction that at the end of this century — this present time —
the struggle would still be going on. Not that all the necessary
battles have been fought and won. But the youths in SNCC believed that for decades to come the battles they were waging — for
the rights of blacks to vote, to go to school with white children, to
sit with whites in restaurants and movies, to check into any motel
or hotel — would persist.[1]

In the Atlanta office of SNCC I heard those youthful organizers and strategists wonder and worry as they tried to estimate how
many volunteers would enlist for a summer of door-to-door can-
vassing, of picketing and marching and demonstrating, of "grass
roots organizing" — a term I never did understand until I went
with men and women as they knocked on doors, asked to be let in,
seated themselves on chairs or floors, talked and asked questions

and tried to establish trust and a shared dream of what might be possible. One day in the midst of planning, a group of us went to the Southern Regional Council (where I had a desk, a place to sit and write or talk with people when I was in Atlanta) to hear Dr. Martin Luther King give one of his powerful midday sermons to the "brothers and sisters in the movement."[2]

That day Dr. King was more reflective than exhortative. He returned to his days as a graduate student, when he had studied philosophy and theology. He asked aloud how we "ought to think of one another" — how we should regard those we opposed in an ordeal that was far from over. He worried about the consequences of the struggle for those waging it, about the constant temptation to get worn down, to become bitter, and worst of all, he felt, to turn on our opponents in the same spirit that informed their hostility toward us and our fellow activists. I still listen sometimes to my tape of the speech, especially to these words: "A big danger for us is the temptation to follow the [leadership of the] people we are opposing. They call us names, so we call them names. Our names may not be 'redneck' or 'cracker'; they may be names that have a sociological or psychological veneer to them, a gloss; but they are names, nonetheless — 'ignorant,' or 'brainwashed,' or 'duped,' or 'hysterical' or 'poor-white' or 'consumed by hate.' I know you will all give me plenty of evidence in support of those categories. But I urge you to think of them as that — as categories; and I remind you that in many people, in many people called segregationists, there are other things going on in their lives: *this* person or *that* person, standing *here* or *there* may also be other things — kind to neighbors and family, helpful and good-spirited at work.

"You all know, I think, what I'm trying to say — that we must try not to end up with stereotypes of those we oppose, even as they slip all of us into their stereotypes. And who are we? Let us not do to ourselves as others (as our opponents) do to us: try to put ourselves into one all-inclusive category — the virtuous ones as against the evil ones, or the decent ones as against the malicious, prejudiced ones, or the well-educated as against the ignorant. You can see that I can go on and on — and there is the danger: the 'us' or 'them' mentality takes hold, and we do, actually, begin to run the risk of joining ranks with the very people we are opposing. I worry about this a lot these days."

As he shared his concerns with us, I remembered what I used to hear from William Carlos Williams in a similar vein. He once talked of the "zeal" with which we "take to labels of all kinds." He explained, "We crave certainty; we love to put a period at the end of a sentence, and that is that. But take a look at people, a real close look, and you'll find inconsistencies and contradictions — and that's where a closer look is needed, not a category or a definition that tells you, that reassures you: all right, you've got it!" He went on, in one of the lively, unabashed polemics I'd come to know well, exhilarating both for him and for his listener.

My thoughts also returned to my mother and my attempts to contemplate with her biblical passages or statements from the Book of Common Prayer. Again and again that phrase "all sorts and conditions" would cross my mind, a phrase meant to describe us in our vast variety, as we come to "common prayer," to our knees in heart and soul as well as body.

It is tempting, and at times not altogether inappropriate, to sort people into a few well-chosen "types" — as I'm about to do. But I urge a sense of the complexity of people on myself and on the reader. I well remember, for instance, those SNCC cadres and that "category" of four six-year-old black girls initiating school desegregation in New Orleans; with them, as with all of us, what Dr. Williams once remarked certainly held: "The closer you look, the more one picture turns into two and three and four and more."

In this chapter I divide service into categories according to the kinds of motives I have seen in the children and youths and older people I have come to know who have chosen to give their time to others. I have tried to do some useful, even necessary, sorting, but I hope I have left room for overlap, for a blend of motives and deeds that, properly, cautions us all against airtight conclusions and formulations.

Social and Political Struggle

As a child I often heard my mother use the word "charity" in referring to her constant involvement in the Red Cross, the League of Women Voters, a Catholic Worker soup kitchen, and in numerous hospital fund drives, as well as in her reading to sick children and helping people in the hospital as a volunteer. Still, my so-called research, which would become a lifetime of observation, of conversations and more conversations and efforts to understand what I'd heard, all began in the South, with the children and young volunteers I got to know there. I have chronicled that research many times, but as I have already indicated in connection with young Tessie, I wasn't always prepared to think of my work as a study of service.[3] Nor were many of the boys and girls and older people who got involved in those momentous confrontations inclined to think of themselves as Tessie did, as people trying to offer what they could to others.

As Stan, a civil rights activist who would later become a VISTA volunteer, declared to me one day, "You keep asking me *why*, why I'm here. I'm here because I believe in something. I believe in racial equality — 'black and white together,' and I'm willing to stand up for it, for what I believe. That's what I'm doing here. You could even call it selfish — it's important to me, and I feel I'm lucky to be here with others, doing this. Do I think of them, the segregationists? [I had asked.] No, I really don't. I mean, I do, of course — the sheriffs, the mobs. But a lot of the time I close my eyes to all of that, to them. I say to myself, Hey, you're here, and you're ready to keep putting yourself on the line, and that's as far as I let my mind go — one day at a time, one step at a time."

He had carried to the South the values he had learned in a white, fairly well-to-do, secular home up North. Or, it might be said, those values had carried him to Dixie, and though he might not have dwelt on them explicitly, they were a part of his life, as he acknowledged, and they help us understand what he was doing, what others like him were doing and continue to do. There he was in Canton, Mississippi, in 1964, amid the frantic activity and constant anxiety of the SNCC Summer Project, stopping for a while to think about his parents and what they taught him, and how that helped to characterize what he was doing with his life.

"I was brought up on the idea that you have to think of others, the poor, not just yourself. My dad is a lawyer, and he makes a good living; but he always contributes some of his time to causes — to people who need his help and can't afford it, or to politics. He joined the NAACP when he was a young man, when that was itself a real political statement, at least in the neighborhood where he and my mother lived.

"Neither of my parents are religious; my mom never goes to church, and my dad says his parents were agnostics, though they went to a Congregationalist church at Christmas and Easter. But both my parents had strong political ideals: they wanted the New Deal to last forever, and to expand, and make the country more egalitarian. They weren't socialists or communists. They were old-fashioned liberals or progressives, but they really believed in political commitments — and those commitments were sort of their meal, the bread and potatoes of their life. I think it was always like that for me too — it really mattered who was president, which party ran Congress, what laws were being passed, how the Supreme Court voted. The ways some kids are all tied up with church calendars or Hebrew school, I was tied up with this law (will it get through the Senate?) or that idea (will the president really push it?), and it's still like that for me.

"I guess you'd say that I'm here because this is a big moment in American history, and it really matters that Negroes get the vote and that the segregationists lose this political struggle, and it matters not only to me as a voter, an American, but to me and my family, [because] that's the kind of people we are, and this is what we believe in doing: to stand up for your ideas, your beliefs, and, like we say in SNCC, to put your body on the line, and if it's dangerous, then you don't walk away then, not if you want to hold on to your self-respect."

He didn't mention the real help, the genuine and important service he was offering every day as a teacher, as an advocate. In the above-quoted remarks and in hours of other comments, his emphasis was always on his politics, his activist purposes, his willingness (indeed, eagerness) to join with others, to link arms in a movement dedicated to those purposes — all on behalf of his principles, which he eagerly discussed at great length. For him, tutoring children in Mississippi, providing health information to families, and teaching a civics class to men and women in hopes that they would take the considerable risk of walking to the county courthouse and attempting to register as voters — all these activities were part of a social and political struggle that he used as his defining compass. He pursued those directions, he kept saying, that served "the movement's ends," a phrase that appeared repeatedly in his sometimes urgently impatient statements.

"I have so damn much to do," he would say over and over, as if uttering mere words — which he liked to do and could do very well — was an indulgence. When I told him how impressive his work with schoolchildren was, he brushed aside the compliment and made a point of indicating the relationship between his teaching and his social activism: "We need to earn the confidence of the people here. We can't just come in and ask them to put their lives on the line — and that's what they feel they're doing when they go into that courthouse, and who can blame them!" He had little apparent interest in acknowledging the worth of the tutoring per se. And given the risks *he* was taking — *his* life on the line! — I felt I could not press the matter.

Over the years I have stayed in touch with a number of men and women who more or less (that qualification is all-important) resembled him with respect to their deeply and proudly felt notion of what they were doing and why. "I'm trying to change the world," a student of mine who became a community organizer in a white working-class suburb once told me. As he talked about his work, he hardly mentioned his deeds of service, which were considerable. He worked hard to get recalcitrant landlords to repair rotting steps, furnish adequate heat and garbage containers, remove dangerous lead pipes, and fix windows that didn't work or screens full of holes or roofs that leaked. But in his mind, all the time and dedication he gave to those important initiatives was simply an aspect of the social and political struggle he was involved in. If questioned hard about the service he was giving needy tenants, he quickly sidestepped the subject.

"You bet these folks are having a lousy time — and they *will* until they all pull together and learn to stay together. That's the trouble sometimes, I hate to admit it; you help to make things just a little better for them, and they think, Hey, things aren't so bad — and they're ready to relax and stop pulling together politically. The really smart landlords are the ones who give their tenants just enough in the way of services to keep them quiet. You see what I mean?"

He stopped to make sure I was following his line of thought. I demurred, saying I doubted that landlords thought that way. I argued that some were greedy and callous and indifferent, others more conscientious and law-abiding, but I doubted that many calculated their actions on the basis of how to keep their tenants inert or passive politically. He didn't really disagree; he only wanted to give our discussion what he called "a political context." And then he made a long, didactic presentation of what needed to be done to reach people so that they would become more "conscious of their interests," after which they would presumably join a struggle that he described as essential and inevitable.

Rhetoric aside, he wanted very much to see the vulnerable, even desperate people he knew so well become better off and have a great deal more say about their lives. At moments he would soften, abandon his political interests, and concentrate on trying to help a particular family. "I stop seeing them as tenants; they become a mother who has a disease — trouble with a valve in her heart —. and I want to make sure she gets the best medical care, and her two children the best daycare, while she's in the hospital. I got to be an advocate of theirs, I guess. You know what? The landlord, he heard about this, her troubles, and me helping out, and he came up to me and he said, 'Hey, if you'll just leave me alone, I'll take good care of her — how's that for a bargain!' I said, 'Nothing doing!' He said, 'What's the matter with you? What do you want? I thought you're interested in these poor people — I thought it's their welfare that's on your mind!' I told him, 'Look, it *is* their welfare — their *long-term* welfare!'

"He just shrugged his shoulders and gave me a look as if I'm crazy. My sister agrees with him; she says it's hopeless to fight city hall, and those landlords are in bed with city hall, and I should go back to school. I'm halfway through social work school, and she thinks I should finish and then do social work, if that's what I want, instead of picketing and having fights all the time with cops. On a bad day, I'll tell you, I agree with her!"

But he did have better days: days when he was able to get a landlord to clean up his act; days when he successfully interceded for a tenant and got the court to rule that some repair must be made — and soon enough it *was* made, if reluctantly, even if the landlord turned out to be a "shadowy real-estate trust with ten crooks the behind-the-scenes owners." He loved talking that way, engaging in such fights. Naturally, I once asked him if he'd considered law as a profession. No, he wanted "to work with people" — he *was* a "social worker at heart," he admitted, as if owning up to a sin, though his intentions were "primarily political."

So they were, yet his everyday behavior was that of a concerned friend who wanted to help families contending with one terrible emergency after another. The longer I knew him and the more closely I observed his work (and heard about it from the children I knew and worked with), the more I sided with his sister's judgment: he had the soul of a dedicated social worker, his ideological passions notwithstanding. Certainly the tenants in that slum section of Boston would vote with his sister.

Often, as I talked with him, my mind went back to the civil rights activists, who also tried to balance their political or ideological interests with their personal responses to human distress. In Mc-Comb, Mississippi, for example, I was at work one July weekend in 1964 when the Freedom House, our home during the Summer Project, was dynamited. Soon thereafter we occupants were arrested — a strange legal logic![4] While we sat in jail and listened to the sheriff's ominous threats, we had some lengthy and emotional discussions. What *were* we doing there in Mississippi — what *were* the purposes of the Project?

The black people with whom we were working were at times as frightened of us outside volunteers, no matter what our skin color was, as they were of the sheriff and his police officers. "We want a better life [the Project's promise], and we want to vote [the Project's stated purpose], but we don't want to be killed," one tenant farmer had told us as we tried to persuade him to work with us and go to the county courthouse to register as a voter. He added, "You folks, you come here from outside, and one day you'll be gone — but we've been here forever and we'll stay forever! After you've gone, we'll have to get along with these [white] folks. They've got the money; they've got the police. What have we got? I know, you want to make it better for us. You want to see us voting, and you want to see us eating better and living in better homes, and walking with our head up high. I've heard you say your speeches many times, and I think you're all fine people, but maybe you should think of *us* more, and not of all the changes you want to make, and if you do, then you'll adjust your calendar — you see what I mean? — so that we all stay alive!"

Plenty of arguments could be made against his point of view, and they were made — and he listened to them. Sometimes only outsiders can dare to take on entrenched power such as that of the segregationist South; and sometimes risks have to be taken and suffering experienced to end an oppressive political and economic status quo. But I noticed that it was easier to argue such a view than concretely to put ordinary people, already so burdened, into further jeopardy, in spite of the possible long-term gains. Many SNCC activists flinched when it came to the actual moment of choice: "I'd been helping those farmers out; I helped with their crops, and I helped them do some building, and we'd become friends, and I'd bring them some groceries from town — and then, when push came to shove, and I had to decide whether to cash in on our friendship and try to persuade them to go there [to the courthouse], I got cold feet. I just couldn't carry through. I mean, I got revved up. I gave them my speech, *the* speech. I talked away — and you know, they were so damn polite and respectful, and they listened hard, and they even nodded and said, 'Yes, sir,' like they do in church, and 'amen.' But I made the mistake of looking at them, looking right in their eyes, and what I saw was fear, fear so deep that it was like looking down a deep well, and all you know is that the water goes way down, and that's what their fear did, go way inside them. One of them said, 'You know, we've been here as long back as anyone can remember, and I've seen what they can do, I've seen them take one of us and hang him from the tree, until he be choked to death.' That's all he said, and that was the end for me — I stopped talking, and I went back to working with them on an irrigation ditch."

There is always tension and alternation between the prophetic and the pastoral, the abstract and the concrete. "I have some grand notions in my head," Dorothy Day once noted, "but they often fall by the wayside when I'm sitting at the table talking with one person, hearing all that has happened in that one life." Slowly that SNCC worker figured out how far he'd prod those Delta tenant farmers and how much he'd try to be of help to them with no questions asked, no requests made — just as Dorothy Day learned to know when she was ready "to push things a little."

To some extent, all those called to social and political activism struggle with that tension between the obvious desire to change a situation and the necessary respect for those who have had to endure hardship and have learned to survive as best they can — and who have a hard-earned skepticism of outsiders, whatever their good intentions. The activists who stay the course longest seem to have figured out how far they can go in prodding others, how deep within themselves they must look. They have a mixture of political insistence and introspective tentativeness that allows them to be effective in spite of the ever-present frustrations.

Community Service

In contrast to the young members of SNCC, today's students are likely to express their lofty political and social impulses and practical desires to change the world through community service, even if in limited or modest ways. I have spent many years — since 1978 — working with college students engaged in community service; they tutor the young, keep company with the elderly, visit the sick, run summer camps, design and implement educational programs in prisons, help the medically needy and indigent get hospital care, and argue in the courts on behalf of tenants or workers.[5] Often those students experience the same conflicts or misgivings that deeply troubled the activists of the civil rights era and that now trouble older people working full-time as community organizers.

"I want to help the kids I know," a college junior told me, but he had his eye on what he called "the larger picture." When I asked him to fill me in on the details of that picture, he was both voluble and impassioned. "This entire ghetto is a breeding ground of crime, and someday it has to go! Don't ask me how we'll do it, but until the nation addresses the problems here in this ghetto neighborhood, we'll keep having the troubles, the riots, the problems with drugs and violence. I tutor the kids, and I try to tell them there's a better life for them to lead if they'll only study and do well in school. But they only half-believe me when they're young, and when they become teenagers, they're cynical — boy, are they cynical. I guess I'd be if I was living where they are. It's hard for someone like me to argue against that cynicism, so I try to undermine it. I try to be as thoughtful and helpful as I can. I try to keep teaching, and I try to show these kids that there's another world out there, and it's not a totally bad one or a totally callous one. I take them to Cambridge, and I show them that world, and I hope it rubs off on them."

His words spoke of an earnest dedication to children, even those whose prospects seemed poor. This dedication was enabled not by a fatuous refusal to look at a grim social reality, or by a romanticism that proposed salvation through tutoring and friendship. That young man had taken a close, hard look at the obstacles and had told himself (as his work showed) that one person could give direction to another in a classroom, on a playground.

On the other hand, doubts and misgivings asserted themselves again and again. "Sometimes I think I'm just kidding myself. I think I should forget tutoring and mentoring, and field trips and summer camps, and just go to work as a political organizer, something like that — try to change the whole system. If I was a lawyer — I say that a lot out loud to myself: 'If you were a lawyer . . .' But I never really finish the sentence, because I've seen the law students come here and take on cases, and what they do seems exciting for a while: fighting against lead poisoning, or dangerous stairways, or rats all over the place, or not enough heat in the winter. But you know, it's like a drop in the bucket: this is a neighborhood of thousands of people, and they're locked in — they just don't seem to be able to break out, and the world I belong to, the white world of affluence and power, that world doesn't really want these folks. Maybe it has no use for them, no jobs for them, though there's prejudice, too, plenty of it.

"My dad says, If a black boy really works hard he can make it, he can go to a good school. He's a trustee of one [a fine New England private school], and he says the school goes begging for black kids, but they're hard to come by. I don't think Dad realizes what those kids have been through by the time they're thirteen or fourteen and old enough to go to high school. A lot of them, they've just surrendered. I've taught them; they're smart, plenty of them are, but they're not 'into' school: it's not their idea of something that will lead to anything. That's what they tell me, and then I talk myself blue in the face, but in the middle I can see they're tuning out on me. That's when I tune out on myself and think of politics or the law — but I'll never go into either."

Nevertheless, he persisted. Twice a week he went to a ghetto school, in spite of an extremely busy academic schedule, to teach math to some fifth-graders; sometimes he would bring several of them back to his college dorm for a meal. The commitment was exhilarating as well as exhausting; he took pride in a child's thank you, a child's declaration that she was doing better in school, a child's wide-eyed awe at the sight of a well-known university, followed by questions about how one gets there and where one goes as a graduate.

Soon we will take a sustained look at the emotional ups and downs of those rendering service, but here I want to describe the efforts of one young woman in college who hadn't considered what community service might be until her boyfriend, a seemingly single-minded premed student, mentioned that he was going to be a Big Brother and do some tutoring.

She said, "We were having coffee at the beginning of school, and he told me he was going to be doing community service. I thought it had something to do with politics, maybe, or some charity, like the Community Fund. I remember looking at him in a different way. I'd never seen that side of him.

"Anyway, the more he told me about community service, the more I wanted to do it. So I volunteered — and here I am. I go to the school one afternoon a week. I sit with kids who are having trouble with their schoolwork. I teach reading and spelling. I try to connect with them — that's the first thing you have to do. If you don't, then you might as well go back home and call it quits. I tell them what's happened to me during the week, and I bring goodies, and I've promised the kids that one of these days I'll teach them how to make these oatmeal raisin cookies I make. I bring in some books I used to read when I was their age — well, younger. I can remember Mom or Dad reading the stories to me. It's so sad, though — these kids have never owned a book, never seen a book in their house, never had anyone read to them. They ask me why my parents read to me. I tell them [it was] because they liked to — and they believed reading is important, and it will make a big difference in your life. They aren't convinced, some of them. Others *seem* convinced, but I'm not convinced that they're really convinced. A few — they break my heart — they're really eager, and they're aching, that's the word, *aching* to get out of the ghetto and live someplace else. This girl said to me she wanted to find 'someplace that's safe, where you can wake up and think you're really going to go to bed that night in your house, and not in the hospital or in a funeral parlor!'

"I really work at the spelling. The kids will ask why — what's such a big deal about spelling the word 'commit' with two *m*'s and one *t*? Why not one *m* and two *t*'s? Why not two *m*'s and two *t*'s? Stop being so uptight, they say to me. I sure don't want to be someone who corrects someone else's spelling, a kid said. How did I answer him? I wasn't sure what to say! I tried the 'rules' strategy: we have to go by the rules, so everyone speaks the same way and reads the same words and spells them the same way.

"The kids really pushed me. They said, So long as you can understand what someone writes — understand the words, then that's all that counts! I gave them a speech about order and predictability, but I remembered my uncle saying that George Bernard Shaw wanted to change the spelling of a lot of words, because spelling is so arbitrary and irrational, and I remembered that Flannery O'Connor hated spelling and deliberately didn't spell a lot of words right. I wouldn't want *her* there when I was teaching the word 'commit' or 'commitment'! She'd probably have spoken up, said, 'Hey, I don't have to take this, the way you're spelling that word; I can spell it any which way I want!'"

Yet the young teacher knew that her students needed to learn how to read and write and count and spell; they needed the same educational competence she herself had long ago acquired. She kept working against her students' indifference and surly distrust — and her own sophisticated qualms, her temptation to join those boys and girls, to stoop rebelliously to their cynicism. She kept reminding them and herself that jobs would eventually be at stake, and a distinctly improved standard of living.

"That's what community service is for me, if you want to know: the nitty-gritty of it is getting right in there with the kids, and not only teaching them how to spell 'commit,' and what it means, and 'commitment,' and how to use the word, but getting down in the pit with the kids, and trying to show them you're not some snotty white creep who's loaded with money and wants to make them feel dumb, and then get them to improve, so *she* can feel even smarter than she did before, and be even snottier!

"I'm being vague, I know. What I mean is, you've got to stand up for what you believe in. You've got to tell those kids, Look, this is the English language, and this is how you spell 'commit,' and if you want to be part of our society, our country, then when you see a red light, you stop your car, and when you see someone who is smiling and saying hello, you say hello back, and when you pick up a book, you read it in such a way that you stop if there's a period, and when you write, you begin a sentence with a capital letter, and you spell the word 'sentence' and not 'sentance,' the way my kids there told me they'd like to spell it, and 'commit,' not 'committ.'

"I think they get the message. They may not agree with me, but they realize that I'm putting myself on the line, and trying to reach them and give them some connection to the world of literacy. I really scored when I told the kids that if they knew how to spell 'commit' right, they'd do well in a job if they had to type for someone — and if the person writing misspelled the word, they could say, Hey, that's not spelled right! They got a big kick out of that — the boss-man falling flat on his face. They're used to hearing their parents talk about the know-it-all whites, and how you can't cross them, no matter what. I think they really took to the idea of learning how to spell so you can trip up some honky!"

She was doing her best to enjoy her community service work while at the same time taking it very seriously. That work eventually led to the end of her friendship with her premed classmate. Once, talking about the teaching they did in ghetto schools, he mentioned that this would help him get into medical school. She was appalled — and he was enraged by her dismay and disapproval, her naiveté. Their falling-out affected her work.

"I had more time for the kids. I stopped and asked myself: what do you want to do — jump fast into another relationship or stop for a while and try to figure out what kind of a relationship you want, and meanwhile spend a lot of time with these kids? That way you're becoming *yourself*, not just defining yourself as a college student, or a field hockey player, or someone's girlfriend.

"It was then [after the breakup] that I figured out a way to teach reading better, and spelling. I took a course, and I put more energy and imagination into the class, and there was a big change in the kids: they could see that I was there with them, heart and soul, and they quieted down. When they started making noise, I spoke right up; my voice got tense, and I leveled with them and told them I wasn't there so we could waste time — I had too much respect for them. I really don't think it was *what* I said; I think it was my attitude — my *commitment* (with one *t!*). I told them I thought of them a lot when I read something or saw something on television or heard something over there, back in college, and so they began to pay more and more attention. And then I started making home visits, and did *that* make a big, big difference!"

At first, it made much more difference to her than to the children she was teaching. Her visits to homes were a measure of a new resolution, a step into territory she had only imagined or heard described by the children themselves or by sociologists. Now she was seeing their world firsthand, and now that world lived in her, even when she left it.

"I'd never seen where these kids live, how they live. I'd driven by, but it's another thing to go and walk up those stairs and be in the apartments. I don't want to be overly dramatic; it's not that I had any trouble, or that what I saw was so surprising or shocking. It's just that I finally began to see, right before my eyes, what separated those kids from me. At first, when I started teaching, I thought that if I could just go back a little to my own childhood and draw on it, then I'd make the connections I needed to make, and things would go well. But once I'd started going to the homes, it sunk in that these kids had to cross lots of bridges to get to me and my childhood, never mind me now. You can read a lot in books about 'the culturally deprived child,' but when you're sitting on a couch in a ghetto apartment building, looking and listening and wondering and worrying, then it's another story."

By her senior year she was a leader in her college community service program. She helped other volunteers settle in, helped them as they stumbled and sometimes thought of quitting. She was not interested in the political struggles of the ghetto where she worked, nor did she ever become an "activist," as some of her friends did.

"I'm a teacher here, and it's enough for me to do the best job I can. I have a friend who now wants to go to law school and fight with the school people and fight with the welfare department and fight with the store people and the real estate people. I guess I'm not a fighter. I wish I were sometimes. I'd like to go into court and sue somebody — anybody — for the sake of those kids I teach. But there's room for everybody, I guess. That's what one of the mothers told me when I said I wish I could go and change the world. She said, 'That's all right, you *are* changing the world!' Hearing her say that was like getting all A's on a report card."

I began to realize that she was telling me of more than a shift in activity. To be sure, she had learned how to become more effective, more knowledgeable about the children she intended to inform and even inspire. Yet she herself was being informed and inspired. It was an awakening of sorts, a change of moral direction.

The phrase "community service" these days commonly refers to the work done by young volunteers: high school and college students working in schools, hospitals, soup kitchens, nursing homes, or prisons. They help at camps and on playgrounds, visit homes and neighborhoods with books and instruction manuals, with basketballs and footballs and baseballs. Older people render community service in those same places and in other ways, too. When I talked with men and women at a General Motors factory in Framingham, Massachusetts, I got to know blue-collar and white-collar workers who proudly mentioned their community service. They described work with Boy Scouts, Girl Scouts, Little Leaguers; they talked about their visits to hospitals and nursing homes;

they mentioned cleanup drives, weekend efforts to make streets, parks, and playgrounds clean and attractive.[6]

A thirty-year-old assembly-line worker spoke with great feeling of his weekly visit to a nursing home two miles from his home. "I got into it by a fluke; a buddy of mine had to put his dad away in one of them, and he got all upset. He didn't have much money, and the place wasn't good. The only good thing about it, some people came and read to the old folks, and brought them cookies and cake, and just sat with them and watched TV with them and talked with them. They'd play checkers or cards, nothing fancy, and show them pictures of their family — shoot the breeze. Then my buddy's dad just suddenly died one day, and that was it. But for my friend it was hard to get that nursing home out of his mind. He talked with the priest; he told him he'd wake up in the middle of the night, and he'd be thinking of his dad — that's normal, that's grieving for you — but he'd be thinking of that nursing home, all those folks. It was sad. So the priest said, Maybe the thing to do is go and visit one of those homes, and see if you can be of help, and that way you'll feel you're doing something good, something worthwhile — and it could be a kind of memorial to the old man. And my friend, he really liked that idea.

"So that was how it got started. He talked to me, and I said yes, and he and I went to this nursing home, and we told them we aren't anyone special, but we like to have fun, and we could try to give the folks in there a good time. We could bring them some cookies, and we can sing — I can sing a lot of songs, and my friend plays the piano (no big deal, but the tune gets across!) and we could always read from the papers, if someone was blind or had the shakes and couldn't hold the paper steady. They were glad we came — they said visitors really help the people, and the staff, too. So we started, and we weren't sure at first what we were going to do, and we were nervous, to start, but we just decided we'd be ourselves and try to be as friendly as we knew how, and my wife made these cookies, and I just went and offered them around, and they all told us to come back, and we did, and now we're regulars and we love it — it's part of our lives. You give something, and believe me, you get something back."

He was too modest to mention that he had urged others to

work with the elderly or with young people in trouble with the law, with drugs and drinking. In fact, he always pointed to the initiatives, activities, and good ideas of friends of his, working men who made it their business to give time and energy to others. When a local paper wanted to highlight his volunteer efforts, he insisted that he be mentioned only as part of a group. And he urged that their work *not* be called community service.

"It's more a person-to-person thing, and it's us trying to be friendly to people who aren't having the best of times. I know, it does help everyone — the community — when you go and visit the old folks, but I don't think, of it as service. To me, service means, like, the military, or you're doing something you've *got* to do, or you've been *told* to do it, or you've been *sentenced* to it, because you got in trouble with the law. To me, what we do is — well, it's us trying to offer something from our hearts, only we all got together, and we're organized about it."

He could have been speaking for many of the college students and older people who have the impulse to engage themselves in a broken world and find a place for their moral energy.

Personal Gestures and Encounters

The service provided by programs in schools, colleges, factories, or offices is distinct from the quite private, idiosyncratic initiatives taken by individuals who make a gesture here or find an encounter there that may or may not be repeated. Sometimes a solitary deed represents a response to a singular set of circumstances.

In 1975, during some interviews among well-to-do families in a study of how "privileged" children grow up, I learned from one girl of a family tragedy: her sister had been diagnosed as suffering from acute leukemia.[7] Amid all the fear and sadness of that illness, her mother was awakened to the needs of others as well as those of her own daughter. Until then an avid gardener and golfer, she turned her energies in a new direction, organizing an ambitious and successful drive to secure donations of blood to the hospital's blood bank, taxed by the needs of leukemia patients. Fortunately, her daughter responded to chemotherapy treatment, and the family was able to resume its ordinary rhythms.

Yet for the mother, a particular incident at the hospital proved hard to forget. She had heard a black child from a ghetto neighborhood talk about how hard it was for her and her mother to get to the hospital for her chemotherapy treatments. With no car, they had to take a bus, then a subway, then switch to another bus. They arrived tired and often late for the dreaded treatments. In their shared jeopardy and apprehension, the two mothers got to talking, discussing their daughters' experiences and the drugs they were receiving.

The nine-year-old girl I was interviewing told me, "My mom has become a little different since Alice [her sister] got sick. She has been going to church a lot, and she doesn't worry about the usual stuff — what we eat and whether she's overspent on her allowance! She goes all the way to Roxbury to help that family; they've become her friends."

The girl mused about this shift in her mother's activities and about her new friendship. "My mom is easier to live with these days. She's lost her [bad] temper! She's calm about everything, it seems! She says all this trouble we're having is for a purpose. She loves going to those people [in Roxbury]; she drives them to the hospital and she waits, and then she drives them back. She says she talks with them better than [with] anyone. Daddy is scared because of the neighborhood, but Mom says the people are very nice to her. She says they're nicer than our neighbors, because the people in this town are always minding their own business, and they don't say anything, just keep moving in their cars, but over there, a lot of people don't drive, and they'll stop you on the street and ask you how you're doing, and they seem to mean it."

Eventually that intense coming together of two mothers and two daughters would end. For the white woman of privilege the entire episode — the illness and all it prompted in the family — was "like a dream," meaning "that everything was vivid and almost unreal, and now it's all gone." But she kept up the connection with the black child and her parents.

Her daughter explained, "My mom kept going there [Roxbury], until they stopped going to the hospital because the girl went into remission. They talk on the phone every once in a while, my mom and that lady. The lady says she keeps praying for all of us, and she hasn't even met us, except for Mom and my sister. Daddy says it's good to have someone praying for you — and it's especially good for us, because we don't pray for ourselves! Mom told us she'd never had friends like those people: it's a different kind of friendship. The lady wrote a note and thanked us for all we've done, but she's helped us a lot, too, Mom says — she has a lot of faith in God, and she teaches you a lesson, that you can be poor and have a good soul."

Those last words were a mother's assertion become a daughter's conviction. As to service, it is hard to decide which of the women offered more to the other. The well-to-do white suburban mother went out of her way to offer a service to the black mother: many days of driving in and out of the city. But the black mother extended her own service to these newfound friends of hers — prayers, occasional dishes prepared, and, most of all, an attitude best described by the white mother.

"She gave me a lot to think about. She taught me to have patience. I'm not religious — I'm agnostic, really, so, I can't say I trust in God, the way she kept urging me. But I learned to trust in each day, in my husband and my children — and in her. It was a miracle — *two* miracles: our daughter getting better and meeting those people and going to their home. Every time she tells me how good I've been to her, I get all teary, and I tell her she's been a tremendous gift to us!"

Those gestures back and forth surely constituted a kind of service all the more impressive for its personal and idiosyncratic nature — indeed, its fateful origins. Barriers of race and class yielded to the imperatives of suffering, of uncertainty, of a parent's terror. ("There are white folks who *care*, there really are," said the blac mother again and again, confronting an incredulity earned through the grim lessons of a lifetime.) Though both mothers resumed their ordinary lives, for a stretch of time each extended herself mightily in the other's direction, tried to be of assistance to and learn from the other — a testimony to the redemptive side of suffering.

"I gave her a big hug," the white woman remembered, describing her last meeting with her black friend. They both suspected they might not meet again soon, or ever, but they vowed to keep in touch, and they did, with occasional phone calls and notes.

This extraordinary acquaintance made me think of other friendships I've known that have continued off and on in spite of the challenge of keeping in touch over time. Service can mean a connection that waxes and wanes, yet somehow lives within the individuals.

In brief moments of caring we can give service an everyday life. For every grand and celebrated project, there are no doubt dozens of quiet movements by one person toward others. I think again of six-year-old Tessie, accompanied by federal marshals to integrate a school. Two months into the ordeal, with the mob showing no signs of letting up, she was beginning to wonder how long her daily hecklers would persist. One afternoon when she came home from school, a letter was waiting for her. She had become accustomed to receiving messages of encouragement and praise from near and far. Her name had been in the newspapers; she had lost her anonymity and privacy. The presence of the marshals was testimony to the dangerous public life she lived. This letter was different, though; it was from her own hometown, not Boston or Chicago or California, and it was anonymous and brief:

> Dear little girl,
> I stand there with them and sometimes I've shouted, along with everyone else, but I feel sorry for you, and I wish all this trouble will end, soon. You're good to smile at us, like you do sometimes, and I want you to know I'm praying this will be over, and my kids will soon be back in school with you and the other two.
> Sincerely,
X

That note meant an enormous amount to Tessie and to her parents and both her grandmothers. Out of all her letters, she kept that one in her bedroom, on the bureau. Her mother read it to her many times, as did each of her grandmothers. "I think of that letter a lot," she told me. "It shows you, people will be nice even when you expect the worst of them! I guess that lady wants to change how her people are acting, but she can't, so she's upset. Now when I go to school, I'll glance over at them, and I'll be wondering which one of them is her; and I'll be wondering if there are others like her, thinking as she does, only not daring to open their mouths!

"In church, our minister read the letter out loud, and he gave us a sermon on it. He said, 'Here is someone who has heard God's whisper, and she's writing because of it, and the letter, it's about God beating out the Devil.' I guess so, but it's about her being friendly, even if she's afraid to say it, so she writes, and then she's afraid to tell me who she is. But Granny said she *did* tell me who she is: she's a nice lady, and she was trying to shake my hand, and help me out, and she did, because that's a letter to remind you it'll get over, all this happening now. It might take a long while, but it'll get over."

For the girl's outspoken, passionately religious maternal grandmother, that letter was even more — it was a sign from the Lord, a prophecy, and, not least, a gift: "We're all in His service. He decides to use us, and He does; and we're sure lucky when that happens. That lady, she must have heard Him calling her to be in His service, and she paid attention, and she sat down and spoke from her heart. It doesn't matter whether she gave us her name. It's not the letter, it's the spirit, like it says in the Book. You can sign your name to pretty bad stuff, and you can hold your name in secret and be good, and the Lord will know you anyhow!"

Two long years later, after many white children had returned to the McDonogh School and the mob had long since disbanded and a normal routine had returned to the New Orleans schools, the mother of one of Tessie's homeroom classmates, a white boy who sat across the aisle from her, came to talk with the teacher during school hours about her son's schoolwork. The boy had been having some difficulty, but of late he had started to improve. The mother wanted to thank the teacher. She told the teacher how strange it was to enter a school that for some time she'd observed from the outside as yet another upset parent, angry as could be at what had happened. The mother and the teacher, both lifelong residents of New Orleans, looked back with relief at the city's recent accommodation to the changes mandated by law.

The visiting mother asked the teacher whether she might say just the briefest of hellos to Tessie. Yes, of course that was permissible — and the woman did so. Tessie remembered, "I was doing my reading so that I could be good if I got asked to read out loud. Then I looked up, and this lady, this white lady, was standing right beside me, right over my head. I looked at her, and she looked at me, and she didn't say anything at first, and I didn't know what to say, so I kept quiet. I was going to smile, but I didn't; and then she did, so I did. Then she looked back at the teacher. I thought she was going to turn around and leave me and go to talk with her, but she didn't. Instead, she leaned over and she said she'd written me a letter a long time ago, and she was glad to meet me, and she was glad her son was back in school and not staying out, like everyone was for all that time, and she was glad he was in the same room with me.

"I didn't know what to say, so I just smiled, and then I told her, 'Thank you,' and then she said, 'Thank you,' back to me, and she went up to talk to the teacher. I tried to do my reading preparation, but I couldn't pay much attention to the book, because while I sat there and looked at her and looked at her, I kept thinking of that letter, and I realized *this is her, this is her.*

"I could barely wait to get home, so I could tell my momma and my dad, and my granny, both my grannies. I couldn't believe it was actually happening, but it was, it did. My granny wasn't even surprised. She said the lady had been wanting to meet me, for sure, because she'd tried to shake my hand and pat my back through her letter, and that's how she had sent her friendship, and that's how God does things: He brings people together in 'strange ways,' and they help each other."

That last description, by a woman who seven months later would die, does justice to a certain kind of service: people brought together in "strange ways" end up being of assistance to one another. The "strange ways" may be chance encounters through good luck or bad, or they may occur under the aegis of secular or religious sponsorship. Whatever the prompting circumstances, one human being responds to another in private gestures that morally inform certain lives.

Charity

An old-fashioned name for much that gets called service is, of course, "charity" — a rubric still used by many people in this country. For some of us the word has patronizing implications — toss "them" something called "charity." But for others the word summons the greatest of moral mandates, for as a biblical word it is meant to convey the essence of concern for others and the act of making that concern concrete and generous. "There is charity in my heart for all those poor white folks, shouting at our black children going into 'their' schools," said a New Orleans minister shortly after riots broke out, at the start of the year-long ordeal he was mentioning in his sermon. And Dr. King, I well remember, offered his heart to those he described as "victims of hate." Sometimes he substituted the word "charity" for "heart."

My mother felt that charity was ministration to or advocacy of someone in distress, and she defined the word by recourse to Christ's deeds: His attentiveness to the poor, the sick, the lame, the halt, the blind, the humiliated, and the scorned. Charity for her meant rolling bandages for the Red Cross, reading to a blind person, visiting the sick in hospitals, serving food in a soup kitchen, sewing clothes for needy children. Most of all, she wanted to match such commitments to a manner of being through a smile, a friendly greeting, concern. My father, on the other hand, was critical of comfortable people giving an hour or two here or there and utterly avoiding taking a hard look at how our institutions work (and for whom).

"We don't want your damn charity" was a refrain I heard from many poor people, black and white, in the South and in Appalachia; they were determined to claim as a right what others offered as a gesture of personal generosity. I remember that when migrant workers demanded laws to ensure adequate housing, some growers, who went out of their way to offer decent housing (plenty of growers didn't do so), were angered at what they thought was an unearned rebuke, a lack of gratitude or, as some preferred to call it, "political posturing."[8]

In some quarters, however, a charitable deed is not regarded as condescension or as an artful maneuver to retain political and economic and social control through the distribution of crumbs to an achingly dispossessed population. When I was spending time with factory workers in Framingham, I spent many an evening at church socials or lotteries whose purpose was, without embarrassment, charity — money for a family hit hard by illness or a financial setback. I heard the word "charity" used as a trumpet call to summon time and ethical passion on behalf of someone in need. Not that these people had that much time or money to spare. Many of them held two jobs, and many were "up to the neck in debt." Still, they rallied around those suddenly at the edge or down on their luck.

"I give a lot to charity," a man told me who clocked in his forty hours at General Motors and another twenty at a nearby supermarket warehouse. When I asked for details, I got a lot of them — the earnest compassion a husband and wife felt toward a number of people translated into money given, activities undertaken: "My wife can't say no to someone who is in trouble. She baby-sits for this woman who got sick. She drives her to the market, she picks her kids up from school, she's always in there. And she writes checks, even if they're small, because we live near the red all the time. She has a heart full of charity, the priest says, and I sure agree. Sometimes I wish she had a little less of that charity in her — and the same goes for me. We can't afford what we're giving! Maybe the church should do more and let us off the hook — or the government: a lot of people fall through the cracks!"

Often I heard him struggle to be charitable in his attitude toward various charitable organizations (the Community Fund, the Red Cross, the Catholic church), and often he edged toward the sardonic, if not the derisive, as he contemplated certain ironies. "I know a guy at work whose brother works for the Community Fund, and he's a really stingy guy who won't give a cent of his own money to anyone who's in trouble, my friend says. And then I'll say, You ought to meet this priest I know; he wants us to give to the church, but he's cold, cold — won't give you the time of day, really, and he wants to lecture you, but he's got no heart, no feeling for what you're going through. 'Charity is love,' my mom used to tell us, but love won't feed people if they're hungry, so charity is money, too — and I guess you need all those charity organizations, because they deliver the goods to the starving people in Africa, or if there's a disaster here at home."

He stopped and looked uncertain, as if he didn't quite believe himself. He returned to the feelings he had on Sundays at collection time, when he was torn between the desire to keep the money for his family's needs or give it to others personally and the claim that institutional charity had on him. He let his employer dock his wages for the Community Fund so that "there would be some dough" in the event of a sudden social emergency. There were limits, he kept repeating, to what any individual charity could accomplish, but charitable organizations had their own failures and blind spots. In that regard, and with some pride (maybe too much of it!), he scrutinized some of his friends.

"I see folks I know who give to these big charities, and they don't ask themselves whether their charity is really being used right. Maybe I'm cynical, but I think a lot of what you give gets lost in the bureaucracy." This struggle, obviously, was by no means his alone, nor were his views utterly consistent. Like most of us, one day he embraced a charity of the individual, but the next day he bowed to institutional giving with gratitude or resignation, or both.

Religiously Sanctioned Action

That factory worker knew, of course, all that his church did, yet the constant requests for donations and reminders of crying needs sometimes made him irritated and angry rather than compassionately sympathetic. In church, on his knees, he would make his reconciliation. "I remind myself that they [church officials] are trying, and it's hard for them, too: they're dependent on us for contributions, and not all of us are rich! So I pray, and I give!"

He was especially pleased with the work of the Jesuit Peace Corps because a nephew of his wife's, who went to Georgetown, gave two years of his life to that corps in South America. I talked with him often of the work I saw young college students do under the auspices of that organization and of Protestant and Jewish groups: schools and homes and clinics built; wells and irrigation ditches dug; roads cleared; crops planted and harvested. Volunteers taught children, nursed patients, helped entire towns with regard to public health and sanitation, and launched cooperative ventures.

When I worked in Nicaragua, Honduras, Brazil, South Africa, and Israel, those religiously sponsored programs that brought American youth to impoverished or hard-pressed foreign lands (and to urban ghettos and Appalachia in this country) seemed singularly hopeful in situations where the difficulties were overwhelming.[9] I think now of the nuns who ran a school in Soweto, where my sons taught; I think of the Jesuit Peace Corps members my sons and I met in Nicaragua; I think of the nuns and priests and American college students working in a *favela* of Rio de Janeiro; I think of the young people of many nationalities and religious backgrounds working on the kibbutzim in Israel; I think of religious leaders and their supporters who have given so much of their lives to the poor in our own country. Religiously inspired action is surely a mainstay of service the world over. I sometimes wonder whether some of the better-known secular efforts, such as the work of Cesar Chavez, or government-supported initiatives such as VISTA or the Peace Corps, would have gone as far as they have were it not for the cooperation of religiously connected people and their prior experiments and projects.

A Jesuit friend in Nicaragua felt terribly torn as he labored on behalf of social and political reform while seeing the corruptions and duplicities of the Sandinistas, in whom he had initially placed so much faith. But he blamed himself, he told me. "There is a great danger to this work — you forget who you are and what you believe in and why you're here. You forget the distinction between Jesus and His disciples and the *commandantes*, the political people who shout, 'The people!' — but they have in mind themselves, their power and their ideas. I was so glad to see one dictatorship [Somoza's] fall that I forget about what happens so often: the reformers begin to resemble the very people they fought to overthrow.

"We are caught in the middle. We want to work with the poor, help them live honorable lives, and yet we disapprove of a lot that the government says and does. We especially disapprove of a dictatorship and of the attempt to turn the church into a ward of the government. But I try to forget all that, and I urge the people who come here to work with us [young volunteers from Europe and the United States] to do the same. The more time we spend arguing about politics, the less we'll do. There is so much to do!"

That exclamatory sentence echoes around the world. In Brazil

I heard those same words from some nuns and the volunteers who helped them run a favela soup kitchen and ambulatory medical clinic. "There is so much to do" — and they welcomed those who wanted to help with open arms. Several Americans just out of college lived in extremely modest quarters at the edge of the favela and worked with the street children who used the favela as a base of operations for forays into Copacabana and Ipanema to hustle various objects (many stolen) or, alas, to hustle themselves.

A recent graduate of Notre Dame, who had lived in a small Nebraska town in a solid, happy home, found the work he did challenging as well as wrenching. "I try to get to know the kids. Once they sight you a few times, you're part of their lives to some extent. They're suspicious, but they're interested: who is *he*, what's *his* hustle? They find out we're hustling food — soft drinks and candy — and if the kids are really serious about eating (and that's a good sign — some trust) sandwiches and soup and a big hot meal. We travel with them all the way up the ladder from a Coke or a Pepsi to mashed potatoes and chicken! We're also hustling clothes, if they want them. A lot of the kids don't trust us enough to take our food, not at first, and they'd like the clothes, but they hold back there, too. They're proud, and they're suspicious, and they're scared, in equal portions. I feel so inadequate at times, but I keep as busy as I can; I keep doing the work."

He and several others were giving a year of their lives to a world that alternately horrified and fascinated them. They were also using the occasion for much soul-searching through religious retreats, daily church attendance, and discussions about the work they were trying to do. Throughout the Third World nuns and priests and lay brothers mix with volunteers in similar programs, and Protestants have their own such projects.

In this country, ministers aided by parish members have rallied across lines of race, class, and region to bring food and clothing to needy "sister" parishes and to suffering communities near and far. Even ten-, eleven-, and twelve-year-old children try to help.

I think of a Protestant Sunday School teacher in a Boston suburb who enlisted sixth- and seventh-graders to carry food packages, collect clothing, and become summer hosts to children living under great duress in an urban ghetto. The minister told me something about what they were doing and why. "It is selfish, I know — *we* are the obvious beneficiaries of all this. Our children escape their suburban cocoon and learn how the world goes for others who are not as lucky as they are. I have to forget that, though; I have to assume that we are put here by the good Lord to reach out to others — that is our mission, as it was His. I tell our youngsters and their parents that what we are doing, this voluntary activity, is an expression of our Christianity. This is who a Christian is: someone who doesn't sit back and say, I go to church on Sundays, so I'm a Christian, but someone who remembers how Jesus lived and tries hard to follow His lead.

"There's a respectful, sensitive way of doing all this, I hope and pray — and that is important for our children to realize. The last thing the kids in a ghetto need is for snotty kids from a suburb to come into their neighborhood — *invade* their neighborhood — in order to show how smugly virtuous they are. We spend a lot of time trying to look at *ourselves*, never mind the black people and the Puerto Rican people we're going to meet.

"I'm often asked what kinds of lessons we teach our children about the inner city and the people who live there. I answer, Most of our teaching is about ourselves. If we can look at the kind of people we are, and what we're hoping to get from this kind of charity, then we'll stand a better chance of behaving ourselves out there with the people we meet. No, we don't emphasize psychology too much. I try to take a lot of the initial burden on myself; these are kids, and they need all the help (and leadership) they can get. I'm personal with them — even confessional, though I try not to overdo it.

"I try to bring the life of Jesus into our classroom talks. I write a list on the blackboard of what Jesus did, and I write down a lot of direct quotes from Him, out of the Bible. Then I ask the children again and again, Who was He, what did He do, and why did He live as He did? I don't have the answers, and I tell them that — but to ask is to begin to know something, right then and there. Once you start taking His life seriously — what He did, and the people He wanted to be with and help — then you're not worshiping Him in the rote way that tempts all of us. A church service can be such an escape; you ignore His warnings and stories and the suffering He experienced and the reasons for it! I mean, all of that goes in one ear, out the other!

"I knew I was getting somewhere — *we* were getting somewhere — one day when a ten-year-old girl said, 'Even if we never go over there to Roxbury, we have to be grateful to the people there for all they've done for us!' There was a moment, after she spoke, of absolute silence — not a fidgety body in that room. Then they all started nodding, and a couple of kids said, 'Amen,' and no one needed an explanation, an exegesis of what that child, that *preacher*, had told us!" The lessons those children learned are important for older volunteers as well, as ministers and priests know.

The Hebrew prophets, too, had intense concern for the poor, the hurt, the oppressed. A rabbi who helps some high schoolers contribute their energies to less fortunate people described his initial task in this manner: "These are really well-meaning young people. They have the Jewish tradition of justice in them. They want to right wrongs, do good, even make amends for the indifference or worse of earlier generations. It's touching to hear them talk — good kids who want to put their bodies on the line for the values they've learned to appreciate and claim for themselves. I'm always worried they'll be disenchanted — they'll go to a neighborhood that is dangerous, and they'll be overwhelmed. They might even get into trouble. I have to keep cautioning them. But somehow we manage! We read from Isaiah and Jeremiah, we read from Exodus, we read from Ecclesiastes and from Proverbs and the Psalms both before and after we go.

"I want to connect our Jewish moral and spiritual tradition to this philanthropy we do, this good deed for the day, a mitzvah! We mustn't be too pleased with ourselves, as I'm afraid I am right now! That is the big risk — the big egos, the self-satisfaction. I warn myself about all the dangers right in front of the kids, and they listen, get the message — sometimes! I try to make clear that we're Jews, struggling to live the way our great teachers, our great rabbis, told us we should live, so if we go to help others, *how* we go matters as much as (maybe more than) what we bring. If we can learn that lesson and take it to heart, we're at least on the right track. God is our witness, so we have to try hard to be worthy of that — I say to myself, and out loud, so the kids can hear. A boy whose older brother is in the Peace Corps said to me the other day: 'I am beginning to see that we're a *Jewish* Peace Corps and that's different from the regular one!' I was delighted. I only added, 'Different, not better!' He smiled!"

As I heard that mix of deserved pride and caution, I remembered how Dorothy Day would acknowledge the religious motivations of her work yet at the same time worry that she was claiming too much for it. Religiously inspired service often has to contend with potential moral jeopardy. Today's men and women want to do good without losing that most important quality, humbleness of heart, whose absence can undercut all the money in the world, all the time a person takes, all the efforts made.

Government-Sanctioned Action

Many of us are keenly aware of the differences between the efforts of religious groups and the secular idealism or meliorism that for thirty years has informed the Peace Corps and, for almost that length of time, VISTA. Each volunteer has particular reasons for wanting to be part of a domestic or foreign program geared to practical good works, although in my interviews with these mostly young people certain themes were repeatedly expressed.[10]

Over and over, my students who have chosen to work in the Peace Corps or VISTA mention the importance of the government's connection to these efforts — and they often do so in an ironic fashion. "I was going to go to some graduate school, professional school, but I decided to hold off. I wanted to be away from the academic world, and I wanted to do something that would take me away from my own endless questions about what I should do with my life. There were lots of possibilities, but the Peace Corps is something that makes you feel proud to be an American — and there isn't a lot else these days [1986] that will give you that feeling! The country has been taking such a knocking for the last twenty or thirty years — the Vietnam War, the assassinations, the CIA plots, J. Edgar Hoover and his FBI schemes, Watergate, Irangate

— very disillusioning! My grandfather fought in the Second World War, and he was wounded. He was so proud to be in the army then. My dad says we haven't had a war like that since — just troubles of all kinds here and abroad, and lots of lies and deceptions and double-talk. When I joined the Peace Corps, everyone in my family was really happy. This country needs the Peace Corps, my grandfather said, because there has to be *something* connected to the government that isn't fake and full of sleaze or waste.

"I'm being too hard on America! We've tried so long to help other countries, with the Marshall Plan and the millions, the *billions*, in foreign aid. But I do think the Peace Corps is a chance for our plain, ordinary people to step up to the plate and say, Hey, I'm an American, and I want to show what this country has enabled me to do: come and be with you folks and teach or help build a road or help make your farming more productive, or your water drinkable, or your sanitation better than it's been.

"I'm not saying I was on cloud nine the whole two years. There were plenty of lonely times and plenty of disappointments, but I'd recommend the experience to my best friends — I already have! — and I'd do it again myself, if the time was right for me. In a way, I've been thinking, it was the only time I really felt I was tied in to my government and to the history of this country — all the 'civic virtues' you read about when you're studying the American Revolution and the Founding Fathers and what they believed: Jefferson and Madison and the Adamses.

"I actually re-read my American history when I was abroad [in Ecuador], and I even taught some to the kids in the village where I lived. I think they would have done all right in a quiz on the Revolutionary War, why it got started, and the Civil War, our struggle over slavery. I showed the kids a picture of Abraham Lincoln, and he became their hero, too. One of them asked me if Abraham Lincoln was the one who got the Peace Corps going! I had to get him to learn his dates: *1860* to *1865*, not *1960*! To those kids, 1960 was a century ago. Actually, to those kids, dates mean very little. They live in the present, and they don't have dates for the present. There is just sunrise and sunset and then another sunrise, and the events that take place during the day or at night. You're not in the Peace Corps long, even as a teacher, before you realize that a big part of your job is to learn from the people you're with: they teach you and you teach them."

His remarks, calling upon sociology and history and anthropology, were not explicitly moral or spiritual. But indirectly he and many others have been prompted to reflect upon what their country means to them, not to mention what they are hoping their initiatives will mean to others. The Peace Corps turns into a place where Americans become as wrapped up in their own country, through their reflections about what they are doing, as in the cultures of other countries.

People who sign up with VISTA are in a rather unique working situation, one that in obvious ways is unlike that of the Peace Corps. To work at home in the midst of rural or urban poverty is to struggle constantly with national politics and priorities. I first met VISTA workers in Appalachia in the late 1960s, and I realized fairly soon how tense and conflicted they could be as they worked *for* their government even though commonly feeling at odds with it.[11] They did not find it easy to accommodate to this conflict, and sometimes it was not possible. Critics of VISTA have been more than a few times proven right in a way. Young men and women volunteers become outraged by what they see and hear, and the result is estrangement or bitterness and defiance; the government — local or state or federal, or all three — becomes the enemy. That is not always or necessarily so, but there is a good deal of tightrope walking.

One woman, a twenty-four-year-old graduate of a southern university, said, "I've been in VISTA six months [in West Virginia] and I wonder if I'll last. All I've learned is how rotten the county system of government is, how corrupt. I never really knew how government works; where I come from, you have very little to do with government. You pay your taxes, and if there's trouble, you call the police or the fire department, and you send your kids to school — unless you choose private schools, and a lot of folks do. Here government is *the* major industry, along with coal — and government is tied up with the coal industry, lock, stock, and barrel. The sheriff is a big, big deal — and he's a crook through and through. No one dares cross him. The people — they are *so* poor, *so* at the mercy of the county folks, who control the school buses, the welfare payments, the road maintenance programs, *everything*. You start acting independent, and your kids don't get to school — no bus comes — and the road leading up the hollow begins to die, and no one does anything, and you begin to realize you've had it! For someone like me, who is apolitical, or *was*, this was quite an education.

"That's why I've been reading up on politics and talking with some community organizers. I can't just tune out — not when I realize this is *my* country, and these people are American citizens like me. Of course, the big point is that they're *not* like me! I now know that. I have a friend, she's in VISTA on an Indian reservation, and is *she* learning the same lesson! She writes me letters that make me realize that there's a lot I didn't learn in those government courses and political science courses in college. Every once in a while I get really down — I remember that I'm just a volunteer, and I'll be out of this soon, very soon, but for the people I'm working with, this is life. If you're in the Peace Corps, you can just say, Hey, I'm lucky to be an American. Here, doing this, there are moments when I'm afraid I say, Hey, I'm ashamed to be an American! Maybe I'm exaggerating a little, but not totally."

The vicissitudes she spoke of reminded me that each effort to be of service offers particular satisfactions and special hazards. Volunteers working under private auspices retain a degree of freedom that those connected to the government may sorely miss. Those doing secular work don't have to contend with the challenges and constraints posed by the clergy in some cases. I think of the volunteers who were appalled by the number of children in favela families and who very much wanted to offer birth control information to the mothers — only to be told no by the nuns with whom they were working. On the other hand, to work for the government is to deal with other constraints, notably the relationship between "our" government and that of the country or county where one is working.

No matter the kind of service being rendered, the sponsorship, the age and background of the person who is volunteering, and the nature (and location) of the work being done, the ultimate worth of the effort will depend a good deal on how a particular person manages to connect with those others being in some way taught or healed or advised or assisted: the chemistry of giving and receiving as it works back and forth between individuals in one or another situation. "Each morning brings its satisfactions, its hazards," Dorothy Day once said of her work. She only gradually learned to distinguish between the two, recognizing the disappointments (some of which masquerade as apparent success stories) and recognizing, too, the moments of mastery, of achievement (which sometimes come across to the volunteer and observers as not very important at all). With hesitation and bewilderment, we struggle to make sense of those ups and downs and of how they get worked into the life of service — not without a nod, however, to a kind of service some Catholic Workers tend to ignore or regard critically, to say the least.

Service to Country

For two years I served as a captain in the United States Air Force. I was taken into the military under the old doctors' draft law, now no longer in existence: all of us physicians had to give time to the army, the navy, the air force, or the public health service. I had gone through my psychiatric residency, had embarked on psychoanalytic training, and so was put in charge of a major unit at Keesler Air Force Base in Biloxi, Mississippi. It was there that I first lived among Southerners, and it was there that my life changed, as a consequence of the riot-plagued onset of school desegregation in nearby New Orleans. It was there also that I began to realize how significantly patriotism can inform a person's life, causing a man or woman to give a great deal to the nation he or she so evidently loves.

I wasn't using a tape recorder in those days or taking notes in response to interviews, but I was talking with a lot of men and women who weren't in the military just because they wanted a job (or couldn't find or adjust to one on the "outside," as civilian life was often called). Certainly there were plenty of those — individuals whose cynicism more or less matched, I regret to say, my own:

I'm here for whatever reason and I'll make the best of it. But there were some whose passion for the United States of America was heartfelt and sometimes eloquently, if informally, rendered.

I still remember, for instance, some of those nights when I had to do emergency ward duty (all of us doctors rotated through that service) — the late-night bull sessions we had: nurses, social workers, administrative personnel, all in uniform, all trying to get through yet another long night. At times we were rushed, irritated, frustrated. But now and then one of the career people (as opposed to a draftee like me) would stop us all for a few seconds, remind us what the air force meant, what we were there to do — sing a hymn, of sorts, to America, and one I sometimes in my mind readily dismissed, thereby ignoring or derogating some powerful and honestly cherished sentiments, even as I was eagerly prepared to listen to the sentiments of people I'd come to know in cosmopolitan New Orleans, who wore no uniforms and had little use for those who did. (In a few years, of course, the Vietnam War would make such distinctions of attitude even more prevalent and significant in our national life.)

As a consequence of those moments, I think I did begin to sense how serious is the devotion a nation can command. Later, as I became the self-conscious observer and interviewer, the researcher, I met, in the South and elsewhere, men and women who were not in the military (some had finished their tours of duty), who made clear to me how the word "patriotism" transcended rhetoric (and its dangers), how it became translated into acts of service meant to honor a nation and respond to its needs.

I think of men and women who bought government bonds not only in their own interest (in several senses of the word) but from a citizen's sense of obligation. I think of men and women who have taken time to clean the grounds of a town's post office or who work to keep national parks clean or volunteer to fight fires in them; who speak of land or water or air pollution not as a private matter but as a national one, to be solved on behalf of the whole country and its people. I think of those who send money to the government apart from taxes, or who cook and serve food to servicemen and women in USO clubs, or who send money to fellow Americans hit hard by disaster, and, of course, of those who in times of national danger declare themselves ready to give their lives, if necessary, on behalf of their country. Nor are many Peace Corps members or VISTA members unable to mobilize such sentiments — a regard for their country's purposes, vulnerabilities, requirements.

Nations summon a range of passions from men, women, and children — and if some of those passions lead to banal exhortation, to the meanest and most parochial of sloganeering, others encourage sacrifice on behalf of people near and far. For a growing number today, the world itself, this planet that we occupy, becomes the biggest country of all — its continued life a source of anxiety, its needs something to be urgently addressed, as I am constantly reminded by students who join organizations meant to protect everyone's environment, the air, the oceans, and natural life the world over.

· THREE ·

Satisfactions

T HE FIRST CIVIL RIGHTS activist and SNCC member I met did not belong to the "office group," as some called it, who worked out of Atlanta, but was a young black student, Dion Diamond, who had taken leave from the University of Wisconsin to work in Louisiana, where he had relatives. A black New Orleans lawyer, A. P. Tureau, had become a friend of mine; he was the NAACP Legal Defense Fund's representative in Louisiana, and he knew well the four black children who initiated school desegregation and with whom I was talking twice a week. I met Dion at Tureau's home and later in a Baton Rouge prison, where Dion had been jailed on grounds of "disturbing the peace" — for attempting to have lunch at a restaurant that wanted no part of black customers. I was to testify on his behalf. Curiously, the local prosecutor had decided to call him "unstable" and possessed of an "anti-social personality," hence his lawyer's decision to ask me to interview him and later tell the court what I thought of his "personality."[1]

As I sat in the prison's visiting room and heard the tall, thoughtful, sensitive, hard-working man tell of the extreme danger he'd been facing, voluntarily, in hopes of seeing an end to segregation in Louisiana, I wondered, first to myself and then out loud, what gave him the strength to keep going. He was in constant danger, and in 1962 there wasn't the national backing and attention that coalesced behind the Mississippi Summer Project of 1964. Often he was working alone, and there was a distinct possibility that one day he'd be found alone and dead.

The psychiatrist in me was posing questions to him, for I knew that in court similar questions would be posed. I said, "Dion, your ideals and values apart, I'm wondering why you keep at this, given the danger and the obstacles." In fact, I had a lengthier wind-up to the question, because I didn't want him to think I was insinuating that there was anything psychologically wrong with his choice of activity — the line of reasoning that the county prosecutor was pursuing. I knew that even in friendly hands, a question about motivation can be regarded as an implied judgment: Hey, you, what *is* your problem, why *do* you behave this way, do these things? (Not everyone is prepared to turn the tables on the questioner: Hey, you, what is *your* problem, always asking people things, always wanting to know why *they* do as they do?)

In any event, I was stopped in my well-meaning tracks by the young man's three-word reply: "The satisfaction, man." I'm afraid my imagination then was rather limited. I could think of few possible satisfactions for him. Dion had been telling me about how tough his work was, how lonely at times, how frightening at other times, and, worst of all, how discouraging — the suspicion he encountered from black people, who knew well the dangers of trying to integrate a lunch counter or a motel and who were not reluctant to be psychologically skeptical of him: Why *are* you here among us, urging us to do what might eventually mean that we get shot at or arrested?

When I asked him about those "satisfactions," he said, "I'm meeting some really fine people. I'm listening to them tell me a lot about their lives. I'm hearing them stop and think about what they're willing to do to change this world here in Louisiana. Isn't that enough — isn't that a good reason to feel satisfied? If you can spend some of your life doing work like this, then you're lucky! There may be a sheriff out there waiting for me with a gun, but if he gets me, I'll die thinking: Dion, you actually *did* something —

you were part of something much bigger than yourself, and you saw people beginning to change, right before your eyes, and that was a real achievement, and that's what I mean by 'satisfaction.'"

Something Done, Someone Reached

To this day I go back to that young man's appraisal of himself and others — of a volunteer effort and its satisfactions. Dion kept telling me what he was trying to *do*; he kept describing for me the various individuals he was getting to know — the lives he was affecting, even as his own life had already been deeply affected. I wanted to know about his earlier life. I asked about any "troubles" he may have had, any brushes with the law (or with my kind of doctor); about the ways he was handling the terrible stresses of being, in essence, a front-line warrior, taking on tough, sometimes murderous, local and state power. He was polite, even deferential, but also determined to let me know how he spent his time and what his experiences had come to mean for him. He was also willing, in his quiet, unassuming manner, to ask me to become a student of his. Several times he asked whether I would be interested in visiting the communities where he had been working, meeting "the folks," as he called them.

I felt that he was trying to divert me from his "problems," his "attitudes," his "feelings," his "mood," his "thought content," in favor of his "daily rounds," as he called them. I wasn't averse to hearing about those rounds, but I wanted to know why he chose such a clinical word: were a lot of the people he visited sick in some way? He laughed, told me he didn't think his friends were any sicker than "the rest of the people in Louisiana." He wondered whether anyone had studied, psychiatrically, the segregationists, the people to whom he was *persona non grata* — the sheriffs and their deputies, the officials who ran the schools and the voter registration offices, the businessmen and professional people in the county. "They're all ready to call me nuts at the drop of a hat, and now they have me in jail, and they're pushing the judge to call me a sociopath or something, a first-class screwball, maybe, but no one is looking at *them*! What's wrong with *their* heads? They're full of hate and prejudice, and they say awful things about anyone who doesn't look like them and belong to their race and their class!"

I was beginning to crumble inside, to share his grave doubts about how my profession is used to sort people, judge them, even condemn them. But for a while I tried to put up the solid exterior of the friendly and interested doctor who nevertheless was firmly rooted in the "reality principle," as it is put in psychiatry.[2] I pointed out that those county officials whose sanity he questioned were people of power — indeed, they had him in jail — and I suggested we try to be rid of them, make a winning case against them, rather than try to confront them as he wished us to do. Anyway, I noted, I doubted that they would agree to subject themselves to the kind of psychiatric scrutiny he wanted.

He agreed, though he clearly was interested intellectually in challenging my mind — which, I only gradually realized, *he* was "evaluating" and, in his quiet fashion, trying to strip down to its bare-bones, class-connected and race-connected assumptions.[3] He did, however, graciously let me press my conventional psychiatric questions (the taking of a "history"), and waited until I was evidently finished to resume his suggestion, variously tendered, that I spend some time with him as a civil rights "field secretary" — see what he was doing, and with whom.

Eventually I testified in court, as did others, and he was let free — with a warning from the bench that he would do well to return to Wisconsin and college life. Shortly afterward, I took Dion up on his suggestion to accompany him. Our visits to the rural homes of the "folks" he had mentioned were not easy ones to make. I left my car in Baton Rouge and went with him in his car — followed, almost always, by a police car. I knew the police were looking for any excuse to arrest him again. He made light of it, called them "my friends." He drove so circumspectly that I became aware of every road sign and of the speed he was maintaining, however low. He kept looking in his rear-view mirror, smiling. When he signaled a coming turn with his left arm and hand, I had the feeling he was trying hard to be the obliging child to fiercely punitive parents, ever ready to take out the strap — or their pistols.

He was also turning the whole exercise into a parody, but not a joke; he was the "suspect," and they were his pursuers, constantly on his trail. He also told me how lucky he was to have me with him: "They know you from the trial. They think of you as a New Orleans doctor, and they'll not want to bother me while you're around." I smiled, but he zeroed in directly on the ultimate humiliation of all this. "They watch their step with you, and even with me — the 'Wisconsin boy,' they call me — but they'd shoot a local Negro here anytime; they've told me that! The Negroes tell me that, too — and when they do, I feel so ashamed for everyone, for the United States and for all the Negro people here in Louisiana, who have to live with the knowledge that their lives have no meaning at all legally: they are noncitizens, I'd even say nonpeople, to the police, to the sheriff and his deputies, the ones who supposedly are 'the law.'"

Nevertheless, Dion was only occasionally given to such grim, melancholy, and penetrating critiques — to a barely suppressed moral indignation, which used irony, and again, parody, most of the time for its expression. As we went into the unsubstantial (sometimes all too flimsy) homes of these small-town and country people, I noticed his face light up. These families, a number of them tenant farmers, were nearly penniless, living hand to mouth. Because of our escort, the police, we brought along plenty of fear and anxiety — as if those folks didn't already have enough to worry about with the daily insults and threats that constituted their experience of "law and order" in that segregationist world.

Yet in no time, as we sat and nursed our Cokes and Pepsis and 7-Ups and orange sodas ("Now, Mister Doctor, what can we do you with . . ."), I began to see legs stretching, arms folding or falling back in relaxation, facial muscles constructing smiles; I began to hear jokes and stories and laughter — some of it the sharp, dry, bitter laughter of people who didn't know whether to be amused by their difficult lives or cry out their hearts on that account. I also began to hear music: people singing, strumming guitars, hitting old upright pianos. I began to hear, finally, plenty of exhortation: the Old and New Testaments summoned lest, as one field hand put it, "we forget all those who knew pain before we were ever even near being born." The biblical themes of exile and return, of suffering and redemption, of mystery and revelation, and the biblical view of the powerful as suspect, the lowly as destined to sit close to God, in His kingdom — these were subjects close to the heart of men, women, and children caught in the most unpromising of earthly lives.

As we went from home to home — it was summer, the weather was hot and humid, and there were no air conditioners to help out — I began to understand how much this young activist from up North meant to the people receiving us and, conversely, how much they meant to him. I also learned to appreciate what he meant when he spoke from deep within himself.

"I tell you, this is a real *privilege*; I am doing something useful with people who are the salt of the earth! Every day I thank my lucky stars — I thank God — for the good fortune to be here, going from home to home, sitting and listening to these folks tell their stories, being fed by them, being taught by them. You asked me yesterday why I do this, and I could recite the civil rights line, and I believe it — that our people aren't free, and that we have to fight for our freedom, especially here in the segregated South. To be absolutely honest, I came here to spend a month working on a voter registration project, but I've stayed here because I love what happens when I go visit these folks. Every day I learn something from them — about gospel music, about how to put in a good vegetable garden, about the history of the Mississippi Delta and upstate Louisiana, about all the tricks of the local whites, and remember, the Negroes here know *everything*: they have eyes and ears in every white home, and the reports come filtering back every night.

"It's what I get accomplished, the people I reach and who get to me: that's why I'm here. We have a growing movement here of men and women who really want to work together to break the back of the whole segregationist power structure. They meet in the basement of a church, and they sing and pray — and they also talk hard, tough politics. 'It's your baby,' one of the men said to me, about the 'club,' they call it, 'the freedom club.' Talk about why I do this work! I'll have to leave — but I'll never really leave for good. The way I see it, this is the most important educational experience I'll ever have. People say, 'Hey, man, you're into fighting with cops.' I answer, If you don't take on the cops, then you're into something else: surrendering to cops! So we're for sticking to our original purpose here — getting more and more people to become voters — and I'm staying because I get the satisfaction of seeing the baby grow and being with all the folks, a huge family.

"You know what? You look at those cops now — they've begun to respect us! They don't give us that big belly laugh anymore, they don't spit at us or sneer at us. They look real serious when they follow us around. And the other day, I couldn't believe it, one of them, he nodded at me and two of my buddies when we came out of the store. It was as if — well, hey, we sure do know each other! I thought I saw just the beginning of a smile on his face — just the start of one. You want to know why I do this work? To see that look on that cop's face!"

Over the years I have heard his sentiments echoed many times — the enthusiasm and pleasure, the exhilaration that accompany action taken, and the consequences of such action: deeds done, people very much touched, and in return, quite eager to return the favor, through dozens of reciprocal gestures, remarks, initiatives.

Moral Purpose

In a modest, unselfconscious way, Dion was regarding himself and that policeman as historical figures: a pair of protagonists worthy of a moment of notice — each of them a witness to social change as well as a participant in it. As I listened to him, I remembered reading *Middlemarch* and *War and Peace* in college — the effort of George Eliot and Tolstoy to render a time, a place, a series of events, through the concreteness of character portrayal, through narrative attention to ordinary people, as well as to the exceptional ones, those with money, power, privilege. Here were two minor figures in an unfolding national drama — yet each of them intuitively knew well what was happening not only to themselves, but countless others: a smile marking a crack in what hitherto had been called "a way of life." No question that for many volunteers the considerable satisfaction that goes with making a connection with a fellow human being is enhanced by the overall context of the service being rendered. They have sought, found, and fulfilled a moral purpose. For this young political activist, the moral purpose was obvious: he was engaged in a struggle against the tyranny of segregation. But all service is directly or indirectly ethical activity, a reply to a moral call within, one that answers a moral need in the world.[4]

The manner in which a moral purpose is worked into a particular volunteer's life will vary enormously. Some volunteers are at pains to insist (to themselves, let alone others) that what they are doing *is* a moral effort and that what they get from their actions is a kind of moral satisfaction or peace — a moral hunger assuaged. Others wave aside the moral underpinnings of their actions, emphasizing instead the friendships they have made, the boredom overcome. Even when pressed about the good they are doing, they demur, as did Gary, a college student who became a Big Brother to a youngster whose family had recently arrived from the Dominican Republic.

"I enjoy leaving this place [a college community] and I love going to the neighborhood where he lives — the sights and sounds and smells. I suppose some people would want me to wear my heart on my sleeve and to say I feel sorry for all the people there and I'm trying to help them — but I don't like that word 'help,' I really don't. When people tell me they admire what I'm doing, I go ballistic; I say they should compliment my friend Juan and his family for being nice enough to put up with me! They let me come visit them. They feed me. They help me with my Spanish. I've always wanted to work in Latin America — a business, a bank, maybe. This way I sharpen my street Spanish. I get to shoot baskets; I learn all about a neighborhood — who makes money doing this or doing that. I know where to place bets. I know where to buy the best food, and where the best places to eat are. When I go to visit Juan, I learn by walking, listening to him and his friends, seeing all there is to see through his eyes and through my own."

Gary also acknowledged the boy's problems and indicated that Juan had an angry, sullen side that could flare up unexpectedly. Once that admission is made, more can be allowed. A volunteer who has insisted on presenting himself as a grateful recipient of the personal and cultural largesse of others changes tack, reluctantly it seems, tells of the darker side of his experiences, even as that narration, ironically, enables him to get nearer to the very real breakthroughs he has witnessed as an older friend to someone who has needed almost desperately what a relaxed but thoughtful student has provided.

"We take walks — that's the best. He acts like he owns the whole world. He points out everything to me — it's better than a lecture here. But all of a sudden, he'll see someone, or he'll notice something in a store window, and he becomes a different person. He looks so grim! He doesn't talk, he just stares ahead. Then I try to draw him out. I talk. *I* start pointing things out. I ask him questions — anything to get him, get *us* out of this mood. It works, but it takes a lot out of me. It's then that I begin to realize how hard this kid's life is. I know that the man he calls Dad is his stepfather, and he beats him up really badly; that his mother is a heavy drinker, and she tunes out, to the point that they all don't know what to do with her. It sounds like she goes into a trance and then, all of a sudden, she clears, and she's back to normal. His sister is sleeping around at fifteen, having dropped out of school; and a younger brother has epilepsy, the serious kind. Not a pretty picture!

"I'll be honest — I'm surprised at myself some days, because I'll hear me giving Juan a really strong lecture. I'll tell him that he's fighting for his life and that if he doesn't watch out, he'll end up drowning. You may think I'm stepping outside my bounds; I'm only nineteen years old, and I'm a history major, and I've never even taken a psychology course, so what do I know! But when you see someone floundering, and you're afraid he's going to go under, then you sure try your damnedest to throw out every lifesaver you can think of!

"I have been trying to be a friend to Juan, and I've tried to give him some direction. I don't mean that I preach sermons, rant and rave. I wouldn't last a minute with him or his neighborhood friends, if I *told* him what to do, told them. But I play basketball with him and his friends, and there are times when we just stand around after some serious playing, shooting the breeze, and it's then that I show my hand. I start in casually, talking about how you've got to realize that you either take responsibility for your life and try to find some direction you're headed for or, if you don't, you'll be at the mercy of other people, and believe me, if *they're* going to be deciding what you're going to do — then *forget it!*

"The gist of my message is that you either get pushed and pulled by all these other folks, or you take charge yourself. That's what I keep hitting Juan with, and he does listen. The more I talk, the more I realize *I'm* listening, too! A lot of what I'll tell him and his buddies — it's what my dad told me, and my mom, and her dad. Basically I'm trying to connect those kids with the middle-class world I come from. I don't say it the way I heard it at home, but the heart and soul of my own values, that's what I'm advocating. I have no illusion that I'm this kid's savior. I'm not sure Sigmund Freud could save him either. There's only one person who can save him — that's what I keep hammering away at. When I come at him like that, Juan listens. He even nods his head. I feel a little optimistic. But hell, I know the odds, and the more I come to see him, the better I know the odds.

"When I'm through, and we've had our pizza or something, and I'm ready to say good-bye, I look him right in the eye, and I say, 'Keep trucking, man'; and he says, 'Yeah.' Once in a while he'll say, 'I will.' That makes my day — my week! I feel I've actually done something with my life — for someone else, not just me, me, me: the big me that we all celebrate in this place![5]

"I don't know how you persuade someone who is a stranger, except for an hour or two a week, to dream about a different life and then go to work to try to get there. But *underneath it all*, that's what should be happening between Juan and me. It's my voice that might be of help — that's the conviction I have to feel. I've got to be as sensitive as can be — as *clever*. I don't mean to sound like a con artist, but you have to figure out how to do an end run around all the enemies — everything that is pulling down, down, down on this kid's life, and to do that, as they say, 'ain't easy, man.' I haven't found the way — but I have found, I think, a general direction. I keep saying my piece, even if I sound like the boring professor who repeats himself every lecture.

"The more I say what I think, what I believe — well, the more I really *do* believe it! That's the big irony, and I'm afraid to mention it even: that all of this volunteering, this 'do-good work,' one of my cynical friends calls it, will end up being a big boost for my morale and my life. That same guy says, 'You're doing that for your brag-sheet.' I get really furious at him, but I don't give him the pleasure of seeing how I feel. It's true — sure, it'll be nice to list this on my CV; but damn it, I could just go through the motions here. I could show up every week — every *other* week, every third week — and buy my way out by going to a pool hall with Juan and playing pool, or playing cards, or just having a Coke, and pretty soon I could say, 'I have to go, Juan, so have a nice week.' I'd have my community service record for the CV. Maybe that's part of what motivates us [to do such work], but it doesn't take long (I'll speak for myself, and I'm not bragging, I'm *worrying*, actually), it doesn't take too long for something else to get going: what I've been talking about. You become a link for these kids, but you become self-conscious about it, and that means you're putting yourself on the ropes, asking yourself the big questions, so you'll be able to do the same with your Little Brother."

Gary kept addressing the irony that he himself was the moral beneficiary of an involvement with a Little Brother. He was looking intensely inward, groping hard to clarify his own beliefs and values so that he could try to stand by them in his conversations with Juan, and so that he could speak not just out of self-knowledge and a common sense that is, actually, fate's, luck's gift to him, but out of a sincere conviction, a moral earnestness, the expression of which he had come to realize might well be his main chance, his only hope, of reaching, of persuading Juan: "Somehow I think I'm trying to get to him, so he'll pick my values, when he's facing a choice, rather than those he gets from the street and, I hate to say it, at home. That's a tall order. I don't mean to put it like that — we're back to this ego thing: a big temptation. But there's a conflict, a struggle in everyone: what do you decide about all sorts of things? I just hope Juan picks up some of the determination I picked up from my parents, picks it up through our time together. I try to tell him what I believe, and I've even told him that when I talk with him, it helps me because I realize that what I believe is important!"

As I've listened to this student of mine I've learned how much stronger he has become as a Big Brother, a tutor, an older friend to Juan. (He would eventually earn a doctorate in education and help teach in an undergraduate course I offer.) It is as if the weekly meetings, often two or so hours long, enable in each of the two another kind of coming together than that of a shared activity, even a shared conversation. The volunteer, on his own, is given pause: what does he uphold to himself, and why? If he is to be a convincing friend and teacher and guide it is such a question he will have to answer — hence the moral introspection he pursues. Juan's need for a kind of moral purpose that will carry him through any number of critical moments becomes for his older friend, who lives across the proverbial railroad tracks, a reason to locate more explicitly and consolidate his own moral purpose as a prelude to sharing it, however gingerly and indirectly.

Naturally, guile always matters in moral exchanges: how do you get something across without souring the entire enterprise by stirring up annoyance, irritation, resentment?[6] That question, too, haunted this young volunteer — how should he "deliver" moral energy to another person? The longer he struggled to convey his moral strength to Juan, and the more clearly he became aware of that moral strength, the more solid his sense of his own purpose in life became. This gift surprised him, even embarrassed him, but he had to learn to accept it if he was to keep at it with Juan. He did indeed persist with the boy, much to the benefit of both of them.

Personal Affirmation

Not all people who work with or on behalf of others become moralists (in the nonpejorative sense). For many volunteers there is obviously a moral purpose at work. Yet those people do not find themselves morally challenged as they do their volunteer work, do not think of it as bringing a moral bonus. Many even make a contrast between the obvious moral nature of their work and their own sense that they are getting "quite a bargain," as one middle-aged suburban hospital volunteer put it.

"I go to the hospital because I enjoy doing the work there. I love the nurses and the doctors, and I love the patients. I feel lucky to be able to spend part of my week that way. I hesitate to say I'm there because I feel I *should* be there. I don't deny that if I were a different person, with other values than the kind I have — we should be useful to others! — I probably would be elsewhere: maybe playing golf all spring, summer, autumn, like some of my friends do. But I have to be honest: I don't really judge someone playing golf or tennis, which I love to play, as doing something any less worthy of my time and energy than working as a hospital volunteer. I don't mean to sound selfish, but if you asked me what it means to me to do my work — why I do it — I'd have to say that I do it because I enjoy the world there, and, frankly, it's a tremendous educational experience. Not a day goes by that I don't learn something from the doctors, listening to them, and from the patients I meet.

"I was always interested in medicine anyway; if I could have done the premed work, I'd have tried to go to medical school. The next thing I knew I was married, and then I had two children to bring up. My husband's career is hard for me to understand; he's a tax lawyer. If there was some way for me to do volunteer work that connected with his work, I'd have done it. It's just as well, though; he's very much in favor of what I do, and he loves to hear my stories after I come home from the hospital! He said to me a few weeks ago, This job is really helping you learn how *much* you can do — and I said I think that's true.

"I used to think I was weak; I had a slight anemia, and my thyroid was on the low side. But since I've learned the ropes there at the hospital, I find myself really pitching in — until the next thing I know, people are telling me it's time to go home! I'm glad to leave, but I'm glad to come back in a day or two. I have to say it: I *miss* the hospital. There's a sense of excitement — lives are at stake! For me, it's a place where I feel myself needed and where I can live up to the expectations of others. Now this job is a big part of my life. I put a lot of myself into it; but I get back so much more. The people I meet who are struggling with pain and uncertainty — they help me realize that you can take things for granted until you get sick, and then you stop and think about what life really means."

What she was saying was not all that surprising. At times she came across as the slightly restless suburban housewife whose service smacked of condescension toward those who have fallen into sickness — their suffering an excuse for her to count her blessings! But when I watched her in the hospital or heard her recounting a most active, exhausting, giving day, it was certainly possible to overlook what she said and remember what she did week after week, often with great tact and sensitivity.

She was perhaps speaking most accurately when she emphasized the discoveries her work offered — all the people she met, all the stories she heard. "I remember what I hear in the evening; I talk to my husband about what I hear, and he says it's changed me a lot, what I do there on those wards." Interestingly, she avoided saying she had changed for the better, nor did her husband mount that claim — a certain modesty in people who were not always able to sustain humility.

Modesty — like arrogance — is no one's exclusive property by virtue of class or race. A woman from a quite genteel world, on her knees cleaning up after a patient who had fallen and then vomited, took the experience to heart and became quieter, less self-regarding, more reflective, more modest. Thirty miles away a tough working-class man, who never pretended to be soft-spoken or self-effacing, found a way to cope with disappointment when his son was born with Down syndrome. To make ends meet, he worked long hours as an automobile mechanic, then pumped gas at night. When his son was first born, a boy at last after five girls, he was not sad, anxious, or self-pitying, only angry.

His wife understood her husband well. "He's always been a man's man — he has his buddies, and they drink a lot of beer on Fridays. Otherwise, he's sober and very hard-working — two jobs, and never more than six hours' sleep. He's been a good husband and a good father: he loves those girls! But I'd be lying if I told you he didn't want a son. Oh, he was crazy for a boy, and when we decided to give it one last chance and he kept telling me he knew we'd have a sixth girl, he knew it, I knew something myself — how much he wanted a boy.

"Then I delivered, and we all were in ecstasy because it was a boy. Then came the news there was something wrong, that the boy, Ben, wasn't so good, that he wasn't passing the tests these doctors have when they examine babies. The rest — it's a nightmare. I don't know how to tell it — all we went through, but especially him."

Soon after Ben was declared retarded ("modestly" so, the doctors said) the parents had to decide whether they could take care of the boy themselves or would have to entrust him to others. They had no real money, so "others" meant a public institution. The father's dreams of raising a son had to be surrendered. The mother, trained as a practical nurse before a busy family life caused her to abandon thoughts of a career, related the gradual changes in her husband, the slow but finally steep decline in his spirits, in his entire way of being.

"He used to be full of energy, and now he's lost a lot of it. He used to jump out of bed, and he'd be ready for the day, even if it was five in the morning and dark, in coldest winter. These days he's sleeping hard, and the alarm goes off, and he wants to go back to sleep. Now, it's me — I'm the one who has to nudge him out of bed. He'll even fight with me; he'll accuse me of pushing him. I don't. Sure, we'd be broke if he stopped working. I keep quiet, though. I never defend myself when he starts being accusing toward me. He'll stop pretty fast — he sees I'm just letting him go on, and he decides it's no use to be like that. He must feel terrible — real guilty, because he's a decent guy ordinarily.

"That's the trouble, this is not an ordinary time! He's heartbroken. We both are, only I seem to be taking it much better. I say a dozen times to myself: God's will. If the good Lord wanted to send a retarded child here, and a boy, then that's His decision. For me the church is a big help. You know something? When he was at his lowest, he even stopped going [to church]. I said, 'It's bad enough, our troubles, and now you're going to send yourself to hell?' He looked at me, and you know what he said? He said, 'I'm already in hell.' *I* was ready to throw a glass at the wall when I heard that! I thought to myself, I'm fed up with all this feeling sorry for yourself that's coming out of his mouth! I just grabbed my raincoat and I left the house, and I slammed that door so hard I was afraid the roof would cave in. Then I realized I'd forgotten my pocketbook, so I ran back in and I grabbed it and ran out, and I slammed the door again, even harder, if that was possible! The only thing was, I saw out of the corner of my eye that he was crying, that he was wiping his eyes with a handkerchief.

"I was in the car, and I was ready to go, and then I said to myself, Hey, stop a minute. What's more important — to go to church and sit there and fume and ask Jesus to feel sorry for you and to condemn your husband or to skip church and go back inside and sit with him and hope he'll really break down and cry and cry, so all that disappointment in him will come out, and then he can talk with me, and we can try to figure out a way that we can pick up from here."

She chose to go home and take the chance that her husband would resolve his growing desperation — his disappointments, as she kept calling them, which were struggling to "express themselves," as she put it. She went into the kitchen and busied herself making fresh coffee, started cooking corn bread for lunch, one of his favorites, and said nothing. Finally he began to sob openly, and they began to talk.

"He didn't need to say much. All he needed to do was show me what he was feeling — I guess you could say show *himself,* because he'd been biting his lip and pushing himself like mad, as though there was nothing eating away at him, when everything he did showed that in a while there'd be nothing left of him at the rate he was going! I just sat there — I was relieved. Funny thing, I thought I'd start crying myself; but I didn't — I was almost happy. I knew this was a turning point.

"All of a sudden, I broke my silence, and I said, 'Honey, you're as busy as anyone in the world can be, I know, but you've got to find some time for yourself, not for me and the kids, as much as we want you and need you. You've got to find some way of doing something that will give you some peace.' He looked up at me, and I could see he knew what I was saying, but he was helpless; he didn't know what to do. I was going to tell him to talk with the priest, but I thought better of it. I knew he wouldn't talk with his friends — he's Mr. Confidence and Mr. Keep Busy with them. I racked my brains, and then I thought, Why not a doctor? I just blurted it out, the name of the pediatrician. I didn't say anything else, I just said his name. I didn't have to go further, or maybe I was afraid to, or I didn't know what words to use."

A week later he and the pediatrician had a long talk. The doctor took the lead, told his patient's father that he needed to become part of Ben's life and that one way to do so was to work with older retarded children. That way, when the boy was no longer a baby, the father would have some experience with children who needed special education. A month later, with the doctor's help, this father began volunteering on weekends at a state school for retarded and disabled children.

"I was 'slow' myself: I was 'disabled,'" he would recall a year later. He was also anxious, frightened, ready to give up and flee or to break down and cry. But he also wanted "some way out of the trap" he'd built for himself. He intuitively knew that his tears were a kind of grief, evidence of a mind in mourning. "I've been crying for all the hopes and dreams I once had — they're not going to happen. It's only gradually occurring to me that the only way out of this corner I'm in — like I keep saying, it's a trap, and I've made it myself — the only way out is for me to find some other place to go, some new hopes for myself."

By then he had already begun to build up some "hopes" — not for himself or, least of all, his son, but for the three or four youngsters he was learning to engage with, challenge to activities, help restrain and excite to action. Pretty soon he and his boys were quite a team — in sports and games and cleanup activities, in doing routines and assisting the staff with other children. Pretty soon he began to figure out ways to connect with his own son, to show the boy and his mother and sisters that there was a lot this busy mechanic could do to fix the way a home was running.

He didn't lose his wistfulness about what might have been. Rather, he let those thoughts ignite in him the fierce willfulness he had always possessed as a worker. Once the sight of boys playing in a Little League game had been unbearable. The time would come when he would organize his own son's Little League team. When a neighbor once called the team "special," he flinched. "I didn't like the way he used that word. I felt myself getting weak. I was a little teary for a second, and my knees felt as though if someone just touched me, I'd fall over. But in another second I was up for anything. I said, 'You bet we're special.' I meant it. Me and the kids, we were doing great, and we'd show him, we'd be thrilled to show him! It was then I knew I'd crossed some big street, and I was walking on the other side and my head was up, not down, and it was working with those kids that did it. They're the ones who got me across to the other side — do you see?"

I nodded, grateful to a man who had shown what it can mean to fall down, then pick himself up, not through hours of psychological talk or the support of a "group," and not even through the healing that time itself offers. In the end, his willfulness responded to his wife's loyalty and affection and to a doctor's sensible suggestion. But in the end, also, his pain responded to the visible, concrete opportunities a few children offered him. The gifts he brought on their birthdays and at Christmas signaled not only what these children had come to mean to him, but what they had enabled him to find and affirm in himself. They walked him "across," to a place where he was able to manage on his own. He became once again the assertive, capable, resourceful person he'd been before his setback, a setback that was followed by a breakthrough. As I heard him talk about the "choice" he had made, as I heard him remember "wishing" with each visit to that state school for the strength to make the best of his time with those children, I remembered the Latin I had learned many years earlier: the very root of the word "volunteer," *voluntas* — a choice — comes from *velle*, to wish.

Stoic Endurance

Some people exert themselves in a manner less directly personal than the man described above. In many years of work among poor families in Boston and Cambridge, I have met individuals who have wondered why they engage in volunteer work, and to what effect. They say simply that they do what they do — but for no particular reason that they care to spell out and with no particular personal consequences. They claim no affirmation for themselves, though an outsider, watching them in action and overhearing what they say, might disagree. They don't even assert the restricted satisfaction of friendships. Sometimes they acknowledge a motivation that does scant credit to their depth of commitment. An aside such as "I just get a kick out of it" hardly conveys the satisfaction achieved from a voluntary obligation taken on with great seriousness.

In Roxbury I met a middle-aged black mother who did her fair share of listening to children. She worked as a bus driver, tak-

ing children to and from school every weekday.[7] After her husband died of a stroke at the age of forty-four, she was tempted to
immerse herself in the troubled lives of her two daughters and
their four children. She had encouraged both daughters to finish
high school and take courses at a nearby community college to
become nurses or computer programmers or teachers, whatever
might catch their interest. The daughters adamantly refused: they
wanted no more school, even though they were not always happy
as mothers. One went dancing a lot (her boyfriend, the father of
her one son, had left her and gone to the West Coast). The other,
who had three children, moved in and out of serious depressive
states, even as she tried occasionally to work in a fast-food chain.
Her husband had been hurt in an automobile accident but received no compensation because he had been drinking and was
responsible for the crash. The other driver had walked away without injuries fortunately. There was no real reason why this man
couldn't go to work — at least work that didn't require heavy man-
ual effort. But he was mostly unemployed, and he continued to
drink.

In these unpromising family circumstances this bus-driving
mother and grandmother went out of her way to keep an eye on
many of the children whom she transported to school. She volunteered at an elementary school as a teacher's assistant, and even on
the bus she did far more than drive. I first heard about her from a
mother whose son and daughter I was getting to know. She told
me that her children's bus driver "taught" her charges all the way
to school and all the way back. A month or so later I was introduced to this woman at a school meeting and told again of her
unusual vocation. We agreed to meet, and we did, many times. I
became another of her students. I was at times overwhelmed by her
memories of specific instances in which children had learned a
lesson or two on the bus or at the school where she did her
"aiding."

Once I took the liberty of inquiring about her reasons for doing
this teaching. She warmed to the question but wasn't sure she knew
how to answer. "I wish I could tell you more," she said almost
plaintively. Then she said, "I want to see these kids make it in life.
I want to see them survive." As she spoke, I thought that she was

also expressing her own persistence, her capacity for stoic survival. She was a wise woman, earthy and intelligent and determined with regard to those children she tried to assist.

What follows are some highlights from several long, intense, taped interviews I did with her a few days after her fiftieth birthday. She had been getting chest pains and needed no doctor to tell her that her heart was ailing. She had arranged a medical appointment and, almost in preparation for the bad news she expected, was anxious to concentrate on what she called "the good side" of her life. No doubt that half-century mark had prodded her to become more than usually reflective, though she had occasionally been outspokenly introspective in the two years I had known her.

"I had an aunt who would come and help us out, she was a maiden lady, my momma called her. This aunt, Josephine, would sing gospel music, and she'd start her declaring. She'd tell us that we had to do something God would notice, or else we'd just get lost in the big shuffle! I can still hear her saying that now. I can still see myself staring at her and getting more and more worried by the second! What would happen to me if God just overlooked me while He was paying attention to some others, who'd been smart enough to make sure they captured His attention? Why, I'd end up in one of those big fires 'down there' that don't get put out by any men with hoses shooting out water!

"So I'd try to figure out how to get His attention, and I had some ideas. One, I'd go to church *alone* sometimes, and that way He'd see me being loyal, and He'd remember me from all the others. Two, if I did something, got a job, I'd try to do it a little better and different from other folks; that way the Lord up there would spot me, or maybe He'd hear from others what I was doing. Three, I'd try to go the extra mile so I could show Him that I'm not just running with the crowd. That's the worst, my aunt used to tell us, when you just sit there and let yourself be traveling like the other folks around you.

"When I'm driving the bus, I call some kids to be up there near me, sitting, and I've done my homework — I've checked into *their* homework! — and I'm ready for them. I'll quiz them. I'll try to give them hints about how to do better in school. I'll teach them about obeying and keeping quiet and speaking out at the right time. If they're doing good, I reach into my bag, and I give them a chocolate bar — and it's extra good, not just the five-and-dime-store kind! 'Made in England' is what it says on the wrapper — and I get them to read it.

"The teachers have called me an 'honorary' one, and that's fine. I go to school and sit there in a class, and try to get those kids to pay attention and study as hard as they can. When a kid does well, I feel great! It's my reward — and I hope the good Lord is taking it all down. A lot of times, though, I don't get my hopes too high — about the kids or about myself, either. A lot of times I'm saying to myself that I've seen so much trouble hereabouts, and it's not getting the slightest better, and sometimes it's worse. So if a kid learns to spell a little bit better, and he does his figuring, his arithmetic a little better, and he writes his sentences right, it still won't prove much down the road, because there's a trap he'll fall into — drugs, or a bullet that hits him even if it's meant for someone else, or sickness.

"A lot of our kids, they fall sick, and there's no good doctors here to see them. A lot of our mothers, they're not taking the care of their babies that they should. I know! I could start being upset. I could raise my fists and pound them. But I've learned some lessons from life. I've learned that we've been walking before God, all of us, since He first turned us loose down here; and there must be some reason for all this, but it's not *any* of us, no matter all the schools you've gone to and the subjects you've studied — it's not one of us who can find out what the Lord was hoping to do when He got all this going down here. Once you know that, you can begin to sit back and be sincere, and continue your work, and do all the good you can — but not be thinking you're going to lift the world up and change everything upside down."

Such a mix of continuing energy, spent generously on children, and a stoic endurance that forswears self-importance or even a conviction of one's significance in the lives of others is not altogether rare in certain older volunteers, even if they don't attribute their condition to the Lord's presence (a threatened presence?) in their lives. This woman took great pleasure in asking children to do a lot and yet not expecting a world-shattering miracle as a consequence of what happened between her and them. She hoped (and prayed daily) for a "touch of wisdom" — a quiet acceptance of what would be. She did hope to contribute to what would be, yet she had a sense of history that was almost Tolstoyan in nature: she was mindful of all the forces that conspire to make us turn out as we do.

Her exertions, her hard everyday labor, most certainly helped shape the minds of many children. Still, there was much else going on, as she noted like a sociologist, if not a theologian: she knew the power of "the streets," the role of chance in the "tricks of the world," and finally, of course, "God and what He might decide to do."

I think of that bus driver when I watch several older people visit sick children in a pediatric ward or when I watch schoolchildren visiting the elderly in a nursing home not far from an urban middle school.[8] Some of the older people are not unlike that bus-driving woman: energetic and forceful, yet glad to feel detached. They try to help others even though they themselves are ailing a bit.

"I couldn't do this work if I was too involved with those children," one woman remarked to me. "I've learned that if you exhaust yourself, if you overcommit yourself, you lose rather than win. The children pull back — and why shouldn't they! You have to learn just the right attitude with them, and when you've got it, then you really can enjoy this work. It doesn't become a chore or a burden, and yet you do get close to the kids. It's a matter of tone, you could say: you know enough to persist, but not feel the world hangs on your every word!"

Some professional people — doctors, lawyers, teachers — also work hard to remain aroused and interested but somewhat detached; then they find themselves better able to enjoy the work they do. A lawyer much involved in legal defense cases for the poor explained that both for the sake of his clients and for his own sake he had to learn how to keep some distance, or perspective, without losing his personal commitment to the work and to those with whom he was working. He was eager not to lose that commitment; he wanted to remain enthusiastic, full of dedication, and even passion. Not least, he wanted to feel a kind of excitement and fulfillment.

"I've been doing this kind of law long enough to know that it can be enjoyable only if you've adjusted your head in a certain way.

I don't have any formulas. I think each person has to find his or her own momentum and speed. But you can't think it all hangs on you. You can't go around with the idea that if you come at the case full speed ahead, all guns blazing, then there will be a legal action and then a victory — or a defeat — and that will be that. You've got to understand that out here, doing this kind of law, there are lots of complications that can make even what seems like an easy case, destined for success, come crashing down. You never really know whether people are going to want to sustain their involvement with you, and if they don't, why.

"Of course, what I said can apply to any client — but here there's a lot of fear, and people appear, then disappear, or they change their minds, and they're not going to tell you why. I'm at my best when I've got a clear idea of what I'm trying to do, and when I've made my best try to work closely and efficiently with my clients. But I'm not sitting there expecting the world to change for them, for us; quite the contrary, I've resigned myself to the realization that this may be a win, or it may be a loss, but at least we're here, giving it a real try, and that's an important step right there. When my head is 'on' that way, I'm feeling right about things, and I won't fall flat on my face if we lose or go into orbit if we win — neither would be justified."

That "resignation" or acceptance of God's will is what Kierkegaard explored in *Fear and Trembling* — not a surrender of personal initiative, not an apathy, not a descent into gloom or despair, but a thoughtful acknowledgment of what can and cannot be done. For Kierkegaard such resignation was a believer's step: I await what the Lord decides. For this lawyer there was a world of obstacles to face, only some of which would yield to his strenuous exertions. He used the word "resigned" in a thoughtful, unsentimental exploration of the possible, the not so possible, and the quite likely impossible (but one never knows).

A Boost to Success

For a person to remain committed to service despite the outcome, he or she must have felt a prior sense of accomplishment. Some people who work at community service or enlist in privately spon-sored or government service programs are also anxious to help launch a career. They hope to become doctors or lawyers or to enter the world of business or to teach. They look ahead to appli-cations, interviews, committee evaluations and decisions. The lad-der upward beckons toward college or graduate school, toward a hospital appointment, law clerkship, business or teaching position. It is not easy to understand the complex mixture of ideas, concerns, and motives that informs the decisions of such volunteers. Any discussion of the satisfactions of service ought to mention the dilemmas many students feel as they balance their idealistic moti-vations with the practicalities required as they contemplate their future occupation or profession.

Not all young volunteers are as forthcoming — as relentlessly able and willing to enter into self-scrutiny and share the results — as one young man who as a Harvard undergraduate worked for two years tutoring children in the Roxbury section of Boston. He worked hard to earn the children's trust, but he still felt he was "on trial."

"A month ago, one child suddenly shot this question at me: 'Hey, what's in it for you?' At first I wasn't sure what he meant — what 'it' was supposed to be. He saw me trying to figure out what I was being asked, how to ask for some kind of clarification. So he expanded his question. 'You come out here a lot, and you're nice to us, and a few of us were wondering, Why does he come here, and what will he get out of it?' I didn't answer right away. I could have spouted a big line: how much it means to me to be able to help others, and the tremendous satisfaction I get when I see someone improving in school, and my parents' Christian beliefs that you give to others, try to do the best you can to share what you have with people who are in need. Then I could have added that I have *fun*, that I like coming here and meeting people, and we have a good time, and I feel better, frankly, when I return because I have a sense of accomplishment, and I've enjoyed being with friends, and I remember the stories I've heard, and the jokes.

"Instead I sat there, and I guess I was silent *too* long, because a couple of kids laughed nervously, and one kid said I didn't have to answer the question. 'Besides,' she added, 'we like you, and we don't care what your reasons are for coming here.' I sure was relieved to hear that! It was as if I did have these deep, dark, ulterior reasons, but they were willing to give me a break and forget the whole thing. No sooner did I think that when another thought came to me: you're being too defensive and suspicious yourself. Just answer the question — be brief and cool! But I couldn't, and now it was too late. I'd hesitated so long that *I* was the one who turned it all into a big deal!

"Finally I said the truth; I said that it was a real hard one to put to me, what they'd asked. I said, 'Look, I like coming here — you've become friends of mine, I hope, and I hope you feel the same way, that I'm a friend of yours. I love getting a pizza and bowling, and I love trying to help out with your work so you can do better, just the way certain teachers helped me out in high school, and before that too.' I said, 'If you can see someone doing better and better in school, and you've been able to be part of that — of the person improving in English or math — then you feel good, or at least I do.' Then I tried to be honest, to level with them. I said, 'Hey, I can't deny that it helps me to come out here. I like doing it and feel proud to be able to be with you and make friends and do the teaching. But yes, I wouldn't want to deny it, I'll put this down on my record, what I've done here, and that will help me — people like to see that, admissions people. I won't deny it!'

"That's about it, word for word, what I said. I was grabbing hard for words, and I was afraid that I was falling down and making a mess of everything! But they were very nice to me. They told me to forget it, and they told me I was cool, and they told me it was time to go get one of those pizzas, since I just mentioned them. That's what we did — we broke off the talk. Frankly, I was torn. Part of me thought we really should stay there and talk some more — this was pay dirt we were hitting: how do you learn to trust someone, if you ever do? But I was also relieved to have the subject changed. I felt a little like a hypocrite, and I was afraid some of them felt that way about me. Later, when we were eating our pizzas, and everyone was talking about other things, my mind was still on that question I'd been asked, and what the right answer to it is, and how you phrase your answer."

He was certainly not alone in the moral quandary he expressed.

He spent a long time trying to settle in his mind exactly what he *was* doing in Roxbury as a tutor and what his reasons and expectations were. Some others who did similar community service, he felt, were "crudely opportunistic." When I asked him to explain, he was terser than usual. "They want to list their community service work on their CV." Then he added, after a very short pause, "So do I. It's self-serving for me to distinguish myself from them — me the good guy, they the clever frauds. It's so damn complicated. I don't know how to begin to look at all this — what our motives are."

We discussed this issue for a long time, and we took it up on other occasions. I mentioned that everything he did — his intellectual and athletic interests, his church activities — could also be placed under the "cloud of suspicion" he occasionally summoned in his mind as he contemplated his community service work. He had turned that youth's question into an excuse for a far-reaching kind of self-arraignment, I began to realize. In a later chapter, I scrutinize how this moral preoccupation can be a prelude to depression and despair. Here it is important to note under the rubric of satisfactions the unquestionable pleasure many young men and women have taken, not only in the value to others of their community service work but in the value it can have for themselves as well.

That value is not only a moral one (so much learned from others in tutoring them) but also a personal one, as this young man said quite pointedly: "This work I do will help me, I sometimes think, more than it will help the kids. I guess I ought to say that the work will give a boost to my success, and that I know it, and that when you ask me about the satisfactions I get from this kind of work — well, if I left that out, I'd be leaving something out that's part of the picture!"

His expression was singularly candid and quite telling. He worked all of the ironies and complexities, really, of a privileged life into a few sentences: the satisfactions of doing community service work and the additional satisfaction that went with knowing that his work would no doubt advance the further work he hoped to do as a lawyer or businessman (he hadn't yet settled that question). In our many further talks devoted to this matter, we brought in other students to ponder the awkward yet important implications of a quite human ethical issue first given shape (speaking of irony) by the question of a boy in a ghetto school who was having an exceedingly hard time of it educationally.

Those who took part in this discussion were outspokenly idealistic and at the same time self-critically assertive of their own rights and needs — a rather tense and complicated attitude. Again and again I heard comments that were apologetically self-serving — sinners proclaiming with melancholy insistence their necessary wrong-doing!

"I live in a world where you have to play all the angles," a young woman announced, and than she denounced such an imperative with considerable vehemence. "I'd like to work at public-interest law, but first I have to get into law school, and so if I work at helping public interest lawyers now, I'll have a better chance of becoming one later." Minutes afterward, those words prompted her conscience to rebel: such talk was "sleazy," she wanted it known, and she didn't so much ask for forgiveness as hope that "one day there will be an end to it [the kind of remarks she'd just made], at least for me. Maybe they [on the admissions committee] see through all this. Maybe they remember their own chicanery." Her good work as a teacher of needy children had now become a manifest confidence trick, at least with respect to what she had intended when she began the service work. Still, the work had its own worth, most of these ambitious, able young men and women remembered, and their tutees would agree.

· INTERLUDE ·

Mentoring

O NCE THERE WERE SIMPLY (and not so simply) those who tried to teach and those who tried to learn — or didn't try hard at all. Now there are "mentors" and their work, called "mentoring." Those who aim to be connected to children and young people, especially, aim to be mentors or, to express it more actively, to mentor. Those who listen and try to learn from these mentors, who take in what is said and make it their very own, are called the mentored — and I have even heard, Lord spare us, of "mentees." Yet even uninspired words that restate the obvious, that try to turn the old art of teaching, which has always been to some extent a mystery and a challenge, into something new (and also challenging) can help us understand the mystery.

I was lucky to have a series of enormously pleasant, sometimes quite touching (and ironic) conversations with Anna Freud in the 1970s, around the time the word "mentoring" began to appear in educational essays and in social science journals. I carried some of these journals when I visited her apartment in a Yale dormitory, for I was always interested in her thoughts on matters psychological, especially when they pertained to children. At that time she was a visiting faculty member at Yale, coming from London, and I had begun teaching at Harvard while also doing research with children in various parts of the United States.

In our relaxed, early-morning talks, Miss Freud could be wryly humorous. We shared coffee and cakes and a memory or two, and her smile occasionally broke into a laugh — or a sigh. When I heard her sigh, I knew her mordant, analytic mind was preparing a skeptical, if not dismissive or even scornful, remark. Sometimes I felt teased. But often, concerned about her own irritation or annoyance, she would clam up after giving a hint of what she *wasn't* saying. "Oh, that is a subject for people who have all the time in the world and no great expectation of learning much that is not already familiar."

Much to my disappointment, those were the words she used when I first broached the subject of mentoring. I had at least expected her to *translate* the word — fit it into established psychoanalytic terminology and theory. But she, too, had been hearing the word "mentoring" a lot, and she clearly had decided not to take an interest either in the word or in what it might express about something happening between individuals. I looked at her usually expressive face for a further indication of her mood and did, in fact, see a thin smile — not the glare of impatience or annoyance she sometimes could fix on a person or on the walls of the room. I responded to what I thought was an invitation for a casual discussion. "It's a word that is used all the time now, but when I was in college, teaching children in a Boston neighborhood as a volunteer, we never thought of ourselves as mentors or as doing mentoring."

She replied, "Right there you are bringing up something: what does it mean when a word like that becomes part of the consciousness of young volunteers? A mentor traditionally was a revered figure, a trusted and wise adviser, counselor, teacher, a source of guidance and inspiration. That is a lot to ask of a young person! It's a lot to ask of *anyone!*"

"Are you suggesting that the word becomes a burden?"

"No, not necessarily — but I do think that words have meaning not only in the ordinary sense but in the psychological sense. If I am called a mentor, and if others are asked to think of me as a mentor, and if I think of myself as a mentor, then people like you and me, whose business it is to take notice of what the mind does under various circumstances, should — well, do just that!"

I didn't know how to pursue the matter further at that time. I frankly hadn't thought of the word "mentor" as a term that would provoke a special variety of expectations (and perhaps, subsequently, disappointments) in those who are mentored. I had regarded the word from the social and cultural angle rather than the psychological one. A particular generation, staking out its own claims on territory hitherto quite resistant to change, had found a kind of password: all those who wanted to work at difficult and challenging educational problems would call themselves mentors. For Miss Freud, however, such a development was not without psychological significance for everyone concerned.

The conversation turned elsewhere that day; but on the drive back to Boston I kept thinking of what she had said. To some extent I was amused — trust an intent psychoanalyst to pick up *that* thread and see that it was important. I had hoped to engage her in a discussion of the actual psychology of mentoring — what happens between the children mentored and their mentors. For me, the "psychodynamics" of being a mentor and being the recipient of mentorship was a take on the old duo of teacher and student.

But Miss Freud (who was, after all, *my* mentor!) had told me that I ought to think of the way in which a social or cultural phenomenon becomes a psychological one. In other words, if I am teaching a child and feel that I'm not only the teacher but the child's mentor, I may well behave somewhat differently. Moreover, a child who feels she is in the presence of a mentor may be looking for a rather different experience than she otherwise might hope to receive. Or so Miss Freud was speculating. I wasn't at all convinced of the worth of that line of thinking. I thought she was attributing to children and to their young (or older) teachers *her* kind of mental life — one that responded attentively and precisely, even relentlessly, to words and their connotations. Nevertheless, I decided I would do the research she was indirectly suggesting. (She was a great one for asking a question or throwing out a modest speculation and looking at her listener as if to say, Might you one day know the answer by making such an inquiry?)

At that time I was working with black and white children in the poorer neighborhoods of Boston and was trying to learn about their moral values, their sense of what matters in life, what is right and wrong, and why. I was also doing some volunteer tutoring in two Boston schools, one in a black neighborhood, the other in a working-class white one, as a way to get to know the children while trying to help them learn. I didn't have to be too ingenious to introduce the subject of "mentoring"; the children were enrolled in a program called Mentors for Future Citizens. The moment I saw the phrase I wondered how the aging but still spry and alert (even whimsical) Anna Freud would regard it. When I heard the children talk about the program, I decided to pose some questions.

A ten-year-old white girl in the program, Maureen, whose father was a fireman and whose uncle was a policeman, said she had a mentor. I knew she meant Susie, who was a student of mine, but I was interested in hearing what a child who had come to know Susie would say about her. What is a mentor? I asked.

Maureen answered, "A mentor is someone who comes from outside — a college, I think. She's taken courses and knows how to teach you, and she's smart. She can tell you how to do things: it's not just schoolwork; it's about stuff in general. She took me to the store, and she told me which food is good for you and which is junk food, and there's nothing in it but sugar, mostly. She took me to the library; I'd never been there before. There were all those books, and I told her, 'I'll never be able to read even ten of them, and there must be a thousand.' She said I was too high on the first number and too low on the second — I should just try one book at a time and not count the number I read, but concentrate on what's inside and what I get out of it, and she said there were more than a thousand books in the library, she was pretty sure."

I asked Maureen whether she had read any of those books. She replied, "You see, you can't just go in to that place and walk out with a book. You have to get a card, a library card. I had to sign up. They wanted all this info, about your parents, and where you live, and the phone number. I applied, and they told me I could have my card in a week — and they'd give me a temporary one right away. Susie said, 'Let's go for it,' but I didn't want to take a book and come home with it without telling my mom and my dad, and besides, I didn't see any book I wanted to read that bad. So we left."

I was waiting to hear of a second visit, of a book taken out. But Maureen was playing with an elastic band and seemed uninterested in what we were discussing. She pointedly looked at the clock and even more pointedly reminded me that in fifteen minutes her study period would be over. Suddenly I came to — we were sitting and talking in the school *library!* I looked at the bookshelves, each of them about half full. I decided to mention this coincidence — that we'd been talking about the discovery of a library, and here we were *in* one. She responded in a wonderfully matter-of-fact way, "Yeah, I know; I thought of that."

So much for this proud ironist, I thought; I had been quite delicately brought up short. I asked if she had ever taken out a book from *this* library. "No," she said — but she tackled me at the pass as I was hurrying too fast for a touchdown. "*This* is where you read the books; they're for here, not to bring home." All right, then. I got up and asked, "Have you read any of these books here?" Now she gave me a look of great pity and lowered her voice as if we were sharing a secret (and pointedly *not* telling the world of my ignorance, if not presumptuous cleverness), "We bring our books here from class and study them here. I never have time to do *extra* reading. If I did, I'd go to the gym."

Suddenly she leaped over my sense of futility and carried me where I'd hoped earlier to get. "I did get my card, and then I took out a book. It was about President Kennedy, and it told of his mother coming from Boston, and his father, and how he grew up and went into the navy, and he almost got killed, and then he became president — but first he was a senator, and then he did get killed, and the whole country was really upset. My mom and dad said they'll never forget that day. It was in November, and they can remember exactly where they were and what they were doing, and my grandma cried a lot, and they all watched the funeral, and they all cried, because it was sad, and my grandma was crying very hard, and even my grandpa."

Maureen had obviously read the book through, and she carried its essence in her still, along with the family stories she had heard when she'd talked about the book with her parents. She told me more details of President Kennedy's life, including some I didn't know (the street in Brookline where he was born, for instance), and then, once more to spare me the next question, she told me of several other books — history books — she had taken out from the public library. She liked history, she told me, and wished the English teacher would ask the class to read history books. Instead, the teacher was "always" (an exaggeration, I knew) assigning poems for her students to read in class and try to explain in "recitation" when called upon. Maureen had no use for poetry, nor did her dad, who went so far as to mock poets and poetry in rather unattractive language, which she shared with me.

But suddenly she surprised me again with this utterly unsolicited observation. "Susie says poetry is really neat. She brought this book to show me; there was a picture of President Kennedy, and he was talking to a poet, a real big one, Frost, Robert Frost. Then she read me some poems he wrote, and she explained them — cool! So, I told my dad, and he said sure, he knew about Frost, and he was a good poet! Then Susie brought me copies she made of a couple of poems, and I showed them to my dad, and he said they're good, and my mom has read them, and I have them in my room."

Her eyes said as much as her tongue; they had an alive look, one of concentration, even fascination. Then she admitted that she had tried to write a poem, without success. Again, though, Susie had intervened and had told her how hard it was to write a poem, especially if Robert Frost was the exemplar. As for the English teacher, *her* poems weren't as good as Frost's, this ten-year-old literary critic allowed. She added eagerly, "Susie says the teacher could be teaching the poems better, and she could be teaching us better poems. But she said you can always find fault with anyone, and then you end up losing, because you miss the good points."

I was at last getting a sense of what took place between this child and her twenty-year-old mentor. I decided not to address the matter any more that day, and we moved on to talk of friends, games, television programs, movies.

A week later, we were again sitting in the school library. I had brought crayons and paper, and I asked Maureen whether she wanted to draw a picture or two, as she had in the past.[1] She assented and looked to me for suggestions, as before. This time I suggested she draw a teacher. I had one teacher in mind, but I decided not to mention the person. But Maureen wanted a bit of help, and I responded: her English teacher.

She quickly began to draw, starting with the orange crayon for the teacher's face, neck, torso, legs and arms, features, and hair. Next she used a blue crayon for the sky, then put it aside for a second before summoning it for the teacher's dress. A green crayon followed, to soften the dress a bit and to put in a rather thick slice of grass. She used the brown crayon hard to put ground underneath the grass. She stopped and looked at what she had done. She was through, I thought, but I was wrong. Rather, she reached for a yellow crayon and began to draw a sun in the sky, then hesitated, replacing the yellow crayon and pulling out the black one. She started to make clouds, which became rather heavy. Then the voice of the weatherman: "It's just begun to rain."

As Maureen spoke, she drew a slanted downpour: the descent of black upon the teacher, the earth, the grass. Now, I judged that she was through. She put all the crayons away, tucked in the tip of the crayon box's cover, and began, slowly, to move it toward me. Abruptly, however, she called the box back to her turf and took out the brown crayon, holding it longer than she had held any crayon before, then began to work. She was making a wall, she announced. It was up to me to figure out what she was doing, she said as she worked. I realized that she was drawing a building, and since it was not far from the woman, I guessed it was a house or a school. The artist took my guess as a challenge and worked to make sure that the building looked like a school. She used the red and black crayons to make a door and to bring plentiful smoke and even fire to the chimney, and she made two lines of windows, closely packed.

Finally she put the crayons safely away. Did I want her name on the other side of the paper? Yes, that would be great. Did I want the teacher's name? No sooner did I nod my head yes than she said, "It's not a good idea." Why? "The teacher might see it, and she might not like it." Why? "Well, she doesn't look pretty." Is she? "A little." In a second I got an amplification: "She could be prettier, if she took better care of herself." How? "If she dressed better, and she did her hair better." When I pressed for details, she said, "Well, her hair is so plain and straight. She should curl it!" She had no comments about the teacher's mode of attire — and then the bell rang: time for that teacher's student to go attend her class!

Two weeks later, Maureen and I were again in the school library, and this time I asked her to draw her mentor. I decided not to use Susie's name when asking for the drawing. Immediately my young artist friend got to work, starting with the brown crayon. She drew two parallel vertical lines, then connected them with a number of horizontal lines to make various angles with the vertical ones — a tree, I realized. She turned to green for the leaves, with a good deal of embellishment. After finishing the tree, she put ground under it, and grass and flowers, all rather attractively arranged — a landscape architect at work. Next she drew a sky and endowed it with a big sun, whose face had a wide, broad smile and rays that reached out pointedly. I noted that no human being yet graced the paper. As if to quiet my nerves, she took the orange crayon and drew the outline of a human form. She used other crayons to help, in a rather exuberant yet careful fashion, and soon the figure was ready to be called "Susie."

Maureen handed me the picture, and as I held it and admired it, she asked whether she should put Susie's name on the paper. I nodded and handed it back to the artist, who promptly took a ruler and a pencil to make, very lightly, two parallel horizontal lines. Then she took a red crayon to make the quite neatly crafted letters spelling "Susie." I had not in a long time seen a child be so concerned about the way a name was rendered. I studied the drawing, then asked Maureen about it.

She said, "She's full of fun! She shows me how to do magic tricks; she's a magician, and she puts on shows. She says she started learning [magic] when she was my age. She's taken me to downtown Boston and to the museum. We joked around, and the guard told us to behave ourselves and not make so much noise, then Susie spoke back to him, and he ended up on our side! She thinks I should try to go to college, but that's way off, my dad says. First I'll need to do better in school." After a moment's silence, she added, "I wish Susie would be a schoolteacher, then she could come here and teach me."

I observed that it sounded to me as if Susie was already teaching her quite a bit. Maureen agreed but said, "She teaches you, but she doesn't hit you over the head. She teaches you by being your friend — like my favorite aunt. It's not a subject; it's the things we end up talking about — that's what she teaches."

Maureen had clearly found in her mentor a person who was able and willing to connect with a child, even be playful with her, to the point that they laughed and joked and carried on as they sat at a soda fountain, in a museum snack bar, on a bus headed for the aquarium, at a movie. I suppose the phrase "big sister" applied, though Susie was perhaps more consciously and deliberately the teacher. She taught this girl not only poetry but arithmetic and spelling and some tips about writing compositions. She balanced her casual, offhand manner with a certain gravity and solemnity that Maureen picked up on and contrasted with the demeanor of her teachers.

"Susie can become really serious; she'll start telling me something, and I can see that she really wants me to understand and remember. She looks right into my eyes, and then she asks me, after she's told me something, 'Do you see?' Then I make sure I *have,* or I ask her to repeat what she's said, so I'll be concentrating harder. She'll say to me, 'Now let's earn our good time' — and she'll whip out some words for me to spell, or we'll do some [arithmetic] problems."

Some Big Brothers and Sisters are similarly teachers as well as companions to the boys and girls they aim to educate in the literal sense of the word's derivation: that is, to "lead out" of a ghetto world that is slowly bearing down hard on the notions those children have of what is possible and desirable. Still, those Big Brothers and Sisters tend to be less self-consciously anxious to teach and inspire the children they know than is the case with the mentors. Perhaps this is because the mentoring program that sent Susie to South Boston had a different stated agenda than the Big Sister organization.

Susie had taken on both roles, and she was quite clear-cut, even sharp, about the differences: "A Big Sister's agenda is to be *that:* a warm, encouraging older friend, who is there to help, in ways the child wants and needs, including to offer academic help, though often it's a relaxed being together — food, maybe a trip to downtown, or athletics. A mentor is someone who doesn't only want a kid to be a friend, but to look up to her, and want to take her advice, and learn from her, and follow her lead down various paths: in school, in the way she thinks about the future, in what she plans for herself. A Big Sister is supportive; a mentor is a guide, a person who has earned a kid's respect, has got enough credibility with her so she's ready to dig in at school and avoid trouble at home and in her neighborhood, on the street. [It] sounds like a tall order, being a mentor, and it is!

"I used to be a Big Sister, and I was glad if I could stay in a good, friendly relationship with the two girls I'd 'adopted.' I used to tutor, and I was glad if I could get the kids to do their homework halfway well. This mentoring program is more ambitious: we're supposed to connect with these kids, like we did as Big Sisters, and teach them — and teach them and teach them! — like tutors do, and more so; and then we're supposed to stimulate them and give them a kind of moral incentive, a psychological spur to aim higher, to look way outside the world they know and aspire to leave it and go to the other world, the one we come from. That's a tall order for *us*, never mind the kids. We've got to lift our own eyes up, before we can get the kids to follow our lead."

Jack was another college student who agreed to become a mentor. Benjy, the nine-year-old black boy for whom he assumed responsibility, was already in danger because he had turned down an offer to make money (fifty dollars a "run," and maybe more) carrying drugs to individuals who worked in bars and nightclubs and "juke joints." Still, he was beginning to "melt" — his word — because he wondered where else and when he'd ever do any better. On the other hand, his grandmother was still a formidable figure in his life and in the life of his ailing mother, who had dermatomyositis, a relatively rare, progressive autoimmune illness that made her increasingly weak, with a reduced appetite and abdominal pain. She suffered from an increasing impairment of her ability to use her legs and arms. Her skin became dry, cracked, infected. She lost her "morale," as she put it, and essentially became her mother's child again. Benjy alternated between a desire to help these two women in his life and a wish to escape — as an older brother had, into the army (he was stationed in Georgia).

In the fourth grade an assistant principal of Benjy's elementary school connected him to a mentoring program, where he met Jack, a black college sophomore from a comfortable middle-class Atlanta professional family. His father was a surgeon, his mother a high school teacher of history and Spanish. Jack excelled in both academic work and athletics — he was a first-rate basketball player and a "fast, fast runner," as Benjy boasted one day. Jack also had had a considerable amount of outdoor experience with Outward Bound and with teachers and fellow students at the private school he attended in Atlanta.

When Jack met Benjy, he found the boy cooperative and anxious to oblige. Benjy explained why. "He's high class, Granny says. He's high yellow, too [light-skinned]. He took me to a Celtics game, and he showed me the beaches up there [north of Boston]. He's got a cool car — it's foreign. So I sure was glad to go and see the world!"

The initial effort at getting acquainted was not followed by a successful academic relationship, however. Jack was strong in the sciences at college, and he tried hard to interest Benjy in biology, chemistry, and arithmetic, but to no avail. Indeed, as soon as Jack tried to interest the boy in anything intellectual, a barrier arose. There was silence, a concerted attempt to find diversions, distractions, and eventually outright hostility — culminating in an outburst of angry suspicion.

Shortly after one outburst, Jack said to me, "He told me he could see right through me! He said I had been taking him places so as to get him to do the studying I wanted! He said I had a plan, and he knew it — to make him into somebody he isn't. 'Who's that?' I asked, and he said, 'Some book boy.' I'd never heard that phrase before, so I asked him what a book boy is, and then he really blew his stack. He told me I was lying to him, and I sure *did* know what a book boy is, because I'm one myself! I wish I'd just laughed and said, 'You got it,' but I was scared I was losing him, and I didn't want to provoke him anymore. I figured I'd hear him out and then retreat a little — go back to our trips and our meals and snacks, and that way we'd get to be tighter, and then I'd very slowly try to get us back on track with the academic side of things."

So Jack pulled back from his efforts to teach. He became involved in Benjy's athletic life, taking him to a gym where he could build up his physical strength. Their trips to various places continued, and the boy struggled at home with the temptations put to him by a street gang with connections to the world of drugs. I had been interviewing Benjy and others in his school for a study of how the moral values of children take shape. In fact I had suggested to several of my college student volunteers that he was desperately in need of the mentoring program.[2] I had learned how fragile and vulnerable Benjy's situation was, how volatile he could be under academic or social pressure. He was fiercely defiant of authority, swearing at others in the classroom, fighting in the corridors, muttering epithets about the school and its teachers. "This boy is headed for the gangs soon," his fourth-grade teacher commented at a staff meeting.

Jack began to feel overwhelmed and defeated. "The ghetto is too much for me, it's too much for the school, it's too much even for the boy's granny — and she drags him to church, kicking and screaming, every Sunday, and so, I'd have to say that God is losing and the 'enemies of Jesus' that minister talks about are sure winning." We decided on this strategy: to risk all by trying again to cultivate an academic involvement, and if Benjy balked, then to hoist the flag of surrender and call it quits.

At that point Jack became truly inventive, even inspired as a teacher. He took Benjy to several computer companies in Cambridge, where he knew people in management. The boy learned about how computers are made and the many uses to which they are put. Jack also took Benjy to Boston's Museum of Science, where quite by accident they ran into a crowd of people headed for the planetarium. Benjy wanted to know what those people were going to see. Jack said he didn't know. When Benjy suggested that they go too, Jack mildly resisted. "I was impatient with him. I had *my* agenda — I thought I'd hook him, maybe, on the dinosaurs. So I said let's keep going, meaning, Do this my way, and go where I'm trying to take us. He said no, he wanted to go to the auditorium. He saw my face register frustration, I'm sure — yes, maybe annoyance! [I had suggested that possibility — and told him I was reminded of certain similar moments in my life as a father, never mind as a doctor or teacher.] But I figured, Hey, let's go. He was delighted, I could tell — he'd *won!* So we went — and that turned out to be a small turning point, I now can say!"

They heard a lecture on astronomy given by a gifted teacher and illustrated vividly by photographs. Benjy became quite intrigued. Jack, surprised, was flexible enough, resourceful enough, to respond to the boy's flicker of interest in a mental activity. They talked about the lecture and about the origins of the world. Jack bought Benjy an astronomy book at the museum bookstore and a week later took him to the Harvard Observatory. Here were the first moments of a child's growing absorption in the stars, the planets, the sun and the moon, the astronauts and their activities, and, not least, telescopes and what they can reveal to us. Jack, fortunately, had taken an astronomy course in college and knew how to answer many of Benjy's inquiries.

There was no dramatic shift in the boy's school behavior or, for that matter, in his street behavior. He flirted with a junior membership of sorts in a neighborhood gang. He argued, as before, with his teachers, and played hooky repeatedly. He was warned, threatened with transfer to a school meant to hold on (as best it could) to "difficult" children. Yet Benjy did begin to quiet down, ever so slowly. He averted being transferred by telling the principal he wanted a "final chance." He angrily began doing his homework in order to "show those teachers something," prove them wrong in their judgments of him. Jack pointed out that the teachers had all they could do to keep up with children who often were quite a challenge; he also reminded his young friend that those teachers weren't being paid a fortune and some of them might well be able to get better jobs elsewhere. The boy argued back, but he did listen, and he was less vehement. He kept returning eagerly to the Science Museum and to the Harvard Observatory with Jack.

Around this time Benjy drew for me the fifth of a series of pictures of his school. Like its predecessors, the picture was a grim one. The building served as background to a portrait of a teacher, but the building dominated the picture, dwarfing the figure. The teacher's short arms and legs were awkward and angular, his eyes too large, and he lacked ears and a nose. This grim, tight-lipped white man, frightened and frightening, held a blackboard pointer, as he often did in real life. Near the school, the artist drew two automobiles.

Benjy's description of what he drew and intended to say went like this: "He's a strange guy; he says he was in the civil rights movement, and he wants to help us, so he comes here, but he's always complaining that we don't do things right, so why doesn't he go back to his own people! He lives in some town where — well, if I showed up there, they'd have police dogs go chase me down fast as can be. He says our school is terrible, and they should build a new one. I agree with him on that score — nothing works right! When he isn't telling us we're all doing wrong, he's going to the principal to tell him that the school should be torn down, and a new one built.

"I was trying to show him and the place where he works. They have cops near the school to keep an eye on us, so we don't fight and so we don't get pushed around by the older kids — they'll come offering us deals. With the cops there, they stay their distance. So I put the cops' cars and the yard and the school and him in the picture."

The picture told a story of a teacher and a building and the police — but no children. A city's institutional life, as it connects with a ghetto's life, was rendered, while the people to be "served," those who are taught and protected, were nowhere to be seen. The building looked to be in thorough disrepair: boarded windows, walls less than solid, a rather sinister, fiery smoke leaping out of a chimney, the door noticeably bolted. There were no trees, flowers, or grass, only the black tar of a yard and the black lines of the street and black patrol cars. The teacher's orange face certainly stood out — a lone, white presence in a world whose darkness was not only literal but metaphysical. Significantly, Benjy had no interest in drawing a sky, a sun, or earth, let alone birds, dogs or cats, or houses. The picture was a stark evocation of a child's dissatisfaction with, and estrangement from, a school and a teacher.

A month or so later Benjy was calling Jack his "pal." By then they had indeed become pals, though Jack still wanted Benjy to do well at school and to aim high with respect to a future education. He kept emphasizing — insisting upon — his role as a teacher. By then, Benjy felt he could talk to Jack. He told me, "I like it when Jack stops talking to me like a teacher and a minister and becomes just Jack, a guy who's not so sure about what he's going to be doing later on. I told him I'd sure like to be an astronaut, when they've built a spaceship that can fly to the planets and then to the stars.

Jack and I talk about space travel; he's not interested. I think he'll be a lawyer — but he says no, he wants to be a teacher. He'd spend the rest of his life struggling with kids like me! No way, I say! He laughs — and then he'll want to get down to the homework I should do! I do it so he can feel he's getting somewhere."

He stopped and smiled, and I smiled with him. He was saying in a nicely indirect, ironic way that the two of them were far from antagonists. When I asked him whether he'd like to draw a picture of Jack, Benjy said yes, but he wanted to know why. I reminded him that I'd asked him to draw pictures of himself, his mother, his granny, his teacher, and his school. He quietly nodded his head as if to say yes, he understood what this was all about.

He picked up the box of crayons as he looked toward the refrigerator in his mother's kitchen. Then he began with the blue crayon to make a huge sky filling up over half the paper. Below the sky he put down a layer of earth with the brown crayon and covered it with green. He created a hill on one side of the paper with the brown and green crayons, then moved back to the sky, using yellow for a big glowing, smiling sun. On the hill, he used the brown crayon to construct a human figure, then used black for the features and to put something in the hands, which were lifted skyward. Switching to brown, he drew another person, bigger. That figure, too, held an object in his raised arms. For a few seconds I thought they were both holding guns (the observer as doubter, suspicious critic), but after I asked discreetly what was happening, Benjy apologized for not explaining. He pointed at the two individuals on top of the hill and said, "I'm sorry I can't draw better, but they're holding telescopes, and they'll be looking at the sky later, when it gets dark. Now they're talking."

He returned to his drawing and put in a naturalist's coda: trees and flowers galore. What would the two figures do until sundown, I wondered. Benjy then put an airplane in the sky and told me the two were talking about taking airplane trips, about places to go to on the earth and in the sky. They, of course, were Benjy and Jack, as the boy nonchalantly told me. If he were a better artist, he said, he'd proudly show the picture to Jack, the bigger of the two figures, on whom he had lavished much attention and care. The two, standing close to each other, looked as if they were in harmonious agreement about their telescopes as instruments of pleasure and instruction.

The more time I spent with Benjy and Jack and with several other children and their mentors, who were college students or medical students, the less abstract "mentoring" became to me; I began to see it as a mix of friendship, instruction, guidance, and inspiration. When I returned to Miss Freud months later, I brought along several narrative accounts of children, the tapes of our exchanges, and, not least, a stack of drawings, including the four described in this chapter. She listened patiently, as always, examined the drawings circumspectly, asked me what I thought, and mused aloud about what she saw and what she guessed.

She also engaged me in a wonderful discussion about mentoring. First, she pointed out, we ought to ask ourselves the derivation of the word. I hadn't bothered to look up "mentor" in the dictionary. I simply assumed that I knew what the word meant: a person who is a respected adviser and teacher and who becomes for a student someone of great importance, one whose example is to be followed, whose way of thinking or doing things is carefully noted and emulated. She, however, *had* looked the word up and had gotten a brief lesson in Greek literary and religious history. Mentor was the friend of Odysseus who became an important person in the life of Odysseus's son, Telemachus. He was an instructor, a moral example, a wise and revered figure. It is said that the goddess Athena entered Mentor, presumably to help him do his work: her divine inspiration became Mentor's wonderfully animated, infectious capacity to help a young man grow and find his way.

Miss Freud doted on that story, and as she gave me her brief but lively lecture, I remembered her father's lifelong and passionate interest in the ancient Greeks, especially Sophocles and Euripides. All very touching, I thought — but not quite to the point of mentoring in late-twentieth-century secular America, with very poor children as our modern-day equivalents of Telemachus and with students in the position of the Mentor of old. When Miss Freud finished her lesson in the classics, she took one look at me and obviously read my mind: Interesting — but so what!

She told me first what I was thinking, then said, "You are wondering what the story of Mentor and Telemachus and Odysseus has to do with these children you know and their mentors — who are young people in college, remember, or well-intentioned adults, and not close friends of the fathers of the children they hope to influence. In the Greek legend, Mentor was godlike; he was trusted by a father and then handed on to the son. He inspired the son, helped him grow up and become the good and decent and brave person the father was and the son turned out to be. It is interesting — the Mentor of the Greek legend is not a teacher or professor, or a volunteer from another part of the city, someone whose job it is to impart information to groups of students. He was closely connected to the family, had that kind of credibility. He himself was inspired, and he wanted to inspire the next generation, and he did.

"Now what are these mentors you know like? They aren't regular teachers either; they're not, as Mentor was, you might say, an especially revered and admired Dutch uncle. Often they are of a different race, and almost always they are of a different class. Even if the mentor was born poor, he or she, by virtue of being a college student, is headed upward — has already 'risen,' you might say. Of course, there must be some mentors — though not in the programs you are working with — who are of the same race *and* class: a person in the neighborhood, maybe, who takes on a younger person and really works to advise and guide and teach and inspire and help shape the life of the younger person. [I thought of some drug dealers I had met, perverse neighborhood mentors of sorts.] What matters, obviously, is the attitude of the young person whom the older person wants to lead. But the question is, Does the younger person want to follow? If the younger person has followed, how come? What enables that kind of relationship? How lasting will it — can it — be? What about failures — do some would-be mentors simply lack the ability to enlist from the young the requisite emotional response?"

She gave me time to think about her remarks, and then we had a full hour to talk about identification, in a one-on-one relationship; about idealization in the young; and about her conviction that only certain children could be mentored successfully, and then only by certain kinds of mentors. She offered a critically important series of observations.

"A child who already has a reasonably solid conscience — however much it is endangered by the drives that adolescence gives such power to and by the social and racial forces at work in the society — that child will be able to connect with a mentor, take in the mentor's ideas and values and add them to those that the child already has acquired. If the child hasn't learned the difference between right and wrong, I doubt even Athena, *un*disguised, will be able to save the child for society! Many of these children, you will note, have no fathers or have very little to do with their fathers. They are not doing well in school, probably because they haven't been given the reason to do so at home, by parents convinced that school really counts, and in school, by teachers who really believe that there is a future for the children they teach — and have not themselves become discouraged. I am simplifying here — we could talk for hours about the educational problems of ghetto children and of their teachers, who can often be in a tough bind as they try to make up for so much that the children they teach simply don't have, haven't acquired: I am talking about psychological resources, apart from the absent economic ones!

"I think those two children whose drawings we've looked at both tell us the same thing: that a child who has *something* going at home — as many children do, even those from very poor circumstances and troubled families — can become engaged with an older person and really use that person to the best advantage: copy, imitate, rely upon, follow in the footsteps of and also [as] a sounding board, a person to test things out on and to plain test, and tease, and challenge, and confront, and get angry at. We are talking about, I think, an intense person-to-person association: a friendship, a teacher-student involvement, a counselor with someone to advise, a coach with a child whose athletic challenge is to take on the world and negotiate with some success!

"Mentors do a lot that you and I do — and receive affections and animosities, attitudes and feelings once meant for parents, and still meant for them, and released toward the mentor through the intimacy, the intensity of the relationship. I hope those mentors you know can take the heat: the one who is so obviously preferred by the white girl to her regular teacher, as her drawings show, and the one who has become a fellow 'seer' of the young boy — the two of them, together, trying to get a bigger view of life, certainly bigger than that offered in the school and the schoolyard the boy sees every day!"

When she stopped talking we looked at those four drawings again and let them silently tell us something of what mentoring can come to mean: a child seeing sun rather than rain; a child finding it possible to leap toward the heavens, to envision a beyond, rather than feel confined to the bleakest and most barren of worlds. Not that either Maureen or Benjy had been easy to get to know or willing to fall quickly or happily into a close, trusting relationship with a mentor. These children were, in different ways, hurt and angry, and the vehemence they directed at their regular teachers and the schools they attended was not fully deserved. No question that plenty went wrong in those schools (what school can lay claim to perfection, or even know what it is?), and no doubt some of the teachers made errors. But both Susie and Jack could testify to the provocations, the disbelief, the hostile withdrawals, sudden and seemingly senseless, that "went with the territory," as Jack put it with a shrug. After he used that phrase, made that gesture, I thought I'd gotten closer to an understanding of mentoring: a kind of resigned acceptance, based on a commitment. The child has been denied a lot, and will make sure you know that, and maybe make you pay a bit because of it, and then, if he or she weathers some storms, the intellect will assert itself, the emotions become less raw and turbulent.

I said this to Anna Freud, and she nodded. She would be the last, she reminded me, to offer elaborate definitions of something as complex as the bond between a mentor and his or her young friend. But she agreed that Jack's shrug probably was a "bigger message" than Jack "may have intended" — a testimony, actually. He was saying, I know I am embarked on a journey that won't be (shouldn't be) brief or without many setbacks, and I've forsaken enough pride (narcissism) that I won't get jumpy and impatient too often, so that I won't take too many challenges (and setbacks) personally, but rather, will keep my eyes and ears open, and wait for the moments when good luck conspires with a ripening connection, a widening and broadening of vision, of responsiveness. Then is the time of the telescopes shared, the first step and the next and the next step taken — the mentor, in fact, surprised, affirmed by his young friend's initiative. Mentoring as one person handing another along until the moment that allows both of them together to envision possibilities hitherto out of sight.

· FOUR ·

Hazards

B Y 1961 I had completed residencies in pediatrics, psychiatry, and child psychiatry and was in training in psychoanalysis at the New Orleans Psychoanalytic Institute. I was the chief of the neurology and psychiatry unit at the United States Air Force Hospital at Keesler Field in Biloxi, Mississippi, and I had worked with many quite troubled men, women, and children. Yet that year I found myself talking with quite normal, solid, and sensible children who were caught by accident in a major historical crisis, the school desegregation struggle in New Orleans, and also with young men and women working for SNCC in the civil rights movement. I have alluded in an earlier chapter to some of what I learned under those circumstances.

As Erik H. Erikson, a teacher of mine, kept telling me in 1962, when I had the first of many conversations with him about the relationship between individual initiatives and social change, those of us who are trained in psychiatry and psychoanalysis have to be careful when we try to understand the thoughts and actions of people who are going about the business of changing the world.[1] We have to be wary of turning ordinary (and, morally, not so ordinary) people into caricatures of themselves by our application of psychiatric and psychoanalytic nomenclature. Viewing them from that perspective is a self-serving reductionist indulgence, at the least; and doing so can even amount to a sadly instructive outburst of name-calling under cover of a social science used normatively to punish those who challenge the status quo. I had to abandon the language and mannerisms of the clinic for a psychology of every-day human activity. If it is true that no one is without problems, it is also true that most people manage to live fairly useful and con-structive lives without recourse to people like me, with our words, our viewpoints, and our judgments, some of which are less value free and more class- and race-connected than we may realize.

I learned this new way of thinking slowly, and not without making many mistakes — often falling prey to the inclination to make those psychological pronouncements that earn all too ready public attention, if not awe. Moreover, some of my SNCC friends began to call to my attention another possible danger in 1962 and 1963. They were concerned that I would bend so far in the oppo-site direction that the clear and crying personal anguish and hang-ups of some people would be brushed aside so as not to label anyone gratuitously, unfairly, with the words and phrases of psy-chopathology.

By late 1962 it was clear to me that in spite of all my reserva-tions about my role in SNCC, a number of young civil rights activists whom I had come to know quite well very much wanted to talk with me about what was happening to them psychologically. They were not asking to be called "patients," they were not asking for therapy or treatment. But they were in some inner trouble, and they turned to me because I was a psychiatrist, and their troubles, rather obviously, had to do with their worries, fears, and anxieties, their increasing "low spirits," as one of them described the way he felt.

I was quick to point out to these young men and women that their psychological state was a consequence, mostly, of what was happening in their lives — the threats, the beatings, the imprison-ment, the constant harassment, the spying by local and state of-ficials, not to mention the illustrious Federal Bureau of Investiga-tion. The psychiatric patients I had worked with in the late 1950s had come to see me in a hospital clinic because they were still struggling with conflicts that had developed during their childhood and adolescent years — the disorders and early sorrows of family life that still had a hold on their lives. In contrast, the young people in SNCC were responding to brutal sheriffs, sadistic jailers, and unrelenting, hostile mobs. The issue was not neurotic distortion of reality based on childhood suffering that persists into adulthood, but the exhaustion and worse that can come from contemporary suffering at the hands of a society that won't relent in its punitiveness.

Weariness and Resignation

I began reporting on this latter kind of psychological distress as early as 1963. The first of many papers I would write about my work in medical and psychiatric journals was titled "Social Struggle and Weariness."[2] That essay reported in guarded but candid language many conversations I'd had with frankly worn-down youths, some of whom described their condition as "battle fatigue" or "exhaustion" of the kind that takes place in war.

At the time, I did not want to publish too much of what they were telling me — that "war" was still actively going on, and the outcome was by no means assured. But many of those who had talked with me urged me to make some communication with my colleagues. As one young woman, Laura, put it, "They should know what happens when you do this kind of work, with the deck stacked so high against you." She was speaking from direct personal knowledge of the "wearing down." She emphatically did not want pity from me or anyone else. Although she and I had many long talks, she did not believe they would give her the help she needed or a recovery. She was self-aware and psychologically sophisticated enough to realize that in her exhaustion she would exhibit her own particular vulnerability, her response to terrible stress. "Who wouldn't begin to crack under all this?" she once asked rhetorically. Then she conjectured, "I suppose we all crack in our different ways."

Laura had not always been politically active or even aware. She had grown up in a well-to-do, conservative Connecticut family, and when she went to Vassar she had little interest in efforts to desegregate the South. Her boyfriend, Tim, a student at Yale, had also been raised in a wealthy old-line family. But in their junior year Tim and Laura read *The American Dilemma* by Gunnar Myrdal (sent, unexpectedly, by Tim's mother), and their eyes were opened. The more they read, the more they saw in the society around them.

Soon Laura and Tim were marching in front of the restaurants of national chains that honored the South's segregationist laws and contemplating further action on their campuses. They met in New York City with representatives of southern civil rights groups, became even more energized by them, and arranged to go to Atlanta for workshops. They became committed civil rights activists and worked to enlist the help of others. By that time their parents (even Tim's mother) were becoming alarmed. The more concerned they became, however, the more radical was the response of the two students. Tim and Laura threatened to leave school, live together without marrying, move to the South, and work in a rural area to try to help Negroes register to vote. (Thirty years ago students did not drop out as regularly as they do now, nor did they live openly as a couple as readily and without notoriety as is the case now.)

Tim and Laura did stay in college and in the good graces of their families. But shortly after graduating in 1961, they announced that they were going to head South and take on the rural sheriffs and the urban police, with their dogs and nightsticks, who were by then becoming familiar sights on national television. Aghast, the four parents tried persuasion, then threats of financial punishment, to no avail. (Eventually both sets of parents would contribute money to Dr. King's Southern Christian Leadership Conference and would reconcile with Laura and Tim and take pride in what they had done — even as the country moved, from 1960 to 1965, toward more and more support for the civil rights movement in the South.) For Laura and Tim, no outcry at home, no withholding of allowances, no stopping of dividends from stock portfolios, would have had any deterrent effect. "We were ready to do what we believed was right," Laura pointed out from the perspective of a year's residence and experience in the South. Indeed, she added, the more opposition the families offered, the more determined the two young people were to go ahead with their plans.

These two activists were regarded as brave, resourceful, and thoughtful by the people with whom they worked. They traveled from county to county, state to state — itinerants of sorts, ever ready to lend a hand to local civil rights people in need of support. As whites, their presence very much escalated the stakes for sheriffs, segregationist lawyers, school authorities, and county officials. "The next thing you know," one high school principal in the Mississippi Delta told me in 1963, referring to Laura and Tim and a few others like them, "there'll be a bunch of their newspaper friends coming down here, checking into our motels, and out on the prowl, looking for any trouble they can find."

It didn't take long for the two to accumulate a jail record. Tim was always ahead of Laura in that regard, much to her annoyance. Time and again the police would arrest him but leave her to fend for herself, though with threats of taking her in if there were any future provocations. She did not heed those warnings, and eventually she paid a stiff price. "We talk a lot about equality here [at SNCC], and we should: 'Black and white together and equal.' I hate to sound like a grouch, but there's another struggle we're going to have to wage one of these days, for another kind of equality! I'm talking about the sexes — and that goes for white women as well as Negro women. The way some men behave . . ."

She stopped abruptly, deciding she ought not to continue. To do so, many would have said in 1963, was to engage in a major "distraction," a word often lobbed across a room at someone who brought up a matter others did not want to examine. Then she resumed, "Here I am worried about lagging behind! My friend has been admitted to many more jails than I have! I'm a victim of discrimination!"

She stopped again, smiled wanly, ran her right hand through fairly unkempt hair, and looked at her fingernails with a faint smile. The last time she had been in jail overnight, the sheriff's assistant, a woman, had come to her cell and told her they wanted her fingernails cut lest she hurt herself. Her nails were not all that long, and she had no desire to use them self-destructively, but they were cut "down so far you'd have thought I was biting them, eating them, as a regular diet." As she told that story and others — about insults she had heard, insinuations, invitations, bargains offered — she lost her ironic bemusement, and a tightness came over her face. Her eyes looked down. She folded her arms and held them high, perhaps to express tension or dissatisfaction or a grim sadness.

Then came her outcry: "I've given up counting the number of propositions I've heard. I've given up even remembering some of the awful things those people say. I used to keep a diary; I thought it was important to try to record what happened so that others could know. At first I felt sorry for those people — the women working in those jails and the women locked up, and even the sheriffs and their deputies: they're all people who are down and out in their own way. For them the Negroes are the one big possession white people have — white skin is their million dollars in the bank, their fortune of self-respect! I'd hear them making all their snide or nasty comments, and I'd say to myself that these folks are in the gutter, and they deserve understanding, if not a little pity. I'd even try to talk with them, and sometimes I'd get somewhere — I mean *we* would.

"I especially remember one woman locked up — she'd stolen something. For a white woman to be in jail, even for an hour or two, was a scandal. The sheriff's wife was watching over us (a boondoggle: she was paid extra for 'white folks'), and the three of us got to talking, and pretty soon we had a lot going. I wish you were there with that tape recorder — though I'll bet if the tape recorder were there, we'd never have talked as we did. I *know* if you — if any man — had been there, we'd have stayed apart from each other, the way it's supposed to be with prisoners, and between prisoners and the guards.

"It all got started when the sheriff came and got sarcastic with his wife. She didn't answer him back, but when he left, she swore like hell at him — and I clapped. She was surprised — then she smiled, and I told her she was right on target. She opened right up. She told me all she went through, and the more I heard, the sorrier I felt for her. Then *she* said it with no help from me. 'He treats me like a nigger.' Then she remembered who I was, and she changed the word right away: 'like a nigra.' I didn't say a word. She just rambled on and on, like a lawyer, marshaling her evidence. When she stopped, the other prisoner spoke up, and she said that there are lots of 'lousy, rotten people in the world,' and 'most of them are men,' and she [the sheriff's wife] agreed, and that's when I said — I decided to take the risk — that the 'colored people,' I called them (to stay in their ballpark linguistically, I guess!) take a lot on their shoulders for others, and they're not as lousy and rotten as a lot of whites who shout and screech at them. Amazingly, they both agreed. They both said, 'Uh-huh,' and then they went further and said they really felt sorry for 'the colored' because 'most of them, they're good people — and they hold everything together for us,' that's what she [the sheriff's wife] said.

"In a few minutes she decided to go get the one colored lady in jail and bring her to the room where we were, and give her a Coke, or an orange soda, like we were drinking. And as she got up to go get her, she said, 'Everyone calls her the town whore, but I'll tell you, there's lots of sleeping around among the fancy folks who live in the big houses, and no one knows what's going on, or if they do, no one is going to say anything, that's for sure.'

"A few seconds later — I couldn't believe it! — we'd integrated the bastion of the county's segregationist power, and we were sipping our Cokes and making fun of men. 'The best women's talk,' they called it, the two white women, 'in a long time.' The Negro woman wasn't shy; she joined them, much to my surprise. She told a few stories that got us all to sit in complete silence — about the white men who came seeking her. 'I don't want to know a word about them,' the sheriff's wife said, but then she changed her mind. She *did* want to know, but she didn't want to know any names. 'Honey, I wasn't going to tell you any,' the Negro said — and I was amazed at the way she spoke: friendly and a little sardonic."

Laura stopped and smiled, then abruptly turned grim. I asked a series of questions meant to draw her out, and she answered tensely. After all, she'd been through plenty of confrontations, at least ten arrests, and five jailings. She wasn't tired, she said, but then she added, "I'm not tired today; I'm feeling all right. But I *am* tired — I'm plain weary. I get the feeling that we'll be at this for years and years, and I wonder — I really do — whether things will change all that much, once we've 'won' these battles, and the Negro has all the legal rights in Mississippi that whites have, and throughout the South, too, and the schools have been desegregated, and Negroes go to the polls without worrying about sheriffs and someone's gun or his truck with dynamite inside it, waiting to be used."

More silence. Picking up on the word "weary," I asked whether she was just in a low mood that day, or whether she was trying to say something broader. Without hesitation, she said yes, the latter. She was describing not only herself but others, too: "People being pushed around a lot begin to wear down, even if they're winning some of the battles they're fighting." I asked her to tell me how that "wearing down" affected them, how it got expressed. She briefly teased me — "You should know, you're the shrink" — but then, quite poignantly, she let me know what she had been noticing.

"After a few of these encounters with the police or a sheriff you begin to know what to expect, and it's not very nice. I'll get up some mornings, and I wonder what the point of it all is. I mean, will it make any difference? I know, I *know* the answer: yes, it will. But I don't feel it in my bones. It's not that I'm physically tired, no. It's upstairs, in my head. I'm sort of resigned. I'll stick with it, but I've lost something, some kind of hopeful, alive confidence. I begin to say our slogan, 'We shall overcome,' on a picket line, but I'm not sure I believe it. I'm going through the motions. We *shall*, I know — but now I can picture new problems replacing the old ones, and after a while, feeling this way, you begin to wonder.

"I snap out of it — I'm not saying I feel this way all the time, or even most of the time. But it's growing — enough for me to be talking like I am now with you. And I see this in others, in Tim, in a lot of the people out there, marching and picketing and organizing and trying to confront not only the white power structure but, let's face it, the Negro power structure, too — all those Uncle Toms who are in the pockets of the big shots who run the towns and counties and cities. The other day Tim and I were talking, and for the first time I heard him being nostalgic about Yale and those stupid drinking places up there — the whole world he was so eager to leave a couple of years ago. He doesn't really want to go back to *that* — but he's tired, too, and he's trying to grin and bear it and stiff-upper-lip it, and *great*, if he can. But I know him too well, and when he sighs a lot, and stares into space just a few seconds too long, even if it's only once or twice a day, then I know this guy is beginning to wonder whether his earlier expectations are going to come about, and whether he shouldn't be thinking of something else to do, some other way to be useful to this fight. I don't know what other way. Maybe by getting a job to report, to write on what we've seen, what we know."

For a few minutes she became intensely self-critical, almost self-lacerating: she was "spoiled," she had no right to speak as she had just done, given what others who had so much less than she had to carry on their shoulders without "bellyaching." "This is temporary," she assured herself and me.

But soon she acknowledged her stress and the exhaustion that was beginning to influence how she thought not only about her own situation but about the prospects of the movement itself, to which she had so closely connected her life. She pointed out that even the veteran "Negro leaders of SNCC" and of the other civil rights groups had shown signs, occasionally, of a similar tiredness or "resignation." Some of them had talked about resigning — leaving their work for a while — only to stop and realize that they were thinking of resigning because they felt increasingly resigned.

She laughed, enjoying the play on words, then began to accuse herself again: she was frivolous and overeducated; this was all a "passing mood." Yet she quickly reversed herself once more with a series of rhetorical questions expressing her confusion. Did others feel this way, those who weren't in the civil rights movement but were trying to make the world a bit better for people near and far?

I didn't know how to answer her questions about how people manage the kind of challenges — the ordeal, at times — she was facing. I hedged with the expectable evasions and qualifications, falling back on individuals and their differences. The truth was that like her, I was just beginning to learn about such matters (from her and others like her), and I didn't know how to think about the psychological turmoil she was describing, other than to try to document it.

*   *   *

In the thirty years since then, I have had many conversations with young activists and volunteers and have often heard remarks surprisingly similar to hers. Their talk is of uncertainty, of "reevaluation of objectives," of doubts about what is to be done. They speak about the need for rest and rehabilitation, for "a clearer formulation of procedures," for retreats where the participants would share their ongoing difficulties, their battle fatigue, their "tendency toward a more passive posture over time." I have culled these remarks from many statements, announcements, and tape-scripts of conferences in which the participants, all involved in community service projects, are also involved in what they so often call the ups and downs of coping with the various stresses and tensions generated by the work they do.[3]

The longer I listen to those "debriefings," those "breaks for reflection," the more I realize that even in communities where reasonably comfortable people are able to do reasonably conventional work without harassment, beatings, ostracism, or jailings, a measure of hesitation, of tiredness, of relative apathy can begin to take root. Of course there are fluctuations — a spell of the old, unqualified optimism will prevail yet again — but all in all, many doing service comment on their second thoughts, their lagging interest in the work being done, their feelings of being winded or out of breath, footsore and just plain beaten.

A student of mine who was working with the elderly in a nursing home spoke guardedly, on occasion, of the burdens the various staff members carried. In this way he could introduce some of his own budding concerns. "I see those nurses and the aides working, and I wonder how they can take it day after day. I only come here once a week, sometimes twice a week, and I've noticed that there are times — well, I sure admire people who do this for a living, and it's sort of nonstop for them. I wonder whether they get down sometimes. I've talked to one of the nurses, and she said, 'Look, it's a job; things could be a lot worse — I could be out of a job!' But I've seen her when she's whistling and singing and cheerful, and she really gets the old people to smile; and I've seen her when she's pretty sour — with me, and with the patients, too. She's reciting rules or telling people she's too busy for this or for that. And I've heard them remind her that she doesn't always say that, and 'only yesterday' — they'll start in with that as an opener, and she knows what they're going to say, and she cuts them right off!

"It's true, it could just be her mood; we all have our moods. But I notice lately I've been having a few down times there. And so I was wondering why. Because when I first started I never felt like that — I was all gung-ho, and the more I did, the more I helped, the harder I worked, the better I liked it! Then I began to stop and think. That's a bad sign, my sister says. [She worked as a volunteer, teaching retarded people to swim.] When you start thinking, according to her, you're going to think it's all too much, and no matter what you do, the same old problems will be out there, so why not just do something, sure, but don't expect too much, and take breaks when you need them, and just drop out for a week or two, now and then, to recharge your batteries."

He stopped, afraid he was going too far — and not just because he was sharing his thoughts with someone else. He started to call himself lazy and selfish and "always tempted to goof off in situations that demand a lot." I hadn't noticed any laziness in him, or selfishness. All along he had been, even when he voiced those unflattering remarks about himself, a rather steady and conscientious worker. He erred, if at all, according to the staff at the nursing home, on the side of enthusiasm and generosity of self, to the point that they had cautioned him that the work could, over time, prove to be draining. Not for him — or so he thought for several months. But now he was less formidably energetic and optimistic. These people *were* elderly, he was beginning to acknowledge, and a lot of them would soon enough be gone.

When he made that acknowledgment, he found it necessary to change tack. "You mustn't emphasize the negatives! We're *all* going to be gone in a snap of the fingers when you think of how much time came before us and will come after we're no longer here! The thing that matters is *today*; that's what you have to think. You should remind yourself that sometimes you have to rev yourself up if you're headed toward a low period. Talk to yourself, that's what I do. I say, Hey, you, shape up and stop letting your feet work so slow, and your eyes begin to droop. Quicken your step and look at people with your eyes as wide open as possible, and be glad you're there with them, and say to yourself, If you can just help one person out during one visit, so the guy or the woman will feel they've had a good day, and they're really more upbeat for a while — I know it won't last forever — then you've done your job, and you can hold your head as high as anyone else. That's how I try to think to myself; but sometimes I need to talk to myself more than that, and there may not be the words."

He was edging toward a fuller discussion of the weariness, the resignation he sometimes felt as he stood at a nursing station and looked down a long corridor at all those rooms full of people nearing the end of their time on this earth. He once had thought about all those people being so grateful for even the smallest gestures, and hence he was rewarded and even stimulated because he had many chances to make them more comfortable. They were glad to engage with him, talk to him with warmth and appreciation. Now, it seemed, he was noticing the cranky side of even those people who were usually cheerful.

Cynicism

One can make too much of a volunteer's spells of weariness and of a resignation that says, Things will go on, and I can try, but it's really hard to make the kind of decisive difference I'd hoped to make. On the other hand, one can make too little of such a feeling, shrug it off as a minor dip in mood. Sometimes what starts as weariness becomes hardened into a form of cynicism — a doubtfulness about the world, about people and their possibilities. I use the word "cynicism" because I have heard others use it rather often, sometimes as an epithet directed squarely at themselves. Indeed, cynicism is often touted as "the enemy" by volunteers as they give themselves to service but worry about the personal consequences.

I heard such a cautionary, self-directed remonstrance from a young woman of Hispanic background from the Rio Grande Valley, a college student who was working with enthusiasm as a tutor in a black and Hispanic neighborhood of Boston. She commented on the pleasure her work with children brought her and made clear, without boasting, that she brought considerable resourcefulness to her work. But suddenly — her remarks a surprise to herself as well as to me, I realized — she slumped a bit in her chair and said, "I hope I don't begin to turn all this into a routine. I worry sometimes when I hear some of the teachers talking — they sound so cynical. They say 'oh, yeah' a lot, as if they mean, We've heard *that* before, or we've seen *that* tried and tried, and it's all the same in the end. I actually heard four teachers talking the other day, and I don't think they realized I was in the next room. The door was open, and I was reading the assignment I'd given my kids. But I couldn't pay attention because I heard them talking away — and I got upset. They said that 'it's a job,' and 'you do what you can, but you're a fool if you think the world will be that much different in the end,' talk like that.

"I wanted to go in there and give them a pep talk! But to be honest, I knew what they were saying — I could understand. Before this, I was a Big Sister, and I used to work in a daycare center when I was in high school. And sometimes I'd wonder why we were all trying so hard with the little kids, because some of their mothers didn't seem to care much about them — they came from work, and they were beat, really beat. The woman who ran the center once said to me, 'Don't let it all get to you, or you'll become very cynical about the world, and that's no good.' I think she could see that it was happening! I'd work hard with the kids, but I knew a lot of what we did in the day got undone at night. The kids told us that when they went home, they'd get spankings for no reason at all — *beatings* a lot of the time. They'd see these big rats running around. They'd see big fights — I didn't want to hear too much, because it did something to me. I'd begin to wonder, What's the use? Like that lady said, if you start asking that question too often, you're getting into some real trouble!

"Even with my little sister — I'm very fond of her, and we get on great, but I go visit her sometimes, and I realize all the troubles she has, her family has, and I wonder whether it'll really make any difference that I'm coming there, and we take our walks and get some ice cream, maybe. I know she likes me and I like her, but will that change anything? That's what I'll wonder sometimes. Not all the time, no. [I had asked whether she felt that way constantly or episodically.] I'll shake off my pessimism; I'll remind myself of what my mom says, that a few minutes with a nice person is like sunshine getting rid of the shadows; but they can come back, those shadows."

Among those engaged in social and political struggles cynicism is no stranger, and that is true as well for Peace Corps and VISTA workers. Sometimes a threat of sorts looms over their intensely committed lives, making them all the more susceptible to disappointment and disenchantment. One Peace Corps member, who as a student had tutored ghetto children, was helping devise a new curriculum for a village school in Ecuador. He said, "I'll be going along fine, and I'm really satisfied that we're getting someplace, and then all of a sudden some bureaucrat says something, and our whole plan is in trouble. I'll come home, and part of me is upset, sad, but part of me is really furious. And then I'll clamp down, and that's when I feel myself getting cold and cynical. I just say, Hey, this is the way the world is, and don't be so surprised, and do what you can, and get what you can out of this experience, but that's *it*. I mean, don't think you're here to change human nature and save the world, because the fact is, people are people, and there's a lot of bad in them, a lot of selfishness and stupidity and, worse, a lot of meanness and spitefulness. But I'm sounding too cynical now. There's a lot of good in people, too!"

The growing tension between hopefulness and serious second thoughts about that hopefulness sets the stage for cynicism. Some individuals, introspective by nature, or given to self-examination as a result of past difficulties, can be quite articulate and knowing as they struggle to achieve a balance that precludes both the fatuous cheerfulness that is blind to all sorts of dangers, setbacks, and obstacles and the gloomy cynicism that can skeptically overshadow any glimmer of hope — to the point that obvious steps forward in a given project are discounted, even discredited. Among the civil rights workers, whose shifts of mood and attitude first alerted me to the various personal hazards of volunteerism, cynicism was not rare, was even persuasive — and much discussed by those who succumbed to it, or yes, regarded themselves, at times, as blessed by it.[4]

A black SNCC field secretary, who did heroic work in rural

Alabama and Georgia, for a time described himself as a cynic and was anxious to urge that point of view on others, as if it was a much-needed remedy. He told me, "I came to all this from Howard University, where I was premed. I really believed in people — too much listening to my mom, who's always ready to buy something from a salesman and who's always ready to pray for someone, because 'that's what Jesus would do!' My father was no help either; he was a social worker, and he had a divinity school education first. So he was always telling us that people can change, they really can, if you assume they can, and if you try to help them, so 'the better part of them will be able to take over.' That phrase, that way of seeing people — it's my father to a tee!

"No wonder I came South with the idea that I'd offer myself to those people, do whatever was necessary for them, and then, by God, they'd take over, the better part of them, and that would be that! Sure, I knew there were social and political problems — what everyone now calls 'structural' ones — that need to be solved. But I think my idea was this: once we all come together and sing 'We Shall Overcome' and start talking and marching and praying — start putting ourselves on the line — then all of that will crumble, and the good side of the world, of people, would begin to appear and it would take over, like my dad would say.

"Maybe I could have kept thinking of life that way if I'd stayed in the nice, protected life my parents had, and they gave to me. People talk about how hard it is to be a Negro, but the black bourgeoisie has had its own walls of protection — and ignorance, and naiveté! Once I got down South, and started meeting sheriffs with guns drawn and ready to be fired, and heard myself called the foulest language in the world, and got kicked in the stomach and the groin, I began to understand how little my parents had taught me about the world — the world I'm now trying to change down here.

"The other day a white kid, just out of Princeton, showed up here. He's got his eyes looking at the sky, and he probably talks with God every night. I shouldn't speak like that, I know. He's full of ideals, idealism. He makes me feel like a first-class cynic. When I talk with him, I try to connect with him — connect with my own childhood. But the more I hear him, the happier I am that I've lost all that. I'm a little callous these days, maybe, and you lose something being like this, like I am, I know. But we're in a fight, and the fight is with a very cynical world, and if you don't have a little in you of what you're fighting in your enemy, then you stand to lose, that's what I guess I feel. The only problem is if you let your cynicism take over — you're down a road that could get you into some trouble that way."

Arrogance, Anger, and Bitterness

When cynicism takes over, other emotions swiftly follow. The young man who spoke of his own cynicism knew (and at other moments had acknowledged) how angry he was becoming, how embittered — not only at bullying, murderous sheriffs, but at plenty of black people who, in their own way and for their own reasons, were resisting SNCC's confrontational policies. He found himself increasingly angry at the moderate to liberal world, white and black, of Washington, D.C., that he had left a year earlier. Sometimes, with an impressive candor, he would spell out the basis of that anger and its serious dangers to his own sense of himself.

"With each struggle here — and the defeats! — I find it harder to keep my composure. I think of all those comfortable liberals up North, saying what they think is 'right' (or is it fashionable?), and full of their own high opinion of themselves, and I compare them with some of these poor folks here, who are risking their lives every day — the good, simple people (there aren't many of them!) as against the loud-mouthed intellectuals, the college professors who taught me and teach in all the fancy schools up there.

"The trouble is, you get angrier and angrier — I do! Then I think back on what I've said, and I'm not so happy with what I remember. I'm condemning people, and I sound like those I can't stand! This elderly [black] woman heard me talking about 'the intellectuals up North,' and after I'd poured out a gallon of rage and disgust, she came up to me and told me she wanted to clean my mouth and aim a hose at me, so I could get a lot of the mud off me! 'You're beginning to sound like the white folks I work for,' she told me. I know who they are — one of the town's lawyers, a snob if there ever was one. I got really mad at her. I said if I was sounding like those people, then she was beginning to sound like someone who has been working so long in a job, she ends up hearing her bosses everywhere, even in her own back yard. She laughed. She told me I shouldn't turn her into 'another enemy.' I wanted to scream, but instead I shut up, and that's what's happening to me, I'm getting more and more silent, and less and less interested in being nice to people." Later he poured out his resentments to a college classmate and felt much better for having done so.

Others have felt an angry righteousness, which can turn quickly to self-righteousness, prompted by experiences such as his or by social activism or volunteerism that may be less dangerous but is no less demanding. One elderly black woman worked hard to help other elderly people living isolated lives in the broken-down tenements of a Boston ghetto. She was quite grateful for the assistance of several students of mine. They did legwork for the agency she represented and drove her from place to place as she investigated complaints about inadequate heat or threats of eviction. Yet she would lose her customary graciousness at times and become not only outraged by the problems she was trying to resolve but heatedly scornful of others who were trying to make things better for Boston's elderly.

Sometimes she turned on the students, much to their chagrin and perplexity. One of them reported to me, "She'll blast the landlords, and we're with her, though not all of them are as bad as she makes them out to be. She'll blast the police and the firemen, and then she'll go after a lot of black people in her neighborhood, the ministers and the elected officials and the business people. If she were white, she'd be called a racist, a really agitated, angry one. Pretty soon you get the feeling, listening to her, that she's the only one out there doing anything! She'll even turn on us, and it makes no difference that we're black: she says the 'college kids who come out here' don't understand what's going on. She's looking right at us when she'll say something like that! We just hold our tongues because by now we know she'll calm down, and then explain herself, and then apologize!"

Not everyone can make an about-face of that kind. A person who can distance himself or herself from bitterness or arrogance by looking at those attitudes unflinchingly has some protection from their corrosive consequences. Some people become all too attached to bitterness, to the constant inclination to put down others — thereby, of course, giving themselves a boost. Not that there aren't plenty of clear, compelling reasons for a civil rights activist, a student engaged in community service, an older person doing volunteer work, to feel enraged or disappointed with, even contemptuous of, people in positions of power — or even those utterly without power.

Another student of mine spoke from his heart about the very real frustrations in his work. "I go to a school [to do tutoring] where the teachers are giving up; they constantly call in sick, or they say things are terrible, and there's nothing that can be done, or they end up really disliking their work but holding on for the security, the job, in a 'bad labor market.' I can't believe what they say sometimes — though I admit, I wonder what *I* would say if I was at that school every day, every week, and that was *it*: my life. I'll feel sorry for them one minute; I'll be angry at them the next; and I'll look down on them, I should add, some other times. Then there are moments when I get down, period. I just feel it's all pretty bad, *objectively*, and if I don't admit how bad it is, then I'm only fooling myself. Those are the worst days, when I'm down in the dumps myself about problems that are real as can be, and not to be upset by them is to be fooling yourself."

Despair

As I go over transcripts of interviews with volunteers of various backgrounds and ages, committed to a range of projects, I find the word "despair" commonly used.[5] "We despair about really accomplishing what needs to be accomplished," a college student said, referring to the academic programs the high schoolers he had come to know really needed and wouldn't ever get, he believed. "I despair for these children," a VISTA worker in Appalachia told me, lowering her head as if to express physically her sense of things.

A Peace Corps member in Africa, a former student who did

much community service while at college, wrote to me, "A lot of days I struggle with despair. I try to do the best I can, but I feel it's one step forward, two steps back, most of the time. The teachers here aren't that happy with what I suggest, and maybe they're right. I worked on an irrigation project and now we have a terrible drought — and besides, the people in the village aren't as happy with all we've done as we are! There is constant fighting over water, over who should get it, when it's available." He moved on to a happier subject — his fiancée's work as a teacher in an American private school — and then hastened to assure me (and himself) that basically he was doing fine, but it was quite clear that hope was no cheap commodity for him during his stay in the Ivory Coast. He had many times wondered whether there was any point to what he was doing, apart from the advantages that accrued to *him*.

That theme is often mentioned in connection with despair: the volunteer believes that he or she will learn a lot, "get" a lot from the experience, but that what is being done will not amount to much. Put differently, the person is not despairing of himself or herself; on the contrary, as my Peace Corps correspondent phrased it in a later letter, "things will work out very well" as a result of his stint of service: he would acquire much knowledge and experience, and in the course of doing so also acquire a "biographical item," as he worded it, trying to be sardonic about his own confessed careerism, which was increasingly on his mind as his two years of service were coming to an end.

This distinction between one's own prospects and the prospects of those with whom one is working may well account for despair in many volunteers. They feel considerable discomfort at the disparity and an increased consciousness of their own good luck; in contrast, the misfortunes of others seem engraved fatefully in stone.

"I come back from that detention center [for troubled, delinquent youths] and I realize that my feeble efforts to teach are a small drop in a big ocean, namely the life they've lived, and *will* live, it seems to me," said one college student. He declared that a sense of "futility" had overcome him, but he felt he must continue doing his work. "I talk about despairing for these kids because from birth, almost, they seem doomed. You read those charts and wonder how they've even gotten as far as they have — such terrible things in their families from day one. But I have to admit I like going over there, and I actually enjoy talking with those guys, and we laugh sometimes, and I figure, who knows, maybe this is a turning point for them — not because of anything I'm saying or doing, but because they've been hauled in and confronted by the law, by society, and so they might decide to change, somehow. That's what I'll think, and I'll say to myself, Look, you're doing all you can, and if nothing will change, then at least you've tried." He walked that tightrope: he despaired for others, yet felt enough hope and promise in life, its twists and turns, to "keep trucking," as he often phrased it — and, of course, he knew how much the work he did meant to him.

Especially among young volunteers, such as college students or members of VISTA or the Peace Corps, despair is commonly evoked during spells of reflection, which are sometimes welcome, sometimes dreaded. I sit with two students, a young athlete, who is a Big Brother to a ghetto boy, and a young actress (and brilliant scholar), who works in an inner-city school as a tutor. They discuss earnestly their hopes for the children they meet (the athlete also works as a coach with other ghetto children). For a while the emphasis is on possibility, on "the silver-lining scenario," as the actress calls her desire to be upbeat. Soon enough, though, that "silver lining" begins to disappear; the room seems to get darker with each sentence — and as if to point that out, and remedy it, the athlete reaches over, puts on a lamp near the chair he occupies. The actress smiles, says, "That's better" — and immediately announces that every once in a while, no matter her "pessimism," a child will surprise her, will show a real and convincing interest in learning, in being helped to learn.

It is those moments that nourish and sustain her, she points out. And then, a vivid description of other moments: "I will leave that school some days, and while I'm sitting on the subway I feel so sad, so upset — I feel I'm not really being of any help to anyone except maybe myself. I feel that God must have His reasons for letting children come into the world, that world of those kids. But I can't figure out what His reasons are. I can't even keep some of the horrible things I hear [from the teachers and guidance counselor] in my mind — it's too upsetting. I just try to forget it all — not the kids, but what's happened to them, and they're only ten or twelve years old.

"I try to 'accentuate the positive'; that's something my dad used to tell us to do. I hear him talking while the subway goes clickety-clack, clickety-clack: accentuate the positive, accentuate the positive. But there isn't much to accentuate — and the other half of the phrase (it's from a song, I think) is 'eliminate the negative.' How am I supposed to do that — how are those kids going to? By the time the subway pulls into Harvard Square, I think to myself, Thank God I'm back here. It's as if I've gone to a foreign land, where the sun can't break through the clouds, and the evenings are *very* long, and there's a shortage of food and clothing, of everything — and now, I'm back to this land of plenty, with long days and plenty of good cheer!"

As soon as that is said, she reverses herself, remembers some good moments she has had with particular tutees, tries to put a smile on her face, barely succeeds in doing so. She turns to her friend and fellow volunteer and asks him what he thinks. He tells her, more to the point, how he *feels*: "I'm down a lot because I had these really high expectations when I started, that I could get along real well with this kid, and we'd become friends, and we'd hang out, and pretty soon we'd be talking about his schoolwork and what he was going to do with his life — and that way he'd begin to think more seriously about things, and it would make a difference. The problem is, he doesn't seem to be going that way — I hate to say so, but it's true. So I'm really sorry I can't see a better picture emerging! I look at him when I go there, and we're walking, and I think to myself, He could be in real big trouble a year or two from now, real big trouble. I even told him that and warned him he was going down the wrong path, with the fights he was having, and not doing his work, but he just smiles or frowns, and I can't really get him to level with me, to open up and talk. That's the worst of it, the silence — I get discouraged, real discouraged. I feel like just ending it, saying good-bye. But you try to hold on — you hope he's listening, even if he's not letting you know, and things might change. But I doubt it."

On that note of gloom, he himself sinks into silence. His fellow volunteer talks about *her* discouragement and, like him, expresses her "hope against hope" that somehow "there will be a breakthrough for the kids." But she, too, ends on a downbeat note: "I wouldn't count on it." We all decide to go have lunch and lift ourselves into another frame of mind.

Depression ("Burnout")

Many of those who respond most heartily and zealously to the summons of a service program slip into a mood that is far more fixed and burdensome than that of those two students. They were able to shed the despair they connected to concrete and recurrent events in the lives of the youngsters they were meeting. They could change the subject, as it were, and either try to find the silver lining or keep reminding themselves that others had found it. They could accept the possibility that what seemed hopeless now might one day give way to a more providential turn of events. Moreover, their despair was linked not only to specific individuals (whose attitudes and actions evoked it) but to their own experiences with those individuals. When told, for instance, that a Little Brother or a tutee had done well in something, the dispirited if not despairing volunteer could quickly shift emotional gears and become at least guardedly willing to keep trying, keep working hard to reach and touch that Little Brother or student. But any number of individuals who have talked of the despair they feel about a child or a grownup or a group they are working with have, alas, gone beyond such pessimism to a more persuasive and tenacious despair — of a kind that shapes their entire social outlook, their view of what is possible and what is impossible.

In my years of working with young and older volunteers, I have heard so many references to "burnout" that I almost expect to hear the phrase in every conversation with someone who is doing community service.[6] The phrase for many is a shorthand way of saying, "This work can become exhausting, and I am on the way to an exhausted state of mind, and once there, I will be 'burnt out,' worn down quite badly, and so not able to do the kind of service I formerly offered." Not that people don't vary in their definitions of burnout, or in the personal stories about what burnout has meant in their experience as they have tried to understand it and overcome it.

Some of the students with whom I have worked use the term interchangeably with "depression" to convey a *general* sense of futility and hopelessness, a paralysis of word and deed — as if there is no point in talking or persisting with one's activities. A senior college student, for instance, warned me (warned herself) that she was getting near burnout in her work at a rest home for the elderly. She amplified her dire forecast this way: "I get to feeling that there's no use to all this. I try hard, and the people seem to perk up, and then I'm happy, I'm pleased. But I've learned a lot this past year. I've learned that the people *do* perk up, but a few minutes after we've gone, the same old problems are at work: the staff is too small, the old folks have a terrible time — they get cold food and inadequate nursing, and they're shouted at and pushed and pulled and smacked. I know because one of the ward attendants called us up and arranged to meet us away from the home and told us the whole story. Maybe I never should have listened.

"No, I was feeling real low before I heard that. I began to feel that there were better things we could be doing with our time. Then I got disgusted with myself for thinking like that. Then I began to think it's an ego trip that we're on: we come there and we expect everyone to make a fuss, and they do, and we feel wonderful, we feel gratified! They tell the elderly to smile and clap at us, and they do — maybe they're afraid of what will happen if they refuse. [She had learned of that detail from the ward attendant.] But even if none of that was happening, we are there with people who are out of it, or they're close to death, and we try, but it takes a lot out of you, a tremendous amount, and after a session or two, you go there real tired before you even arrive, and you leave feeling you've lost five quarts of blood.

"I'm selfish saying this, but I'd better just tell it like it is. The fun has gone out of it all, the surprises, too. And the cold, hard truth is that we're not making nearly as much of a difference as we'd hoped. I know that sounds spoiled of me, to speak that way. But it's how we've begun to feel — really useless and helpless a lot of the time. When a woman I've been visiting and talking with and helping to nurse for a year keeps asking my name each time I come *and* while I'm there — even though I know full well her condition — there comes a time when I just want to cry, and I have, and I want to run away, too."

She wanted me to understand that she was aware that she may have sounded silly or self-pitying or self-indulgent. When she began she had not expected miracles. She had a clear-headed sense of what she was doing at the nursing home and why. She was quite knowledgeable about Alzheimer's disease, about other forms of dementia, connected to strokes, renal disease, diabetes, various neurological disorders. She expected to receive only the small satisfactions an elderly confused person could offer: a grateful nod or smile, a moment of recognition followed by a moment of expressed gratitude — and maybe, a week or two later, awareness on her part that those moments, those memories, had disappeared into the aching darkness and dissolution of elderly oblivion.

Now she was unable to have that perspective. Now she was constantly troubled by her senses — what they brought to her mind's consciousness: the groans and cries and screams; the smell of excrement and urine; the sight of faces and bodies twisted, contorted, bent over, with skin wrinkled, paper-thin, sore-ridden. Now she felt her energy leave as she arrived at the home and return as she left — the opposite of what had once been the case. Now, in fact, she felt herself leaving the nursing home when she entered it — her mind took flight so quickly. For a while she thought she was getting tired or troubled as she noted her growing reluctance to do the work. But now she possessed a phrase that explained everything: "I've become burnt out; that's what has happened to me. I've reached a point where there's nothing left inside me. I go through the motions, but there's no energy left to give. I'm a burnt-out case!"[7]

She generalized about her condition and said she was not even able to contemplate doing another kind of service. She needed a break from all such activity. Maybe her spirit would return, but not until she'd had "a good dose of R and R." Yet immediately she was ready to condemn herself and ask with a certain rhetorical disgust why everything was getting to her.

I reminded myself of the nature of the work she had been doing, not only talking with the elderly and reading to them but cleaning up after them. She had been going to the home twice a week. Perhaps, I wondered aloud, she should cut back on the frequency of her visits or switch activities. But no — she was stopping everything in the way of community service activity for "the term." Several times she assured her coworkers that later she'd be stronger and be able to start in again. For now, she had her mind on helping with a children's theater group run by her roommate and on playing tennis. A week later she insisted that she was not "squelching" her social conscience — that her tennis games and her new interest in golf were part of her "R and R." She had read an article about burnout in a magazine and remembered the advice: do something relaxing, that makes no emotional or moral demands, that simply lets one recover and get that needed rest.

Nevertheless, in narrating her new interests she *had* made a demand on herself, a moral one. It was a challenge to her conscience to come to terms with playing golf, especially — golf was a reminder of her father, a lawyer with no great interest in community service work. "I think of him when I lift my iron and try to hit the ball hard," she declared with embarrassment. She had never wanted to play golf, and the idea of hitting golf balls rather than reading to the elderly or doing some other kind of service troubled her.

In a poignant analysis of her unhappy condition, she said, "I must be pretty depressed — out of it — worrying about whether I should or should not be playing golf! I hope I'll get back in harness one of these days soon!" A year later she was tutoring children and feeling fine doing so. She wondered how she had succumbed so long and hard to what she now called a depression, which she felt she had caught from the elderly people with whom she worked — many of them obviously melancholic.

Yet many individuals who work with children, as she was doing with evident pleasure, or who become involved in social and political struggles, or join the Peace Corps or VISTA, even those who do the more limited, genteel work of hospital volunteering or work for the United Way or the Red Cross, complain of an exhaustion that takes over their spirits. In the days of the civil rights struggle

I saw person after person, black and white, of poor or rich background, lose their ability to work. They felt tired or bored or utterly disappointed and had a strong wish to stop that effort and begin a new kind of life, at least for a while. Some talked openly of depression and of the anger that informed (maybe set in motion) the depression. Some talked of severe frustrations, of constant irritations, and, more ominously, of "betrayals," of the manipulations others contrived — hence the disgust and the wish to make a break, try another kind of activity. Rarely was burnout the result of segregationist violence — the jailings, the beatings — per se. Such experiences, to be sure, weakened men and women and gave them plenty of second thoughts, but they also stirred them to an even more idealistic stance — indeed, to a self-sacrificing one.

But as one of SNCC's leaders told me in 1965, when that organization was increasingly torn by conflict, "We've become our chief enemy! We beat the sheriffs and the Klan, but we couldn't beat ourselves! We 'overcame' the opposition, and what is left is our own troubles with each other, and they are destroying us, I'm afraid."[8] At the time there was much talk of burnout, meaning, as that SNCC leader put it, "the exhaustion that comes with a long, tough fight, even if you win it!" But he had majored in psychology at college and had experienced psychiatry in his early twenties. Once, as we discussed burnout, he became a psychiatric pathologist and insisted on making some distinctions. "You can get down without being in a state of burnout. The people who are burnt out are really wasted. They're depressed: they are in trouble the way you are when you're depressed! They're also pretty angry — and I think what happens is this: they become like the people they're fighting. They call each other names; they fight all the time; they've become victims now of each other. It's a pretty sad sight. You tell me, what comes first — the squabbling or the depression? Do we fight with each other because we're tired and depressed, or do we get tired and depressed after we start forming our cliques and going after each other?

"I've been here [at SNCC] from the start, and in my mind, it's been the bickering and meanness that came first, and then the real moodiness, and then the talk of burnout. I think a lot of folks took seriously all the swear words thrown at them, and the bullets, and now that we're on top, they feel relaxed enough to let loose on each other and on themselves, the way others used to let loose on the movement! But maybe it goes the other way — that people get more and more drained and overworked and strained, and finally they begin to snap, and when they snap, they start snapping at each other, and that's what we've got now."

I could have argued the matter either way with him psychoanalytically — not a rare phenomenon. Several times I told him that my answer to his either/or formulation was "probably both." A mixture of self-laceration and mutual recrimination takes over in response to all the battering people have endured and the consequences, physical and psychological and sociological, of such assaults. At a certain point the police brutality; the exile and scorn imposed by a segregationist society; and the chronic fear, anxiety, and terror all weaken us, bring out the "primitive," even the "crazy," in us and the capacity for depression we all have. Soon enough, having been hurt by others, we strike out; we blame, we accuse, as we have been blamed and accused. In this way we try to protect ourselves, get ourselves off a psychological hook, out of an impasse.

Burnout is a surrender, Dr. Martin Luther King once said at a conference in 1964. A lot of us were sitting at a table talking about the subject because we had witnessed it in others and in ourselves. He explained his somewhat startling choice of words this way: "We have just so much strength in us. If we give and give and give, we have less and less and less — and after a while, at a certain point, we're so weak and worn, we hoist up the flag of surrender. We surrender to the worst side of ourselves, and then we display that to others. We surrender to self-pity and to spite and to morose self-preoccupation. If you want to call it depression or burnout, well, all right. If you want to call it the triumph of sin — when our goodness has been knocked out from under us, well, all right. Whatever we say or think, this is arduous duty, doing this kind of work; to live out one's idealism brings with it hazards."

I have often thought of Dr. King's way of seeing things as I have talked with college students working in ghettos, in prisons, on the serving line in soup kitchens for the homeless; or when talking with VISTA workers or members of the Peace Corps; or when talking with ordinary men and women, living their lives as factory workers, as office workers, as professional men and women, or businessmen or women, as housewives, as retirees — all the people I've known who have become involved in one or another kind of service, many of whom have heard talk of burnout, of battle fatigue, of depression, related to the demands and rigors of volunteerism. There is no question that each of us brings his or her own mind and personality, with its own strengths and weaknesses and vulnerabilities, to the tasks of service, so generalizations must at some point yield to human particularity.

No doubt burnout *is* a hazard of voluntary commitment, although people who work in any sort of job can tire of it, can want out. "I've been working with the homeless for two years and I've got to stop for a while," a twenty-three-year-old woman, a former student of mine, told me. When she said she had become "incapacitated by burnout" and said further that she was depressed, I asked her to explain the connection between her psychological state and the work she had been doing. She hesitated a long time before saying, "I hadn't really thought about the connection; I just assumed there *was* one, a big one, cause and effect — you get tired, you feel sadder about what you're seeing and hearing, and finally, some light inside begins to dim, and you're in a pretty down state of mind, and that's burnout, people tell you, and so you've got to take some time off, and recharge your batteries."

The longer she looked into the matter, however — the closer she looked at her own life — the more she realized that *her* burnout had its own distinctive history and character. She had fought with her stockbroker father for years: her decision to work with the homeless was not unconnected to the anger she felt toward him. She had never felt appreciated or respected by him, and he strongly disapproved of the kind of work she was doing. Her mother, who had a "drinking problem," had her own difficulties with her husband, though she was all too fiercely and abjectly loyal to, or afraid of, him. This is of course a condensation of a long and, as is so often the case, melancholy clinical story, a family's story.

This young woman, a wonderfully decent and giving soup-kitchen worker, eventually learned that the homeless women awakened in her a certain moral and psychological vulnerability, a "homelessness," that she and her mother had experienced. The more she talked with forlorn, even battered women, learned of their alcoholism or psychosis, their sadness of mind, heaviness of heart, and inability to deal successfully with life, the more she struggled in her dreams and reveries with her own angers and resentments and, not least, with the "low times" she had occasionally had long before she became a volunteer.

At a certain point, what had been an intermittent state of mind became steady, relentless, overwhelming: through constant exposure to troubling external circumstances, an internal set of difficulties consolidated into a mood that tightened its grip enough to be called burnout, rather than "a period of feeling low," or "a downer," or "a spell of moodiness," or "a moment of despair," or "a cynical outburst," or a "bitter" one, or "a feeling of resignation," or "weariness." As I listened to her, I was tempted to postulate, with the grandiosity of a theorist, a series of "phases" or "stages" that people march through — from weariness through bitterness to arrogance and then despair, and finally, the devastation of depression or burnout. Such a progression certainly occurs in ordinary life, not just among those who test themselves in community service or social activism. Nevertheless, we ought to let each life have its own complex unfolding, as it affirms itself in such activism and, sometimes, gets into trouble in the course of that service.

Burnout is by no means inevitable, as some who have avoided it will attest. Nor will a handbook of do's and don't's and how-to's and how-not-to's spare us the ironies and complexities and inconsistencies of human nature as they connect with the experience known as service. Indeed, a person's commitment to service, as well as the nature of its satisfactions and of the hazards suffered, endured, all become part of a person's life. The call of service is a call to a new chapter of a life — its earlier story, its prior chapters, with their achievements and losses, will surely come to bear on what happens in the future, though each person's idealism can have its own surprising victories, some of them achieved against the great odds of a particular past. "My whole life before I started the [service] work was a long stretch of burnout," a student told me, offering a much-needed ironic perspective on the subject. When we single out the low spells of volunteers, we forget that for others (as writers such as John Cheever and Walker Percy make eminently clear) life itself may be a sadder story than the passing low points that are called burnout. Youthful activists are often able to use such low points to become more realistic and reflective and, in the long run, sturdier in the community service work they usually continue doing.[9]

· FIVE ·

Doing and Learning

HEN I WAS A COLLEGE STUDENT I did "volunteer work," as we then called it. I tutored some boys and girls who lived in what would now be called a ghetto neighborhood and who were having trouble with their schoolwork. I left one part of Cambridge for another, often on foot, so that I could enjoy what my father had taught me to call "a good hike." When I returned to *my* school, scenes I had witnessed and statements I had heard would stay with me and would come to mind now and then as I pursued various courses and lived my late-adolescent life.

Often, when I went to visit my parents in their suburban home, they inquired about my extracurricular teaching life. As I have mentioned, my mother was inclined to be religiously sentimental: she felt it was good that I was helping out some youngsters in trouble. For her the sin of pride was around any corner. It was important to escape that constant pull of egoism — to work with others on behalf of their lives, with our own, for a change, taking a back seat. My father, a probing scientist, commonly took a different tack and asked me many times the same question: "What did you learn?"

I was never quite sure how to answer my father, and often I had no need to do so. My mother was quick to reply for me, emphasizing her notion of the education such tutoring can afford a college student: "the lesson of humility" — a favorite phrase of hers. If any amplification was necessary, she had another well-worn piety: "There but for the grace of God . . ."

My father's question often came back to me. What *did* I learn? What was I *supposed* to learn? After all, I was the teacher, not the student. Anyway, these were elementary schoolchildren, and there was nothing new in the ground I was covering with them every week. But I had listened to my father too often, on long walks through various cities, to let the matter rest there. During his boyhood in Yorkshire, England, he had been a great walker and a great observer. He was also an admirer of George Orwell long before *Animal Farm* and *1984* were published — the early Orwell who wrote *Down and Out in Paris and London, The Road to Wigan Pier,* and *Homage to Catalonia.* In those books Orwell explored relentlessly the world around him and described it carefully yet with dramatic intensity.[1]

My father had introduced me to those books before I went to college, and as I did volunteer work, I would recall a scene, some words, or, more generally, Orwell's social and moral inquiry. I began to realize that Orwell was a "big brother" for me in the sense that he was helping me make sense of my experience. His wisdom gave me pause, prompted me to scrutinize not only the children I met and, occasionally, their parents but my own opinions and attitudes.

At college I read the poetry and prose of William Carlos Williams, including his long poem *Paterson* and his Stecher trilogy: *White Mule, In the Money,* and *The Buildup.* Williams tried hard to evoke the rhythms of working-class life in America, the struggle of ordinary people to make their way in the world, to find a satisfactory manner of living and regarding themselves. He knew how hard it was for someone who was well educated and well-to-do to make contact with people who worked in factories, stores, or farms or with those who have no work or are intermittently employed.

In emphasizing his search for an American "language," Williams was getting at the fractured nature of our nation's life: the divisions by race, class, region, and culture that make us unable to comprehend or even be aware of one another. Often, as I did my tutoring, I heard words I had never known, heard words used in new and arresting ways — and I learned about the memories and hopes and habits and interests of people in a neighborhood that was unlike my own. I thought of Williams's poems and stories and realized how much he owed to the humble people of industrial northern New Jersey. As he once told me, "Those house calls [to attend his patients] are giving me an education. Every day I learn something new — a sight, a phrase — and I'm made to stop and think about my world, the world I've left behind." He was reminding both of us that "education" is not a one-way affair.[2]

I fear it took some of us volunteers a good deal of time to learn the lesson Williams was stressing. At my worst, I must admit, I had a sense of *noblesse oblige*, a conviction that I was sharing certain intellectual riches with "them," the children I tutored. Only when I went with Williams on some of his house calls and observed him paying close heed to the men, women, and children he visited did I begin to realize how much his mind grew in response to his everyday experiences.

Now, many years later, I offer courses for undergraduates and for students in the professional schools of law, medicine, business, and education. I work with many young people who do community service, teaching in urban schools, perhaps, or offering medical or legal assistance to needy families. At times I stand in awe of some of those youths, with their determination, their decency, their good-heartedness, their savvy. I also notice that they need time to discuss and reflect on what they are doing, what they would like to be doing, what they are having difficulty doing.

A college senior who did volunteer work in a school near a large low-rent housing project said to me, "I started this work as something apart from my courses, my life here as a student. I wanted to be of use to someone other than myself — and in a really honest moment, I'd probably add that I was also being selfish: it would beef up my brag-sheet when I apply to a graduate school. But hell, I'd been doing this kind of work since high school as part of our church's activities, so I shouldn't be too cynical about my motives.

The last thing I expected was that I'd come back here and want to read books to help me figure out what's happening." He was then reading Richard Wright's stories and Elliot Liebow's sociological study *Tally's Corner.* "I've designed my own private course, and it helps. I can anticipate certain troubles because I've learned from the reading I do, and I get less discouraged because I've seen a bigger view, courtesy of those writers."

His remarks made me realize that some social scientists and novelists and poets and essayists have offered that student so very much: their knowledge, their experience, their sense of what matters, and, not least, their companionship, for their concerns are similar to those of the youths working in volunteer programs. Put differently, those writers or filmmakers or photographers are teachers, and their subject matter is an important one for students engaged in acts of public service.

Our institutions of higher learning might certainly take heed, not only by encouraging students to do such service, but by helping them stop and mull over, through books and discussions, what they have heard and seen. This is the purpose, after all, of colleges and universities — to help one generation after another grow intellectually and morally through study and the self-scrutiny such study can sometimes prompt.

For a number of years I have taught undergraduates a course titled "The Literature of Social Reflection." Several discussion sections are reserved for students doing community service, who can use the assigned reading as a basis for reflection upon what they are experiencing in their work as volunteers.[3] These "community service sections" call upon books such as James Agee's *Let Us Now Praise Famous Men* and George Orwell's *The Road to Wigan Pier* in a quite special way: they connect the intellectual and moral issues posed by the readings to the students' everyday struggles to figure out what they are trying to do and to what effect; how they are to learn about people who are different from themselves; and, not least, how those people regard them and their purposes.

I remember seeing in the Freedom Houses of the Mississippi Summer Project copies of Agee's book.[4] Both blacks and whites were reading the book, Agee's extraordinary effort to learn about the rural South in the middle 1930s. The two well-educated cosmopolitans from New York City — Agee the writer and Walker Evans the photographer — try to understand the way Alabama tenant farmers, dirt poor and without schooling, manage to live their lives. But the book also shows how being with others can help us learn about our own assumptions, blind spots, purposes, and limitations. On the first page of *Let Us Now Praise Famous Men*, through a scene from Shakespeare's *King Lear*, we are given an ultimate context and reminder and caveat: a father and his children can't comprehend one another, are victims of misunderstanding. As we worry (and well we should) about who can know with any accuracy about another, especially across barriers of race, class, gender, culture, nationality, and age, we would do well to keep the wisdom of Shakespeare (and Tolstoy and George Eliot and other writers) in mind: their capacity to tolerate the paradoxical — indeed, to insist upon the ironies, ambiguities, and contradictions of life.

From Agee's distinctive writing about the rural South and Orwell's earnest, cranky, shrewd, provocative journey among coal miners in Yorkshire and Lancashire, my undergraduates move to William Carlos Williams's view of working-class urban America in his *Doctor Stories*; in his novel *White Mule*, which evokes late-nineteenth-century immigrant life in New York City; and in *Paterson*, a lyrical examination of a nation's values and hopes and worries, worked into a language all its own. We also call upon Tillie Olsen's short stories in *Tell Me a Riddle* and Raymond Carver's stories in *Where I'm Calling From.*[5] Williams, Olsen, and Carver bring us very close to the ordinary people of America, whether they are dressed in factory clothes or starched shirts and ties or everyday dresses. They ask us to understand the misunderstandings that take place among people who can take little for granted as they try to make do.

In stories such as Williams's "The Use of Force," Carver's "Cathedral" or "A Small, Good Thing," and Olsen's "I Stand Here Ironing" or "Hey Sailor, What Ship?" we are asked to look not only at others (how to know them, how to know the effect of our presence among them) but at ourselves. Who *are* we who visit others and try to get on with them? These three great twentieth-century American storytellers give much thought to the dilemmas and confrontations and impasses that occur between those "doing" community service and those "receiving" it, those who are visiting a neighborhood and those who live there. The stories are not necessarily about service; rather, they shed light on how we are likely to misinterpret people's intentions, on how we might learn to see others more clearly — a lesson that anyone leaving one neighborhood to work in another needs to keep constantly in mind.

In the course we move on to Flannery O'Connor and Ralph Ellison and Zora Neale Hurston and Dorothy Day and Walker Percy,[6] who help us understand the people of the rural South; black people and their struggles as migrants in Florida or as residents of Harlem; the poor who came to Catholic Worker soup kitchens (and those who served them); and the well-to-do, who have their own trials figuring out how to live with self-respect and decency.

We also go back to the nineteenth and the early twentieth century, to Dickens, George Eliot, Hardy, Tolstoy, and Chekhov — masters of the novel and the short story, who tell us about the powerful and the weak; the healthy but desperate in spirit and the sick; the dying, who still have a chance to find meaning and purpose in life. These writers have wisdom to offer anyone who pays them heed. They have a shrewd, keen sense of how people get on and a marvelous ability to evoke the nuances and subtleties of character and social background; they show how the great mysteries of fate and chance and circumstance connect with character to produce a particular destiny.

For students doing community service and for older people working as volunteers, some of those books can be a means of looking inward, of stepping back a bit, taking a break to think about matters broader than the day's hurdles or challenges. A student in that course, who also worked in a nearby church's soup kitchen all winter, used some of those books, and the class discussions devoted to them, in the following manner.

"I stand there in that soup kitchen, and I wonder at times what I am doing there — whether it makes any difference at all, other than to me. I know *I* feel better for being there, but often the people I'm waiting on get mean to each other, to me. They say rude things, crude things. I get discouraged, and then I get fed up with myself for being so critical sometimes — of the people who run the kitchen and the people who come there, both!

"At such times I'll remember some of Williams's stories — his admissions of what went through his mind, how he really felt. He presented himself as the good doctor, who was out there to help people, but he was also, every once in a while, demanding, impatient, prejudiced, angry, preoccupied with himself, vain, and indifferent to others, because [he was] rushed and hectic, with other things on his mind. [Sometimes] I want to go back to my room and read Williams or Tillie Olsen or Raymond Carver or Dorothy Day or Tolstoy — all of them look at people in real trouble, but they don't make you feel 'sick' because for a moment you wanted to scream back at someone who is screaming his bloody head off while you're trying to offer him a bowl of soup and some bread!

"I shouldn't feel like that; I shouldn't feel angry at people who are alcoholics or schizophrenics or both — or at others who are trying to help them, and help me help them. But sometimes I can't help myself. Sometimes a person is being mean and spiteful toward someone, another homeless person, never mind me, and I think to myself, Am I really helping this person by trying to ignore what I see or hear, or downplay it, or turn dispassionately psychological? — 'You seem to be upset' or 'You seem to have some hostility in you' — [when] the guy has whipped out a knife or he's crashed into someone, knocking the person's tray to the floor.

"There's a counselor who comes to meet with us. She has no sense of humor; she's full of herself, with all the psychological ploys that have become so ticlike these days; and she makes us wonder whether she really does have any psychological judgment, because she doesn't know how to come down strong on anything — only ask those half-baked questions that are funnier (and dumber) than the people who ask them ever realize! It's then, listening to her or looking at her, that I go back to Dr. Williams and Dr. Chekhov and Tillie Olsen and Raymond Carver — stories that give you humor and good clean anger and a moral point of view and plain common sense, not 'expertise' offered in jargon and more jargon. 'You seem to be ambivalent,' she told my [girl] friend the other night. [His girlfriend had described her anger at one of the men on the meal line.] She gave it back to her: 'I'm *not* ambivalent — I don't like that man!' The man was pickpocketing, and he was roaring drunk, and he insulted the people serving him supper — and they'd said nothing to him."

Perhaps this was an intemperate assault on a well-meaning "group facilitator" who was voluntarily giving *her* time at the behest of a pastor enamored of the benefits of "counseling." Yet this student was not averse to looking inward or to seeking help from others. He badly wanted a kind of psychological advice and instruction he was not receiving from the counselor. He found it in the wonderfully subtle, textured, knowing psychology that informs the exchange between a mother and her therapist in Tillie Olsen's "I Stand Here Ironing," or the boldly honest autobiographical narratives Williams presents in "Life along the Passaic River," or the wisdom Tolstoy and Dorothy Day offer in acknowledging moments of confusion, perplexity, irritation, and anger. These writers have no need for the strings of psychological names that actually conceal a reprimand, a not-so-hidden chastisement.

For a while I wondered whether the three Victorian moralists whom I call on at the end of the course — Dickens, Hardy, and Eliot — would be of any practical use to students doing community service. Not that I felt that any book assigned had to pass such muster: the books have great value in and of themselves, obviously. We try not to anticipate what might be "practical," since students have told those of us who teach that course many times that they are stunned to discover what ultimately helps them — for instance, Agee's use of *King Lear*, mentioned earlier. From the very start, however, Pip in *Great Expectations*, Jude in *Jude the Obscure*, and Dorothea Brooke and Dr. Lydgate in *Middlemarch* offered substantial succor to those readers who were volunteers.[7] The story of lowly Pip's ascent to London's higher realms, courtesy of the wealth a prisoner, exiled in Australia, secretly bestows on him because as a boy Pip fed that prisoner when he was on the run, appeals to people who are trying to inspire children to aim high.

"All the time the kids tell me it's no use; they'll never be able to break out of their world," a young woman named Miriam told her section leader during a discussion of *Great Expectations*. Yet Dickens shows how character is shaped by destiny — and not always for the good, even when a supposedly favorable event takes place. He is far from naively hopeful in the novel. He examines the workings of class; he shows how people can lose their bearings, can become all too taken with the glitter and pomp of the world of wealth.

Miriam used the novel to address her concerns about her tutees in a Boston ghetto. "I think of Pip when I tell them that lots of things can happen that you never can foresee or expect. But I try not to grab at straws the way some of the kids do. In a strange way, they *do* expect miracles — they expect that some big drug deal will happen, and they'll be kings for life! When I read of Magwitch [the prisoner who becomes Pip's benefactor], I think of some drug dealers I know. They take a liking to a kid, use him for running their deals, shower him with dough, jewels, a hi-fi set, records by the ton; and they promise him more and more — the fanciest car in the world. The kid begins to turn into a Pip, and all the other kids now feel they are even poorer than they ever were before!

"The kid who's on the rise begins to find out something, though — he learns that there's a price for all he's got. No, I don't mean that he gets into trouble with the law. [I had suggested that possibility a bit too hastily.] Let's face it, a lot of these kids *don't* get caught, not right away. That's what I'm getting at: something happens to you when you're catapulted from one world into another. You can lose your way morally. Pip lost when he gained! Things went to his head; he became — Dickens has him say so — a snob. He became ashamed of his past, including the very good part of it. A lot of the kids I teach tell me they have no hope, no 'expectations.' Then they qualify: they say that if some big guy, meaning a drug dealer most likely, took a shine to them — well, they'd be on easy street, like Pip was in London.

"All right, I ask them, what would it be like on that easy street? They laugh and say, 'Easy!' Serves me right! I ask them to tell me more about the easy life — and they sure know what to say. They've seen it firsthand, never mind on TV or the movies. They paint a picture not only of wealth but of trouble: fights, jealousies, abandonments of friends, lovers, family, losses, cynicism, isolation, paranoia — people with lots of hundred dollar bills, with gold watches and Mercedes convertibles and suits that cost more than some people make in months and months of work, but people who don't know who is the one to trust, to enjoy as a friend.

"'I'd like to have the money of the drug people, but not be like them,' one of my students said, and then we got into a big discussion as to whether that is possible. It was one of the greatest times I've had in class, and I kept thinking of Charles Dickens and that novel *Great Expectations*. We were, essentially, arguing as to whether Pip *had* to become the highfalutin dilettante he was for a while — and would have been for a longer spell, had his 'savior' not returned to England and confronted him. It was a real time of reflection — and I sat there and thought to myself, 'Hey, Charles Dickens, hey, Pip, this one is for you, and I thank you!' That's what I thought — because it was the novel, reading it and thinking about it, that got me going with those kids."

This was not the only moral moment in Miriam's teaching. Tillie Olsen and Zora Neale Hurston and Dorothy Day — each so different, yet all three strong in their convictions and their interest in the travails of the poor — influenced her teaching enormously, especially with the girls she met, many of whom, at eleven or twelve, were already far along into sexuality. She would meet individually with these girls and get into deep talks with them, and in so doing, hark back to moments in *The Long Loneliness* or *Their Eyes Were Watching God* or a story such as "O Yes" in *Tell Me a Riddle*.[8] Those books provided her with an awareness of psychological complexity, of the nuances of human character, uncluttered by the ponderous language and condescensions of the clinic. Those books provided her, too, with an awareness of the moral complexity that informs the choices we consciously make, as well as those we unwittingly make, all the while believing that more leeway is available to us than there really is.

Miriam thought of the young Dorothy Day as she taught, and of Janie in Hurston's novel, and of the children in Olsen's story; she thought of the choices before those children and before her as their teacher. Even more, she read from *The Long Loneliness* to her students. She asked them to read "O Yes" and read long passages of the powerful, evocative *Their Eyes Were Watching God* to them. This was a middle-school class with reading difficulties. She was not about to assign a novel, even Hurston's, so lively, so vibrant and compelling in its language, nor even, without preparation, Olsen's story.

Figuring out how to connect her own reading and its lessons to the reading of her ten academically vulnerable students was a challenge. "I asked for their help. I told them about the [Olsen] story, how much it meant to me. I summarized it. They suggested I read it to them, and then they would try reading it. A good idea! It's not easy to read Tillie Olsen's stories — she can be elliptical, poetic, dense with meaning. But I'd go through a paragraph, and if there were questions, we'd try to answer them, and then [we'd read] the next paragraph. It took time, but we got through.

"I'm not saying I didn't carry most of the load. It wasn't easy to get the kids into the story 'O Yes.' And there I was, a white woman, and the subject of the story is the ways that black and white kids, at a certain age, begin to 'sort'! But thanks to that story we talked about race, and who you can trust, and what happens when people get older — how friends separate after being so close for a while.

"I'll never forget the black girl who wanted us to stop and think about 'O Yes,' imagine it being written differently — as a story of two girls who stuck together, even with 'all the forces trying to push them from each other.' Had she ever had a white friend, a girl sitting beside her wondered. 'Oh, yes,' she replied unselfconsciously, and everyone laughed — a nice 'moment of recognition' for the class. Her mother had a white boyfriend for a long time, and he had a daughter, and she and his daughter became fast friends, and they were 'like sisters,' and even when their parents split, as they did after five years together, the two have very much stayed in touch."

That story caught the close attention of the entire class and got more attention for the Olsen story. "It was a big lesson for me, how you can use a story to get the kids going about their own lives, their stories. Sometimes we try to get our students into an analytic frame of mind so they can figure out what we've been reading, and we wonder why they get bored after a while! I've had great reactions from some of the kids when I do a summary of a story, and then ask the kids if that story gets any bells going in their heads — gets them thinking about their own lives. That's when they start paying attention, and that's when they'll speak up."

In a sense, the books that college student was reading became intermediaries, ambassadors — points of connection between her and her class, seventh- and eighth-graders categorized as failures in need of special assistance. The books obviously prompted her to think carefully about questions her class posed by their very presence: about what it is like being poor, and how we can try to reach people who are different from us. The books gave Miriam many ideas she wanted to share with her tutees. The books offered her a curriculum for her students even as they were part of her own curriculum. As she talked to her students about what a particular novel or collection of stories meant to her, she was telling them that they were her compatriots, sharing common texts, mulling them over together, jointly profiting from their messages, their narrative pleasures and surprises, their moral thrust.

Her growing authority as a teacher, then, was due in no small part to the courage and confidence she felt as a result of her own life as a reader who called upon certain books as sources of intellectual and moral energy. And that "double function," as she termed it, had yet a third side: "When I come back [to college] from my teaching and tutoring in Boston, I'll be thinking of what happened, what I did, and what I didn't do, and what I should have done, and what I shouldn't have done, and suddenly — it happens all the time! — I'll go back to those books, those stories, and they'll really help me to think about what I'm trying to do, and how I might improve or change my approach. And they also help me sort things out, so I understand the kids a little better, and the world they live in, and what life is like for them. I do a lot of that kind of thinking in response to *Invisible Man* and some of Baldwin's essays and Hurston; and Agee and Orwell keep influencing my thoughts and my teaching, even if they were white men working with white people a half a century ago. Some of the issues they bring up — how you, as an outsider, try to make contact with people when you arrive on their turf — are important for all of us doing community service work."

The three functions Miriam mentioned have been noted by others who have read and learned from the books and recommended reading listed on a syllabus, then brought that learning to their community service, and returned to those books as a means of thinking about what they have experienced. Of course, each volunteer will favor certain books, based in part on the kind of service he or she is pursuing.

A young black man, Alex, not surprisingly, found Ellison and Hurston of special interest, along with stories by Richard Wright and James Baldwin's polemical essays, especially *The Fire Next Time*. He was less taken with Tillie Olsen than the student just quoted — found Olsen's stories powerful, but in places dense and inaccessible, and he found Dorothy Day, on occasion, sentimental and even self-indulgent. He liked Hurston's novel and some of her stories, but found her at times provocatively hard to comprehend and, like Dorothy Day, "romantic" in excess.⁹ In his college class he wrote cogently and tersely about those writers and others assigned; he was headed for law school and would clearly be a good student there.

Alex was doing volunteer work at Boston City Hospital, a large public hospital that regularly received the poorest of the urban poor. He'd made that choice because his mother was a nurse in New York's Harlem Hospital, and she had urged him to choose such an activity. (His father, an army sergeant, had been killed in Vietnam.) When he read Tolstoy's "The Death of Ivan Ilyich," he found himself bored at first, then increasingly taken with the story, and, at the end, stunned and enthralled, for reasons he explained at length one evening: "I've been seeing people die these days, lots of people. Kids come in shot, bleeding; there's not enough blood in the world, it seems, to make up for what they've lost. The doctors fight to save them, but the kids, they're smarter, they know they've had it. I got into a talk the other day with one of them; it was by accident. I was assisting while they tried to save him, in the E.W. [emergency ward]. He was thirteen, I think; he called me 'brother,' and he asked me to take his hand! Here he was, this tough gang member, wounded in a shootout over drug turf — and now he was like my little nephew, trying to hold on to someone. The doctors wanted me out of the way, but he wouldn't let me go. So I tried to calm him. I kept telling him we see a lot of people hurt bad, real bad, but they pull through. I told him our staff is the best in the city; they really know their business. I told him he was young and strong, and he'd make it — don't worry.

"But he wasn't buying a word I spoke. 'Hey, man, this is it for me' — that's what he kept telling me. We'd been trying to find his grandmother. She was the only one he wanted us to call. He said she was his family — no one else. I asked if that was really true. Then he really caught me off guard. He asked me, 'What's family? What does a family mean?' I was going to give him some fancy answer out of sociology or psychology, but I suddenly realized he wasn't looking for that. He was talking from deep down inside — the bottom of his heart. I found out later that his mother was on cocaine, and she'd had all these different men fathering her five kids, and there were miscarriages and abortions. She was a regular patient at City.

"The poor kid — the sweat on his forehead, his voice getting softer — I began to lose my cool. I thought, What a waste of life! I asked myself, What does all this mean? Why does someone like this kid end up dying in a crowded, dirty E.W. with old drunks vomiting and pregnant women, pregnant *girls*, his age, screaming more out of fear and ignorance than pain in the earliest stages of labor? But *he* was asking questions like that too! He said it to me — I can hear him now: 'What a waste, my life!' I didn't know whether to nod my head or shake my head. I just stood there. His grip on me was getting weaker; I could tell he'd soon be going. They were pouring in blood, but he'd had an artery injured, and they were trying to repair it, but he was going into shock — he was in and out of shock.

"Then he told me to tell his grandmother he was sorry, and he told me he wished he'd known all his life what he knew right then. I couldn't just keep quiet. I was trying to get him to rest, but when he said that, I was too curious, I had to ask him. I said, 'What do you know now, man — what?' He didn't waste a second. He told me; he said, 'I know I'm going to die. I know I'll never have another chance. I blew it, man — that's what I know. I know that when you really blow it, you don't get a second chance.'

"I gave his hand a squeeze. He tried to squeeze back, but he was fading; he was really going now. He was looking around the room. I thought it was the look of fear on him, terror — that he was dying, and he knew it, and he was scared out of his mind. But he took me by surprise again. He kept staring at the ceiling, and he was moving his eyes, and then I realized he was following a fly up there that was going from place to place, landing and taking off and landing and taking off, one of those nervous flies that won't settle down, even when it's safe on the ceiling. Then the poor kid spoke again, he actually spoke to that fly. He said, 'Hey, you, get out of here, you can do it, I can't.' Then he looked at me, and he said, 'That fly is in a lot better shape than I am!' I was really moved. I thought, He's near death, but he has a sense of humor, and he's able to get out of himself, and he's giving the fly some advice! I didn't know what to do! Then I had this crazy thought — that I'd try to chase the fly out of the room as a favor for this poor kid, who'd been watching it and had just warned it to get out of town before it's too late!

"You know what? I told him I was going to let go of him for just a minute to go help that fly! And you know what? He heard me; I mean, not just literally, but he heard what I was meaning. So I moved fast — I went and got a newspaper in the waiting room, and I got on a chair, and I didn't try to kill the fly; I chased it — and I got it, I got it to go through the door: *out!* Then I closed the door. Then I came back, and I took his hand, and I told him what I'd done — but he already knew. He smiled. He didn't say anything, not a word. He was conscious, I could see, but he was slipping some more. The nurse had looked at me as though I was nuts, but she and the doctors were all tied up with saving the kid's life. Meanwhile, he knew they weren't going to succeed, and he'd said about all he had to say. I thought he was trying to say more; I thought he might have said, 'Thanks, man,' when I came back to him. But to tell the truth, I don't think he said anything. He had this smile — almost as if he knew it: a life had been saved, even if it wasn't his; or maybe in his head it *was* his — like Flannery O'Connor said [in the title of one of her stories], 'The life you save may be your own.'

"He had no more time for that, for thinking, for being symbolic — that's how I thought about him later. He was getting even nearer to the end, so he stared at the ceiling as if he was making sure (dead sure!) that the fly had gone, and then he looked at me, and his eyes just stayed there, staring at mine. It was as though he wouldn't let go of me with his eyes, now, rather than his hand. I mean, I was holding his hand again, tight, real tight, and I could feel his hand letting go, and it was cold and sweaty; but not his eyes, they didn't let go, they held on, and I was really uncomfortable, and I wanted to shift my look. (I've never been a great one for staring and staring at people!) But I knew I should never, never break the hold he had on me with his eyes, and so I just kept looking, and so did he; and then I heard him gurgling, and I realized that this was it, this was the end, and it was.

"The doctors said so, and next thing, the nurse started in, pulling out the IV and the catheter and getting him ready for the morgue. In a few minutes, that's where he was — and I was trying to do more E.W. work, but I couldn't keep my mind focused; I couldn't concentrate. I'd be thinking of that kid, and then I'd think of Ivan Ilyich, and I got the two mixed up; they merged, almost, in my head! Ivan Ilyich, putting the 'death' in his life behind him as he lay there dying, and that kid trying to do the same as he was dying. I got teary, and I wasn't working up to snuff. I'd see a fly, and I'd want to stop everything and go chase it, to get it outdoors and free — in memory of that poor kid.

"Finally, I went and told the nurse in charge of E.W. that I had to go home because I was feeling sick. She wanted to get a doctor to see me, but I told her it was just the flu, I knew, and I'd be okay in a day or two. So I left, and on the bus, all the way back to Cambridge, I kept thinking of that story, of Ivan Ilyich, and what Tolstoy said, and of that kid, and what he said, and the fly. I was going to write my paper on that; I was going to write it out, but I couldn't, for some reason I couldn't; I don't know why."

Later Alex shared some further thoughts on the matter. He had concluded that he was reluctant to "take advantage of that experience for academic gain." Such scrupulousness — *I* can call it that with no inhibitions! — is best respected rather than probed with a view to undermining it. That is how I have come to feel after many conversations with students who are troubled by the "advantages" that come to them as they do their work. One such advantage is the approval they get from others, including admissions committees. But they also see as a problematic "advantage" a kind of enlightenment that can accompany certain experiences.

"He's gone, that kid," Alex told me, "and here I am, with another story in the bank, another account of what I went through, which I can tell to people, and write about — and be rewarded, maybe, for the effort with an A for doing two great jobs, first, being out there with the kid, and second, writing it all up." He squirmed in his chair even as he felt quite torn. He was obviously a more reflective, knowing person for the experience, but he was self-accusing as well.

A medical student doing a summer's volunteer work in a shelter for homeless women constantly struggled with similar concerns. By the end of the season she felt her idealism waning. She felt plagued by monetary preoccupations that were like attacks of lust descending upon a nun. That comparison was hers; her Catholic sense of sin hadn't deserted her, even though she had stopped going to church in protest against various positions staked out by Rome, especially with respect to birth control and abortion. She had read *Middlemarch* in our medical humanities seminar, and now, in a conference on medical students as volunteers, she was ready to share the meaning that novel had for her in her work at the shelter.[10]

"I never thought of anything I read most of the time; I was too busy doing my work. In fact, I was *so* busy doing my work that I was beginning to have insomnia, and I was losing weight. I was feeding other people, and I couldn't find time to eat myself! I began to have this one daydream, again and again — I think it was a dream, originally, and then it kept coming back to me while I was working. I am in a really swank apartment in New York City. There is a room full of comfortable furniture, not flashy or fancy — how do people say it? — quietly elegant. I usually don't give a damn about furniture — yes, we have pretty primitive furniture there [at the shelter], and some of it is always giving way, the chairs, especially. In the apartment there are all these waiters, serving me coffee and pastries and asking me if I want anything. I don't know what I want! I guess I want everything, because I just sit there and eat away, and every once in a while I go to the window and see the city out there: it's early evening, and I'm looking at all the skyscrapers lit up — beautiful! I'm feeling good — and then I get this call. Would you believe it: one of those waiters comes and tells me that George Eliot is on the line! I begin immediately to wonder if

I'm maybe losing my mind — and then I stop the daydreaming and get back to work!"

She was able to smile, in retrospect, and come up with her own shrewd exercise in self-analysis. When she read *Middlemarch*, she'd wondered through much of it what would happen to Dr. Lydgate, the physician who started out so full of good intentions, so convinced in his idealism, and ended up as a society doctor of sorts, well-to-do and quite unbothered by the suffering of those who could not afford his care. She kept promising herself that she would not turn into another Dr. Lydgate. She didn't really feel in danger of being thus compromised. She had gone through a back-breaking, exhausting summer; indeed, she had been near the edge at times because of the long hours, the strain of the work, so maybe she did have that Manhattan fantasy, as she put it, to "let off steam." Who wouldn't want to be waited on hand and foot in a plush, air-conditioned apartment rather than work in the sweaty, broken-down place she and the homeless women she attended were occupying that summer?

Yet the longer she thought about that mysterious call across an ocean of time and space from George Eliot, the more she considered another interpretive possibility. "The character in that novel who got to me — she's the central character, Dorothea Brooke. I never thought I'd be interested in her, because she seemed a little too driven in her idealism at the start, and naive, really naive. And that stupid marriage to Casaubon — talk about a dumb decision! But she goes through plenty of trials, and she begins to soften and get some plain common sense in her. Once, when I was thinking about that George Eliot phone call, I suddenly thought of her [Dorothea], not Lydgate, and I think I know why.

"I was a little nuts this summer. I was determined to give myself totally to that shelter, and that's all I did. I didn't give myself any time — and no one else, either, only the women in the shelter. When I spoke to friends I must have sounded like a zealot, some fanatic, or, to be nicer to myself, someone who was consumed by her tremendous good will and charity and idealism, and all of that! 'You're so far away from us,' my closest friend told me, every time we spoke on the phone. 'You sound like you're on another planet!' I was! I guess in my daydream I was trying to tell myself to soften a bit, enjoy the comforts of life, or else I'd become one more slightly kooky ideologue — and that's George Eliot's message to us, through Dorothea Brooke: you can lose your common sense; you can get so caught up in something, you end up becoming ineffective."

She continued her exercise in dream interpretation for over half an hour — a thoughtful, knowing look inward. She was able to use a novel she had read in an intensely personal way; allow it to become a teacher, indeed, a psychoanalytically sophisticated teacher. George Eliot warns us, by implication, that a high-minded devotion to the call of service can turn into a nightmare of sorts, with unexpected and self-defeating consequences. Such a single-minded commitment comes at a high personal cost and doesn't even further the cause in question. This student realized that her mind was telling her (the call of George Eliot!) to stop, take stock, and go a bit easier on herself, lest she become more and more driven, self-preoccupied, inaccessible to family and friends, and, worst of all, smugly self-righteous.

This message (like so much that happens symbolically in the mind) became a bit overwrought, with the obvious exaggerations of Manhattan's plush, self-serving, and self-indulgent life — a way, perhaps, to italicize the problem, underline it as a warning: you *really do need to heed* the subtly rendered but quite clear and deliberately dramatic remonstrances and warnings that inform George Eliot's *Middlemarch*. So let her "speak" to you, let her teach you her lessons, and meanwhile, as she talks to you, give yourself a break, and let those who are fond of you (and share your ideas and ideals) take care of you, give you affection and nurturance (you who are giving so very much to others and quite clearly ignoring your own ordinary human needs).

In a sense, at a critical moment in her own doing, what she had been learning as a reader came into important play. She took to heart a novel's "news." As the derivation of the word "novel" suggests, the purpose of such a book is to bring the reader what is new, what is news, through stories. In the course I teach on the literature of social reflection, we do not try to make the fiction, poetry, autobiography, documentary writing, and personal essays servants of a social or political cause. All of us, teachers and students alike, are trying to learn from these wise, wonderfully suggestive writers. Inevitably, they speak to each of us in different ways, though they also must be acknowledged as having *their* particular points of view — *there*, on the pages of print, waiting for us to come and take seriously and use in our own ways.

Those students who are engaged in volunteer service are not in any way violating the spirit of the academy by linking what Dickens tells us in his novels with what they are doing as volunteers in a ghetto school or a prison. Dickens's early life was one of harsh poverty, and he even spent time with his family in debtor's prison. He did not write *Bleak House* or *Little Dorrit* out of a knowledge obtained in libraries through "research"; rather, he drew upon the firsthand experiences of his childhood, which were worked indelibly into his remembering life.[11] His talent enabled him to do more than retrieve those memories of pain and suffering and vulnerability; he shaped what others might have been glad to forget into his "news," which he offered to England's readers. He mixed recalled facts with his rich store of fantasies in one evocative, subtly suggestive, arresting story after another.

We, his readers, are meant to enjoy, to be given pause, to learn, to make use of what Dickens tells us as we go through our day. He is addressing, entertaining, and instructing us, and through the narrative order that a gifted talent can construct, we connect this nineteenth-century writer's thoughts and memories and reveries to our twentieth-century thoughts and memories and reveries — and, not least, to our ongoing experiences. I assume that not even the most academically conventional person would want readers to keep Dickens's novels at a remove from their own lives.

Another student, Julia, an undergraduate who worked in a shelter, presented an interesting view of the relationship between Dickens, Eliot, Hardy, and the academic life. "I'm all for interpreting these books. I'm an English major; I've learned how to do that fairly well. But since I've been working in that soup kitchen and that home [for homeless women], I can't just draw a line and separate what I read and learn in school and what I do in my life. The women in the shelter are always asking me what I'm studying, so I tell them. I even tell them what books I've been reading for the courses I'm taking. I don't talk about the science course or the economics one, but I sure tell them about the stories and novels in this course. One or two of the women are well educated; they haven't read most of what's on our reading list, but they've read Dickens in high school, and one of them had read Hardy's *Jude the Obscure*, so I talked with her about it. She'd actually forgotten the entire plot, but that was a good excuse for me to bring it up and tell her a lot about the novel, because I'd just finished reading it, *and* I'd read some essays about it!

"It's a tough novel for a student going to a place like Harvard to read. It makes you nervous, because Hardy brings this decent, idealistic farm boy, Jude, to Christminster, which is Oxford, really. He's hungry for knowledge, and he has dreams of finding his way into the university, but he doesn't, he can't. So he finds work in the town, and he watches the students and professors, and Hardy clearly is on his side when he has Jude speak with bitterness and disappointment about the university people — they are smug and full of themselves, and they don't give ordinary people the time of day. They know a lot, but they aren't kind or thoughtful. They're all stuck on themselves — arrogant prigs! In fact, a lot of the novel centers on that subject: knowledge in and of itself as not a solution to life's problems or a source of moral energy or spiritual salvation, but all too often a temptation to evil — the sin of pride.

"I told the one woman I was talking with about all of that, and a few others joined in, and we had a good talk. A couple of them had lived in Cambridge, and their reaction to Harvard was like Jude's — they looked at those walls and gates around the Harvard Yard as though heaven was inside them! But they also observed people who went in and out, and they overheard what those people were saying, and they got to feel like Jude. I loved hearing them speak up that way and make that connection [between their experience in Cambridge and what Hardy was describing].

"Suddenly, while I listened to them, I realized that I hadn't thought of *my* world when I was reading that novel — and now, with the help of *those* 'obscure' ones, I was making a new connection, a pretty obvious connection! Hardy had himself in mind when he brought Jude to Christminster. He was a working man. He was a mason, a stonecutter, just like Jude. When I first read Hardy's *Jude* I didn't read it the way I did later; working with these women sure helped me be a little of the outsider, and feeling that way, I read *Jude* differently! Sitting in that shelter, with all those really hurt women, and talking about *Jude*, and all the pain in him and in the women of his life — their pain and frustration — it makes me realize that where you read a book and when and with whom (as your fellow readers) can make a big difference!

"The point I'm trying to make, it's this: you can learn a lot when you do this kind of work, and I guess everyone would agree on that — learn sociology and psychology and economics and politics. But you can also learn about yourself, your own psychology and politics and values; *and* you can learn about your own way of reading books; *and* you can read them again, with this new experience, and take note of passages and whole chapters you might not have given the same degree of attention to before. And so while you're doing, you're learning, and when you go back to school, to college, when you resume learning, you can do so differently, because of the doing — you can be a different reader. I'm not saying a better one!

"Maybe I'm saying, in my case, that it took this experience, this work in that shelter, for me to be able to do some of the thinking, some of the learning, that's come to me this fall and winter, now that I'm here studying. It's not so hard for me to get people to agree that when you work in a shelter, or a ghetto school or a prison or a soup kitchen or a nursing home, that you're learning a lot all the time, even if it's not classroom learning; but it's harder for me to make this other point — that what you learn out there then becomes part of you, *and* it gives some new assumptions or attitudes to you, some experiences that become, collectively, a new lens, and you see through the lens when you do your reading."

Julia kept circling around the subject of the reciprocity and continuity of human knowledge and experience obtained in various ways. She wondered aloud whether I should try to do a different kind of teaching, one that focused more specifically on community service as a subject matter — not a course on how to do service or one given over to "group discussions of feelings" or "debriefings" (a term she had picked up as a volunteer), but a seminar in which we would read novels, poems, stories, reportage, and social science texts in the light of our ongoing experiences as volunteers. We would discuss what we had learned by doing, but we would also connect that learning to the learning found in books and films.

The point is *not* to ask that academic credit be given for community service work (I have not suggested this — nor have my students asked for it) but, rather, that the lecture hall and classroom be places where books are read not only as sources of instruction but also as guides and mentors with respect to work being done among people similar to those whose lives are rendered in the books. Maybe, she suggested, if we read those books as returnees from those worlds that are the very subject of the books, we would learn in a new way.

It is not just a matter, Julia reminded me, of an enlarged sensibility and awareness (one hopes and prays) being brought to the academic setting, but of a broadened mind and deepened heart (again, one hopes and prays) being brought back to the place where community service is being done: *now*, thanks to those books and those lectures and those discussions and the thinking that went into those papers, I see and understand what before eluded me. As a result, *now* I can work with these children, with those folks in a soup kitchen or a shelter, with perspective and a bit more open-mindedness or thoughtfulness. I can acquire some plain old savvy from those authors and filmmakers, for their knowledge and experience do count for something.

Julia's suggestion, her challenge, really, provided the stimulus for an undergraduate seminar titled "Community Service." In that course we read books, watched films, and discussed the assignments while connecting them to the community service work we were all doing, and we drew upon our own service work as we considered each book, article, or film.[12] We started with J. Anthony Lukas's *Common Ground*, an extraordinary telling of "a turbulent decade in the lives of three American families" involved in Boston's 1970s school desegregation struggle. Many of us who have worked in Boston's schools have gone through, in our own ways, some of the challenges and difficulties Lukas presents. Once we were in the middle of that long book, we found it hard to leave, so powerfully did it spur us to share remembered incidents. But we had other books to meet, and we knew we would return to some of the important issues Lukas brought to the fore.

Some of the other books we read were Piri Thomas's *Down These Mean Streets*, William Junius Wilson's *The Truly Disadvantaged*, Gloria Naylor's stories collected in *The Women of Brewster Place*, John Langston Gwaltney's *Dry Longso: A Self-Portrait of Black America*, Jay MacLeod's *Ain't No Making It*, Nicholasa Mohr's stories in *In Nueva York*, Richard Rodriguez's autobiography, *Hunger of Memory*, and James Baldwin's *The Fire Next Time*. We reached back to earlier fiction, to Jack London's *Martin Eden*, to Hubert Selby's *Last Exit to Brooklyn*, and to the fiction I teach in my "Social Reflection" course already mentioned. A recently published collection of short stories by James Lasdun, *Three Evenings*, has an extraordinary tale, "The Volunteer," that would have fitted perfectly into that seminar.

It was important to introduce the writing of John Dewey and William James to these students, for those two American philosophers emphasized experience as a tool, a way toward knowledge — the empirical angle of vision.[13] A novel such as Hawthorne's *The Blithedale Romance* would be appropriate because of its tough examination of utopianism and its discontents. Ignazio Silone's haunting *Bread and Wine*, which I use in the "Social Reflection" course, is also valuable, for it engages with the frustrations, moral dangers, and even disasters that come in the wake of a lifelong struggle with social and political power.[14] These novels and those of Joseph Conrad, such as *Under Western Eyes* (which is about revolution against the state and withdrawal into a community that stands resolutely apart from the ordinary communities of a nation), remind us on a larger scale about a question any volunteer must consider: where do I want to stand in relation to the established order of things?[15] As a lady of great means who worked modestly and quietly as a Red Cross volunteer said, "Even the Red Cross is doing something our society hasn't chosen to do on its own." Perhaps she was needlessly postulating, then dramatizing a distance between an organization and what she called "society." However, many volunteers find themselves picking up the slack for a city, a state, a nation unwilling to attend to many important matters that directly affect thousands, even millions, of people.

* * *

Many volunteers also find themselves increasingly aware of the difference between themselves and those who do not choose or do not care to join their company. When I hear them make that distinction, I also hear some of the themes Hawthorne and Conrad and Silone bring up in their fiction — the dangers of self-righteousness, the temptations of social isolation as a means of social assertion, the gloom that comes at times when idealism is not rewarded by victory but is defeated.

A college student, Brad, taking the "Community Service" seminar, wondered out loud, a week before the end of the class, whether he'd get involved with volunteer projects in the future. "I get worn out from the work, but harder to take is sitting in the dining room listening to the silly talk of some people. I want to get up and run away — who's making out with whom, and what bar is the best place to pick up someone, and gossip about the tutors, and the pluses and minuses of Ivy League schools, and the parties coming up, and what courses are really 'guts,' and what courses seem to be, but they can trip you up.

"I shouldn't talk this way — Mr. Perfect, Mr. Serious, Mr. Above It All! But after a long afternoon and evening in Roxbury, I come back here and I feel as if I'm from another planet, and worse, I feel glad that I'm apart from all of them, my fellow students. I used to sit with a bunch of people and laugh it up. I'd go down at 6:30 or so, when the [dining] hall was most crowded. I liked that — sitting with a lot of guys and girls. Now, I sneak in early, when no one is there; or if it's late, I skip the hall and go get a sandwich someplace. That way, I can think about my work here [at college] or there [in Roxbury], and I'm not feeling myself become more and more misanthropic, and more and more low. And I have to admit it, I get a bit of pleasure out of feeling that way! It's as if to be moody and to be scornful of people living in my dorm — it's as if I'm defining who I am by feeling like that! I can't explain it any more — any better — than I just did. Maybe I'm just a little worn down, but when I read those books, I realize others have felt the way I do — outside the usual social scene! I identified with a lot of what Hawthorne was saying: if you get involved with something that's outside the cultural or political mainstream, something that takes you away from your own community, then when you go back, when you return, you're likely to feel betwixt and between, neither here nor there. I know those are clichés; I know Hawthorne didn't have community service in mind, and Conrad didn't have it in mind, and Silone didn't — but they're all talking about *departures*, and then *returns*, or the temptation to return!"

Brad ended his soliloquy because he saw me looking puzzled. I hadn't thought that the drastic, sweeping "departures" depicted by those three novelists quite merited comparison with his weekly trips across town, however challenging, unsettling, exhausting, and nerve-racking. I tried to explain that point of view, and he was quite annoyed at me. *Of course* he didn't intend a literal comparison; *of course*, he knew the difference between radical political activity and community service. I was missing his point — his use of literary symbolism to convey some psychological convergences. The theme of departure does connect those three novelists, and it brought to his mind his own sense of taking leave of a world.

"I go to the subway station, and it's not like going to the subway to get to Fenway Park to see the Red Sox, or Locke-Ober's to eat in a small private room, with the ghost of F. Scott Fitzgerald or John Cheever or someone like them smiling cheerfully down on us. It's foolish to make comparisons like that, I know it. The fact that I do, and that I'm more of a loner these days — well, what I'm saying is: I can't stop seeing connections between what I've read and how I'm dealing with my 'community service experience.' I hate it when I read that phrase! I saw it in some brochure about volunteerism and I wanted to throw up! That's what my dad calls a 'package phrase.'"

Mention of his father reminded him of his father's political and social conservatism and his almost heroic rise from poverty to affluence. Brad began to talk as if his father were speaking through him, and he connected what his father might say to some books we had read and talked about during the seminar. "My dad doesn't really think I'm accomplishing much, doing this work. He doesn't agree with a lot of these writers — he thinks they are bleeding-heart liberals! He came from a very poor family. They had nothing — zero dollars in the bank or anywhere else. My grandfather had no work during the Depression. He had to go on the WPA — but he couldn't take the idea of getting money for doing what he called make-work. He wanted a regular job! So he went to an apartment house one day and found out when the landlord came to collect his rents. He was there, waiting, and he approached the guy, and he asked him, please, to let him clean the halls and the stairs and take care of the garbage. I guess the people were supposed to do it all themselves.

"The owner said no, he didn't have the money, and half his tenants were behind in their rents, and he was having trouble paying the mortgage every month. My grandpa said all right, but he lived nearby, and he'd come and do some cleanup work anyway, and if there was any problem with the plumbing or an electrical problem, he would help, because he was pretty handy at fixing things. And if he didn't get paid, that wouldn't bother him, because he needed something to do. I guess the landlord thought my grandfather had lost his mind!

"After he started doing the work, the place really improved — it looked great, my dad told us. The landlord was impressed, and he started paying my grandfather a little, five dollars a week — that was pretty good then. My grandfather went and found other small jobs, and that's how they got through the worst of the Depression. With the war, he got a job in the Navy Yard, working on ships as a mechanic. My father grew up believing in *work*, just like his father, and in going out and finding something that would work for him, like his father. No wonder he became so successful. He saved, and bought property, and repaired and improved it, and sold it — and bought more! He believes in *will*, in *drive;* and he believes if you're sitting and waiting for handouts, then 'you're dead.' He wishes he had the education I've got. He's lived through me, being here — a big deal. He's worried now, though. He says, 'All I've built, you seem ready to let it go and not keep adding to it.' He's afraid I'm going to be headed downward — downward social mobility!"

In reference to books, Brad mentioned the power of Jack London's novel *Martin Eden* and, in the same vein, Dreiser's *An American Tragedy.* (The movie version of Dreiser's book, *A Place in the Sun,* added some emotional emphasis to his family remembrances.) London and Dreiser knew the fierce ambition some people on the rise can experience amid the thralldom of poverty. When he read those books he thought of his grandfather and his father — and he could understand how those two men, who managed to leave behind one world and enter another step by step, would wonder why *he* would spend so much time with poor black children when he ought to be readying himself for law school, taking part in competitive sports, or socializing.

"Dad says part of success is who you know, and part of success is being on your toes, and able to beat out the next guy, so he's all for my playing hockey and meeting a lot of people who are as well-to-do as we've become. I say 'as we've become,' and he says 'as we are.' Dad isn't interested in the social history I've studied here! I thought of him when we read *The Hidden Injuries of Class* [by Richard Sennett and Jonathan Cobb] — some of those workers who dreamed of breaking out, rising up, making it. Well, Dad did, and now he's afraid this 'community service thing,' as he calls it, will push me down, *un*make me! 'You have got to keep ahead, stay ahead, or you fall behind' — that's his worry, his ethic. In a way, he's still poor in his head, the way my grandpa was in his wallet all his life. I think of them when I read books, and I think of them when I tutor the kids: why aren't they driven, like grandpa and dad? Is it fair to put the question that way? White is not black!"

Brad and the others in that seminar did indeed connect the books they were reading to their experiences as volunteers. A moment in *Common Ground* could trigger a two-hour discussion of class and race, of "forced busing," of the federal courts and the privileges of suburban life, where no judge intrudes with mandates. As the students noted, the ultimate privilege is to be able to avoid a moral test of one's commitments or prejudices. Their own values were tested, they also noted, by the work they did; they were tempted at times to throw in the towel, as one family did in *Common Ground.* Again and again, books evoked memories of service: an incident during a day of tutoring helped a student understand more fully what Ellison or Baldwin, Olsen or Carver, was writing about. A student asked, "Would I have asked that question [about the London novel] if I hadn't heard a kid dreaming of 'being poor no more one day'?"

We now move to a more abstract, intellectual, and psychological question: what shifts take place in the mind as it responds to

courses taken and to events weathered through visits to soup kitchens, schools, nursing homes, and prisons?

I did not usually hear a lot of boasting or egoistic insistence
upon special regard, as if "we" had earned a special affiliation with
characters in the books being read, or with their authors. These
young men and women were, by and large, not strutters, not
satisfied with conquests and ready to gloat intellectually: I've been
there, I know *that* through direct observation. Rather, they confessed to confusion; they acknowledged being apprehensive and
anxious. Their questions indicated indirectly a heightened interest
based on personal awareness and involvement.

For the first time in my teaching career I was asked by the students in the "Community Service" seminar if we might write more
than the two papers I'd requested, in addition to a longer final one.
After a long discussion we agreed that keeping a journal or diary
would be an important element in the course. Each student entered introspective daily or weekly reflections, and we held several
extra classes to discuss certain entries. In each of those personal
accounts, the student made a telling bridge between a point made,
an incident described, or a character evoked in a particular book
and an experience in the writer's volunteering life — a scene witnessed, a comment overheard. Usually, the student would also
write about a reaction or memory that did not easily go away.

As one student reminded us, there are "hidden injuries" other
than those based on class (something Freud long ago learned). But
there are also, ironically, "hidden injuries of class" that arise when
students so privileged cross social and racial borders to render
service; they experience their own kind of hurt, the turmoil (sometimes even danger) that goes with learning by doing under circumstances altogether different from classrooms and lecture halls. All
the more important that they be offered a chance to return to those
classrooms and lecture halls with the various injuries not only
(inevitably) on their minds, but kept in mind as worth consideration in a high school, a college, a university: for their sakes (an
educational opportunity), as well as for the sake of those teachers
who might have a lot to share (or discover!) with respect to what
has been done — even as there is, always, much to learn through
reading and writing.

· SIX ·

Young Idealism

W HEN I WAS AN UNDERGRADUATE, I tutored some children in English and math. Billy, one of the youngsters with whom I worked, was eleven years old, I remember, and in the sixth grade. His parents had been born in Boston's North End neighborhood, though all four of their parents had come to the United States from Italy. They were hard-working people, and they were ambitious for their children and grandchildren, I began to realize, in more than a social or economic or educational way. They wanted Billy to be a decent, honorable, conscientious person.

As for his future, if he were to become the tradesman his father had become, that would be wonderful — so the boy himself told me one day as we chatted. Indeed, several times he reminded me that schooling was not all that essential to his plans and that soon enough, in his teens, he'd be contemplating which of the trades he'd pursue. At the time, I recall, he had in mind becoming an electrician.

I bring up that encounter of long ago because it had a much stronger impact on me than I understood at the time. Again and again, as I realized how very intelligent Billy was, I tried to persuade him to look carefully at his life, develop some second

thoughts about what he might do with it. I talked to him about
going to college and even about attending a high school that would
give him a good chance of being accepted at college. I talked with
him about the opportunities particular professions offered. And I
kept reminding him how bright I felt he was; his poor schoolwork
was a result, I'd figured out, of general lack of interest.

He listened politely but said little, and he constantly tried to
change the subject. We'd usually end up talking about automobiles, a great passion of his. He loved the sight of them, the challenge of identifying their make, the relative virtues or flaws in one
or another company's products, and, always, the speed a particular
car might achieve on an open highway uncluttered by traffic.

One afternoon, after we'd finished our arithmetic lesson and I'd
made yet another effort at persuasion, I found myself decidedly on
the defensive. Billy said not a word in reply to my comments until
I was through, and then he put this question to me, one I still
remember after all these years and have thought about rather
intently and with some perplexity. "I was wondering something,"
he began — and then he paused politely for me to give him the
nod that meant yes, I'd love to hear more. With that signal, he
asked, "Why do you come here?"

Though I was usually able to talk with some fluency, I was
suddenly utterly quiet. I looked across the table at a wall (we
tutored in a school's "visiting room," where parents met with their
children's teachers) and then toward the window, whose view of the
playground and some nearby apartment houses I can still see. I
avoided the boy's eyes and was unable to reply for so long that we
both became embarrassed. He didn't repeat his question, but the
comment he made escalated the matter, I later realized: "I was just
wondering." Since _I_ had often spoken that sentence as I tried to
keep words between us flowing with some ease and frequency (he
was quite reticent, occasionally giving only monosyllabic yes/no
answers to my inquiries), he had managed to confront me with a
solid moment of irony — and I was still quite unable to muster a
sound, let alone a coherent reply. Finally, ever tactful and considerate (more so than _I_ had been, with my constant stabs at self-im-
portant, self-serving propaganda on behalf of college attendance),
he said, "Well, I guess I shouldn't ask."

By then I was ready to insist on Billy's right to be as inquisitive as he wanted to be. (Hadn't I been telling him so all along!) I spent much time assuring him along those lines, but all the while I was trying, in vain, to think of an answer to his question. He never pressed the matter further — and a loud bell, telling us that everyone in that after-school program ought to be leaving, saved my neck for that day.

Billy's question stayed on the top of my mind on the way home, however, and it was still on my mind the next week, when I went to see my college adviser, Perry Miller, a professor of American literature. Professor Miller was *my* tutor: he assigned one book a week — novels of Hawthorne, Melville, Dreiser, essays of Emerson, Thoreau, poetry of William Carlos Williams — and we discussed what I'd read along with any stray subjects either of us wanted to bring up — the weather, the trials of the Red Sox, politics. When I shared that boy's question with Miller in his university library study, he immediately asked what I'd said. "Nothing," I answered tersely. He wanted to know, naturally, what reply I'd make if I were given a second chance when I next saw Billy. I had to answer the truth of my confused, almost blank mind: "I don't know."

After that confession Professor Miller and I had a long talk.[1] He didn't jump on my statement; rather, my anxiety lessened somewhat as I described my confusion, and he nodded his head several times and said, "Yes, yes, I understand." Then he delivered an extended, memorable disquisition on education — on how important it is that teachers remember, always, that our students can teach us a lot, though maybe not every day. They offer us factuality or prod us with respect to intellectual ideas, and sometimes they stop us in our tracks in a most telling way, as that boy had stopped me. I should add that this professor of American literature at Harvard didn't once use a psychological or sociological word as he made that point. On the contrary, he could, on occasion, pour scorn on a densely abstract, theoretical social science that failed to offer what he kept calling "instances" — the specificity of moments and examples. His mind was set on a moral direction — a quaint direction for us today to consider, given the influence of so-called value-free social science in much of our thinking. He wanted to uphold the pertinence of Billy's question and also the reason (even the desirability, he would argue) for my quite apparent muteness.

He wanted me to consider this — and I have certainly kept in mind the gist of his reasoning: what we do on behalf of others may be a big puzzle to them, perhaps because we patronize them, condescend to them, convey to them our sense of lofty *noblesse oblige*, even hector them with it, while refusing to acknowledge (to ourselves, perhaps also to them) our own purposes and reasons and, very important, our own needs. He concluded with these words, an odd and compelling mix, I thought then and still do, of relatively fancy talk and quite earthy talk: "There's a moral asymmetry that takes hold of us teachers rather too commonly — we think of ourselves as offering service to others, giving them our best, and forget what's in it for ourselves, the service that we're receiving from our students."

I think the reason I still have his message word for word in my head is because I realized gradually that he'd hit the nail squarely on the head concerning my attitude as a volunteer tutor. The next time I saw Billy I used my own words to echo my professor's. I said I liked coming to that school, liked leaving the place where I lived (a college dormitory filled with talkative, aspiring, and not always humble young men), and I liked, especially, stopping on my way back to that world for some strong coffee and some Italian pastry at a nearby eating place. Billy liked that last bit of information, liked my thoroughly indirect suggestion of the nurturance I was getting — or so I interpreted his big smile much later in my life. He was telling me indirectly that he hadn't wanted some long-winded, introspective *apologia* from me, or some big-deal analysis and explanation. He wanted only a sign that I was a human being, flawed and even voiceless, like others, like him, and capable of plenty of confusion, as he knew he was, and, yes, as hungry in my own way as he was.

Now, decades later, as I still work in an elementary school near Boston, do my volunteer work in its classrooms only a few blocks from the college campus where I'm called a professor, I sometimes find myself thinking of that moment and of the education I received with the help of an eleven-year-old boy. Billy was an important teacher of mine, whose question, I hope, I won't forget.

My answers to it still come and go, change direction, get dressed in different words and phrases. Most of all I remember a break in our conversation — the moment when he gave me a lusty laugh and told me, you bet, the pastries are good in that place.

Although Professor Miller was a busy teacher, he took the trouble to keep inquiring about that boy and my efforts with him. In his course "Classics of the Christian Tradition," Miller had on more than one occasion lectured us on the high ideals of the various Christian writers and apologists we were reading: Pascal, Calvin, Kierkegaard, Saint John of the Cross, and, closer to our time, Simone Weil and Reinhold Niebuhr and Dorothy Day.[2] I didn't at first realize how much this teacher wanted to connect the writing and thought of those men and women to our everyday lives, to our struggle to figure out what mattered to us and how we should or would live our lives.

When I told Professor Miller about the pleasure I got out of my weekly visit to the Italian bakery, he noticed and took heart. He joked, "You can't feed others if you don't take good care of yourself!" I can still remember cringing as I heard that comment. It was one thing for me and my young tutee to share a casual moment such as I have just described — a teacher leveling with a student, telling him he's a human being, too, but it was quite another to hear the concreteness of a moment conveyed as a story, fitted into a generalization about education and psychology, a formulation about what is possible and desirable in the life of a volunteer instructor. I knew nothing then about psychiatry or psychoanalysis or even academic psychology. I was taken aback, I would later understand, by Miller's directness, if not bluntness: here is what you are doing, young man, so, naturally, here is what you need if you care to do a good job.

Perry Miller was a wonderfully wise and knowing teacher; he also had a spirited sense of humor, a large capacity for irony, and an earthy side — a willingness to be direct and forceful in his conversation with students and others. He saw immediately that I had been knocked off balance by his comment and, like a good psychoanalyst, he watched me closely to see how I'd respond. But he observed me with a kind look on his face, as if to indicate that he was not intending to be insensitive or crude. I had a rough time knowing what to say, and the silence between us was longer than usual.

I now suspect that he tried to help me settle down, feel less confused, angered, anxious, and alarmed, by saying, "It *is* a kind of nourishment we teachers offer others, I think." I recall appreciating the gesture (the high compliment!) of a declared affiliation between us, and I must have been soothed by the tentative manner in which he rephrased his analytic proposition. In turn, he must have seen my tensed body relax a bit, my wary, gloomy face give way to the start of a smile. I still had no words to offer. He continued, "Even the most idealistic of people — some of the people we're reading in the course — have the same appetites and needs you and I have."

There was nothing surprising in his words, but they (and our preceding talk, which had become abstract, on the subject of motivation and idealism) stuck in my mind vividly. What Professor Miller said continued to be a subject of great interest to me during my psychoanalytic training and in my many discussions with those teachers whom I would probably call mentors today (back then they were my heroes). A teacher's thoughtful yet casual remark had to do, in a rock-bottom way, with the overbearing, unequivocal demands we let idealism make upon us.

It was one thing for me to get to know Billy, learn to tutor him reasonably well, and learn also that he was himself and not a stand-in for me and my assumptions and aspirations; thereafter, I learned to relax with him, share with him the kind of person-to-person talk that resulted in his finding out about my sweet tooth and my discovering that he, too, had an insistent sweet tooth. It was quite another thing to take a careful, head-on look at what idealism meant to me, and how I lived with its requirements in my then young life of twenty years.

Some of the writers Professor Miller had assigned us, who were far older when they struggled with the ideas they wanted to share with others, had certainly tried to keep idealism on the "high" (ascetic) pedestal I clearly had used. I doubt Simone Weil would have appreciated Professor Miller's remark, at least at some moments in her difficult life, so challenged by the demands she made of herself.[3] Maybe Pascal, in a more learned and high-minded way, would have constructed a pensée to do justice to the truth Perry Miller was addressing; Kierkegaard might have written one of his trenchant, ironic essays.[4] Saint Augustine's *Confessions*, which we also read, took up the matter of idealism, but he was a saint writing in the distant past, and he treated his mix of emotions not with Miller's urbane, sophisticated understanding but with a great deal of moral anguish, scrutiny, and, at times, despair.

I was being told, Enjoy yourself, or it will be hard for you to give of yourself to others! I think that at the time I could have written an Augustinian indictment of Perry Miller's dictum, which now makes such good sense to me! I also think he knew that some of my awkwardness was the result of a young idealism buttressed by an intensely demanding morality, itself connected in no small measure to a strongly influential religious life. It was as if all my mother's fulminations against pride and egoism and self-preoccupation, so reminiscent to me of those uttered by Saint Augustine and others in the Judeo-Christian tradition (going back to Isaiah and Jeremiah and Amos and Jesus of Nazareth) had suddenly been set aside, firmly and with suggestive imagery, as not quite to the point: be practical and unpretentious and sensual rather than ostensibly so lofty and ascetic in thinking about yourself.

A year later I was in for an even more unsettling experience: accompanying an old, crusty, outspoken physician, William Carlos Williams, who also happened to be a writer, on his visits to hard-pressed families in New Jersey. Poems were his great passion. I had written my senior thesis on the first two volumes of *Paterson*, an idiosyncratic, lyrical examination of a country — its people, their history, and their efforts to make a life for themselves and find some sustaining purpose. I had sent my thesis to Dr. Williams at Perry Miller's suggestion (that idea, too, was not easy for me, although by that time I had decided to become a doctor) and had received a friendly response.

I was anxious to meet this person whose words and thoughts would come to mean so very much to me, but on the day I showed up he had no time for talk. He had work to do, and if I wanted, I could come along. Up and down tenement house stairs we went. After we saw one sick child and before we saw the next, he would give me a rundown on the families and would occasionally sound

off. He blasted the "big-shot medical centers" and their smugness,
ranted at the way some young people get educated and at the
arrogance and self-importance that are not rare in academic life.
He spoke of how students can pick up, unwittingly, a sad "pay-
off" from teachers trying to bribe them to follow their example.
"They'll grade you not only for what you get to know," he insisted,
"but for your willingness to have a certain obedient attitude toward
the kind of behavior and the kind of knowledge they are peddling!"

Most shocking of all, he would occasionally deliver a tirade
against some of his patients, against the callous, mean, stingy side
of life to which he was witness. I sat in silence — unnerved, a little
afraid, dismayed, disappointed. How could a *doctor* be so outspokenly critical of some of his *patients?* He clearly admired, even
loved other patients, and he pointed out the virtues of those whose
vices he denounced. He offered explanations for the faults he described, indirectly invoking history, sociology, and psychology.
Perhaps most important, he worked hard to be fair and honorable
with all of his patients, no matter his private opinion of any of
them. And he cared for many who never paid him or who could
give him only a small share of what he had requested. He sent out
quite modest bills, and often wrote them off: so-and-so just won't
be able to find the cash now or in the foreseeable future.

Still — why such rancor? Or was the rancor precisely a doctor's
response to a financially inadequate clientele? I had read some of
his "doctor stories," published originally as *Life along the Passaic
River.* I knew he was not loath in those narratives to confess to
moments of annoyance, irritation, excitement, or affection. Similarly in *Paterson,* he occasionally turns on his own self-absorption,
conceits, and capacity for self-deception in a manner worthy of
Saint Augustine — spells of prose (as in the prosaic) that interrupt
the exaltation of the poetry.

How to make sense of all those contradictions? Here was a doctor much given to helping others, often selflessly, or so it seemed
to an outsider, yet here was a mind, a voice that could turn gruff,
if not fault-finding, even disparaging. On another visit, when he
noticed a look of perplexity on my face, he addressed me with
sincerity and no small amount of emotion: "The last time you were
here you told me you wanted to do this kind of work when you

become a doctor. If you do, I hope you won't get sentimental about the poor — or yourself as the one who's working with them!"

I looked at him in surprise, obviously, and concern about his doubt, if not implied criticism. He explained that sentimentality about others or oneself and about one's obligations toward others was a form of "idealization" — a burden to carry that is unfair to others, for they become the means by which one's mind sets in motion the idealization.

We were being rather intellectual, though he was never high-falutin in that regard. He shunned big-deal theory ("no ideas but in things" is the refrain through parts of *Paterson*) in favor of the vernacular, albeit the lyrically vernacular, the particulars of every-day life, both contemporary and of the past. He wanted very much for me to see what he was getting at, and I did, but only to a limited extent — and he could see that. Without being patronizing, he let me know that he understood both his difficulty and mine.

He went into a soliloquy about time's burdens and also its gifts. He had been "several different kinds of doctors," he told me. I initially thought he was referring to the specialties or branches of medicine he'd pursued successively, but he was referring to shifts in his expectations of himself and of his patients, even as he'd re-mained essentially the same hard-working, attentive physician all along. He didn't characterize himself that way; rather, he said that he had always "tried to do the best" he could. Yet he had come to his first patients, he said, with a "tremendous desire to help them out, and a tremendous desire to see them in the best possible light."

I nodded, relieved to hear that. But he took us further and told me that gradually he found himself no longer quite as confident about what medicine, even the best medicine, could offer people, and he was no longer able to avoid seeing some of the "warts" his patients presented to him — "warts and worse," he added. (I kept a journal of our talks, and later on, as a doctor myself, I taped some of our conversations.)[5]

He went on to explain that none of us lives up to the ideal — and that an "idealism" which fails to remember that is in "danger." I wasn't sure what he intended by that last word. He replied by bringing us full circle: "the danger of sentimentality," he said, which he defined as a kind of "misreading of things," a kind of "distortion." How those words stuck in my head — and yet how hard it was for me to feel, honestly and clearly, what he seemed so willing to acknowledge as a part of himself, a truth within his heart and mind.

Eventually, during those years when I was taking premed and then medical school courses, we both agreed to drop the matter. Once, in a moment of impatience with me (how I understand his feeling now!) he told me to go talk with Dorothy Day about idealism and put some of the questions to her that I'd been posing to him. He knew I'd been working in her Lower East Side soup kitchen, and he joked that she was an "expert" on such matters — an observation whose sardonic aspect I failed to recognize at the time!

In her own fashion, Dorothy Day, despite her long-standing interest in idealism and her belief in the obligation to do good works, could be quite evasive about definitions and explanations. When I asked her about her reasons for living the kind of life she had chosen, she would talk about her "struggle to obey God," or her conclusion that "Jesus had such a life in mind for many of us." Yet she would almost immediately observe that she "failed often" to live up to such standards, even if she was doing the best she could. "I'm slipping and falling all the time," she once insisted. When I asked for a single example, she gave many — instances of her failure "to meet halfway" some of the poor people who frequented the Catholic Worker soup kitchen. Later, when I was trying to study her ideas for a biography, I found it hard to figure out what her notions of idealism amounted to, even though one would think her life had earned her expert knowledge on the subject.[6]

Indeed, she could be rather dismissive of that word "idealism," though she always hastened to amplify, even to correct herself. "I don't know how to describe us all here. Maybe a group of sinners put here by the Lord! When I was younger — before I ever dreamed I'd end up living on the Lower East Side trying to scramble up food every day for people who are called Bowery bums or derelicts or the homeless — I'd probably have called myself an 'idealist' or I'd have hoped that others would have. There is such a thing as modesty! To be 'idealistic' was to be, I guess, what the cynics call a 'do-gooder.'

"I shouldn't be so negative, though! I should say that when I was young, there was a great desire, a strong desire to help others, and it was a desire that took over my life. I ended up in jail protesting and demonstrating for the right of women to vote, or the obligation of our country to feed the hungry, take care of people who had lost their jobs and were at the very edge of things. You may think it odd that we demonstrated and were arrested for demonstrating over such issues, but we're talking about the early 1920s, and even before that. [She was born in 1897.]

"For me, back then, to be idealistic meant to take certain political stands, to have certain social attitudes, and to be willing to put yourself on the line for those beliefs. No, we never tried to quantify! [I had earned her impatience, if not disgust, by attempting to find out how far on the line one had to be in order to call oneself or be called idealistic.] We were all trying to live up to the same ideals, and no one was out there clocking us or judging us! But we *would* make distinctions, even if, in looking back, I'm quite embarrassed by what we thought or said. We'd call some people materialistic, a big putdown, as people would say now! The opposite of materialistic was idealistic, a big slap on the back, a big hurrah!

"My friends would often call each other idealistic, and by that they meant someone who shared *their* ideals — I'd better mention that! — and who was doing something to live up to those ideals. It was the 'living up to' that was important. But I'll have to admit it: if someone had ideals we didn't like, then we didn't call the person idealistic. We called such people plenty of other names, I guess! We called them materialists, as I said, or people out for themselves only, or people who surrendered to the rat race. None of us took the time to stop and think that maybe those people had ideals and were working very hard to live up to them!"

She stopped, and I felt quite uneasy; maybe I felt quite properly reprimanded. I was, of course, considerably younger than her, and as we sat there in silence, I realized that she was talking about herself at an age not much different from mine at the time. Moreover, she was indirectly bringing up a very important matter, one Dr. Williams had also been trying to broach with me: the danger that idealism can be a cover for a naive or unwitting complacency, a self-satisfaction that does little justice to the truth of one's own life or the lives of those whom one works with or helps or tries to enhance in some way.

What Williams meant by "sentimentality" was just what Dorothy was getting at in referring to the self-congratulatory appropriation of the word "idealism." He had learned to beware in *himself* of a kind of self-delight that was blind both to his own shortcomings and those of his patients. She had learned to beware in *herself* of the arrogance that enabled her to see clearly her virtues and those of her friends while giving the back of her hand to others.

Of course they both merited the description "idealistic" in an old-fashioned, commonsense version of the word. A reasonably well-off doctor (both Williams and his wife, Flossie, had some inherited money, though they were not rich) decided to locate his practice among poor immigrants when he might have confined himself to New Jersey's affluent towns. He also became a vigorous spokesman for the vitality and integrity and decency of the ordinary people whose lives he attended. A young journalist spent her time, from late adolescence on, fighting on the streets for what she believed to be right, and she wrote constantly on behalf of causes to which she was deeply committed. Yet each of them, later in life, warned themselves and me about having an uncritical attitude toward the very idealism that clearly mattered to them.

Not that young people aren't able to be self-critical of their own idealism (and that of others occasionally). I used to be reminded of my own naiveté or ignorance when I talked with such older self-doubters as William Carlos Williams and Dorothy Day. But in recent years, as I have listened to certain youths reflect upon their values and aspirations, I am both surprised and impressed by what they see within themselves as well as others. Perhaps this century, with its various disasters, with its increasing psychological and social sophistication, has made it easier for young people to shed their illusions. Certainly more and more of them are taking part in a level of political activism and a degree of community service unheard of years ago.

At the height of political struggle, detachment from the passions of the day is not necessarily desirable — and it is not all that common. I remember many a civil rights bull session among the members of SNCC in which immediate concerns and struggles took priority over any misgivings or doubts about the larger significance of what was taking place. By then (1961 to 1966) I had completed my medical, psychiatric, and psychoanalytic training and was presumably a little less naive than when I'd met Dr. Williams and Dorothy Day.

However, I was taken aback on more than a few occasions — for example, by the willful daring of one young man, Alan, who was a graduate of Morehouse College in Atlanta and the son of a conservative black postal worker. At a meeting in the basement of a black church in Georgia, Alan challenged a number of veteran activists, saying, "It's not easy staring those sheriffs in the face, but the worst times for me are when I have to stare myself in the face!" With that one remark, it could be argued, he showed more personal courage than was required to take on the segregationists.

He stopped after speaking those words. He got up to get some water and looked out the window. I sensed that he was not only reluctant but unable to proceed. Yet he had piqued the interest of the seven others in the room. Through a dramatic, implicitly confessional remark, he had managed to quell what he surely knew was the desire of others to talk and talk. These were articulate men and women who had a lot on their minds, who were under a great deal of stress, who were very much used to sharing ideas and emotions with one another. Now they waited for him to continue rather than pursue their own agendas.

Finally he sat down again and started talking, haltingly at first, but with increasing energy and conviction. His voice, quivering at first, picked up strength as he went on: "I don't always like what I see in the mirror. I'll turn on all the racists and the 'segs' [segregationists] but I'll suddenly catch myself being pretty mean about people. Maybe it's not white-Negro meanness — maybe it's just me trying to shore myself up by being pretty tough on everyone else. I like to think of myself as an idealist. I don't really know what the word means, though. I know it means 'living up to your ideals' — but who decides which ideals are ideal? Do you see what I'm saying?"

He paused for an answer, but none was forthcoming. Usually several people would have jumped in and begun sharing their ideas, but his engaging seriousness on a matter that was of great importance to all of them seemed to stifle their urge to respond to his invitation. He tried to answer his own question. "I guess it's everyone's job to decide on what's important, and then go and live the way you believe — I mean put your life where your faith is, or your values are. If you do, though, you can still wonder whether you have any right to take yourself so seriously that you end up dismissing other people, who have *also* tried to do the same thing. That's what bothers me — people having opposite beliefs, and yet they both seem idealistic! Maybe if I'd majored in philosophy, then I could figure out who's right, or what's right, and then I'd know who's wrong — and why! But I have a friend who majored in philosophy, and he says the philosophers argue and fight, and they can talk big and then be as mean and nasty as anyone else!

"Actually, I *do* know what I believe in, and why I think it's right. But look, even with us — look how often we get into real tough arguments, angry arguments, and we're all together and we're fighting for something we believe is so *obvious!* Sometimes when we knock others on our side of things, I think to myself that we're not so nice, and maybe we're not even as nice as some folks who don't seem to care about this struggle the way we do — and I mean Negroes as well as whites."

He stopped once more, and I thought that this time, surely, he would have his respondents, and outspoken ones at that. But an almost eerie silence had developed in the basement of that church, punctuated only by a comment meant to prod the iconoclastic speaker to be even more forthcoming: "Go ahead! Give us more of your truth!" The comment — echoing the black religious tradition of the audience's refrain contributing to the speaker's sermon — worked well. Alan spoke more urgently, boldly: "I don't want to criticize anyone. That's the problem, I believe — we're getting so critical of people, there's only 'us' left. Pretty soon we'll start turning on each other! Then all the people we're fighting, they'll be glad: we finally got them segregated! They're locked up someplace calling each other the bad names we like to call them!

"The other day I was sitting in this home — it was a tarpaper shack way out in the pine woods. The family is dirt poor, obviously; the man is a tenant farmer, and if he keeps his wife and their seven kids away from starvation each year, he considers himself a big, big success. We got to talking. He knew why I was there — to get him to join up and go try registering to vote. We were chewing the fat. He was telling me about his problems with a horse. He said, 'She's a good mare, Susie is. She's grateful for the food we give her. I can see it in her eyes, when I feed her.' He must have seen a look cross my face, so he answered the look: 'You think I'm making it up, don't you! Well, I'm not.' That's how we were talking. I'd never told him I doubted that Susie was actually grateful, but he knew the story: a guy who isn't superstitious and who thinks *yes, of course* Susie is glad to eat, but gratitude — that's a little too much to put on a horse!

"The next thing I knew, he was telling me that Susie had been given him by the boss-man because he thought she was going to die. So he and his wife had taken care of her — and to everyone's surprise, she lived. When the boss-man heard that, he came over with some bales of hay and some pellets — a gift! Every once in a while, he comes and visits Susie still. When the two men talk, standing beside Susie, they are friendly. Once the boss-man told his colored tenant: 'You're the best folks in the world — the way you saved our mare!' I hear this and get sick. A powerful land-owner, loaded with money, is telling a man he ruthlessly exploits — 'He drives a hard bargain, that boss-man' — how good he is. Talk about a phony compliment! Who needs that kind of paternalism!

"So I get ready to say something. But how do I say the right thing? The man I'm sitting with is so proud of what that boss-man has said to him! What do I do — blast away at the white guy and try to push the Negro so he recognizes what an Uncle Tom he's become? I couldn't say anything. Then we got onto me — whether I'd ever been on a horse. No, I hadn't. Then, he asked me if I wanted to try. No, I said, I was afraid I'd fall off!

"He laughed, and he said to me, 'Young man, you won't go on my horse for fear of falling, but you want me to go riding on your horse [register to vote], and if I told you I thought there was a pretty good chance I could be shot off the horse even before I fell off, then you'd tell me it's up to some of us to die. The only thing is, I've got a wife and seven little ones, and I don't think God put me here to die on them, so I can tell people I'm a brave man and I've lived up to the best ideals in the world! Like our minister says, 'If you can go from dawn to dusk, and you've been good to your family and friends, then you've got a head start on being on the Lord's side.'

"I was really angry at him! I could see I was getting nowhere. I didn't say what I just said out loud. But my face said it, and he picked it up — written in my eyes and on my forehead and around my mouth! That man has spent his life reading the faces of people who tell him to do this and to do that, and he's really literate at face-reading, even if he can't pick up books and figure out what's inside them. I just shut up for a while — and he did his whistling and his chores.

"Then he suddenly turned to me and asked me what my ideals are. I was taken aback! I asked him what he meant — what I believed in? He nodded. I'd realized how patronizing I'd just been to him. The truth was, I was surprised to hear him put a philosophical or moral question to me. I was surprised to hear him use that word 'ideals.' If I'd stopped and given some thought to the matter, I'd have realized that this man goes to church on Sundays, every Sunday, and he sits in that church for two hours plus, and it's not air-conditioned. He listens to every word spoken, and he says amen a lot, and he loves to sing. Why *shouldn't* he use the word 'ideals'! But that's *my* word — and here he was questioning me about something I'm supposed to know cold: how to be idealistic! All the stories about us tell people how idealistic we are — 'young idealists,' the [Atlanta] *Constitution* said, quoting Dr. King. Of course, the paper's editorial writers aren't convinced. When the polls show more people are on our side, that's when the editorial folks will step up to the plate and tell everyone that it's the holy truth: we *are* 'young idealists,' just like King said!

"But I wasn't thinking of that man, I was thinking of myself, and I was thinking of the newspapers, and I was thinking of Dr. King, and what he says. I *was* an idealist; I *am* an idealist, and this man here, filling up a pail of water for his mare and cutting some rope with his knife and whistling — well, he was in my way. He wasn't paying me attention, the way he damn well should; and now he was quizzing me on my ideals. After a minute or two, I said my biggest ideal was equality: we should all have the vote, and we should all be able to go into a movie house or a restaurant, and the schools shouldn't be separate, they should be integrated.

"He nodded — but I wasn't sure whether he was telling me he'd heard me and he understood, or whether he was saying, Yes, you bet. Then he asked me if I knew any rich folks. I said not real well — I knew them from afar, and I'd gone out with a girl from Spelman, and her daddy had a lot of dough. He ran some hair salons all over Atlanta and in Augusta and down in Macon and Columbus. Then he asked me if I had met him, and I said, Yes, a few times, and I didn't like him because he thought he owned the world, not just those lousy hair-fixing places! He laughed, and he said, 'The folks who have a lot of money are like that.' I thought, We're not getting very far. This guy will never sign up for our voter registration drive. He's a coward! I didn't quite think that! I'd never call him a coward to his face, and besides, I didn't really believe he *was* a coward; I was just angry at him for not going along with our drive and for being so frustrating to talk with!

"But he told me that he was with me — he believed in equality, too. He said that was the idea Jesus had — and the sooner the better. Great, I thought, we're getting somewhere! But then he said, 'It'll take Jesus Himself to get my boss-man and your hair-fixer friend up in Atlanta to agree.' I hadn't thought of connecting the two! Actually, there's no reason not to connect them, though his boss-man is white and my hair-fixer friend is a Negro. He was telling me that the way for me to put myself in his shoes is to try to think of people in my own life who have a lot of wealth or power. The fact is, that hair-fixer didn't like me one bit — and his daughter broke with me because of it: she told me that she couldn't handle the tension! He said I was 'uppity' with him! Can you believe it — one Negro to another!

"I started getting impatient. He'd given me a jab or two, and I wanted us to get down to business! I told him my ideal wasn't the word 'equality,' it was deeds — that we all show respect to each other, and I hoped he'd help us get nearer to that time by signing up with our voter-registration drive.

"He stopped what he was doing, and he told me he would like to be up there with me, 'living up to the same ideal,' but he just couldn't, because *his* boss-man would have him killed, and mine

just took my girlfriend away. 'That's the difference,' he told me —
and boy, did I get angry. This guy, illiterate, stubborn as his horse,
was telling me about differences!

"It was only later that I looked myself in the mirror, like I
mentioned. I realized how snotty I'd been with him. He's an intelligent, hard-working, God-fearing man, and while I was talking
with him I was dismissing him in my mind both psychologically
and intellectually. His ideals were to try to be a good husband and
a good father and to get through the life that fate had given him
as best he could. 'I'm here,' he said, 'and I'll probably die here —
and I hope when I do, it's because God called me, not someone
who's got it in for me; and I hope when I go, I can say that I did
all I could, *all*, for my family and my kinfolks and my neighbors:
that's my ideal.' For me, it was one big rationalization. I thought,
He's *evading*; he's *dodging*; he's *afraid* even to tell me the truth.

"But I now think I'm as scared as he ever was — maybe more
scared! My ideal is to bring equality to him; but when every redneck is gone, and every law is changed, federal and state, I'm not
sure I'll have brought equality to him — because it's in my *mind*
that there's a struggle going on, not just in the society. The boss-
man has economic and political power over him — and he's white,
so he has racial power. I'm just a field secretary for SNCC, and I'm
a Negro, and I've been thrown in jail seven times now, and I have
no power over him. But in my mind I *do* have power — to see him
as he is or to see him as it suits me to see him. It's *me*, not just any
member of the KKK, or his boss-man, who looks right past him:
my eyes are on the voting lists in the county seat and on this
meeting right here, where I'll either have a few names of people
I've 'rounded up' — hear me? hear that phrase! — or I won't."

Alan stopped abruptly. He'd brought his story around to the
people sitting in that room, and out of courtesy, I surmised (and
maybe a little apprehension), he had decided to rein himself in,
await their comments and, maybe, criticisms. One of his closest
SNCC friends, Dick, said, "Where are you taking us with this —
what are you trying to say?"

Another friend, Tim, spoke before Alan could: "He's taking us
right smack in the face of ourselves, that's where."

"Hey, I'm not arguing; I'm just asking," Dick said.

Then Alice, one of two women there, said, "You guys, you

always have a hard time thinking for yourselves! There's always some professor inside you telling you who's smart and who's dumb, and who's being evasive, and who's being mature, and who will be a 'hero of the civil rights movement,' and who will be a big failure, because of fear, or 'cowardly instincts,' and who can talk intelligently about idealism, and who is just a country hick or honky, if he's white, or a 'victim of segregation' if he's a Negro, but both ways, you don't think the person is up to a serious conversation with you, with us!"

Alan seemed uninterested in saying anything more. Alice watched his face carefully, and when she saw him unfold his legs and stretch them forward, she apparently decided that he was still banking on a respite. She told her friends that she had a few more thoughts to share. The room's complete quiet — interrupted only by a car engine being gunned outside — gave her permission to go on, and the car noise, it seemed, gave her energy and direction.

"You hear that? Someone's got to get someplace *fast!* It's *his* car, *his* gas pedal, *his* life! You want to get in his way? Who are *you?* What's *your* problem? You want him to get out of his car and get into yours? You want him to move over so *you* can drive, so you can go where you think everyone should go — and pronto? You think he's making too much noise, and you can get that buggy going in a more 'refined' way: the Morehouse way, the Harvard way, the Meharry way, the SNCC way? Shape up, you kiddo — take lessons from us. Don't waste your machismo on that car! Give it to us, and we'll anoint you a hero! A civil rights hero! So will the white folks, mark my words, in a year or two: that's where we're heading! Better get in with us real quick, though — the white folks don't have too much room for Negro heroes, and to tell you the truth, neither do we, because like my momma used to tell us kids, 'The colored and the white, they're all the same; scrape their skin and they're all sinners!'"

She paused, unfolded her arms, let them hang at her sides. No one said anything. She looked to Alan, but he still seemed lost in his own thoughts. Alice plunged on. "This talk of idealism, and being idealistic. That's what it is — *talk!* We got all this [SNCC] going to get away from that, I thought. If we're going to end up like some of those professors, telling people who *is* an idealist and who *isn't* one, based on some fancy definition which *we've* made up — then what's the use of it all! I took a course in philosophy — no, two of them [at Columbia University], and we were learning all this stuff, ontology and essence and existence, and we were given these 'ethical dilemmas' and had to write essays on what you should do, and why you should do it. But it was all talk — and tests! Did we have the slightest idea what that professor was like? For all we knew, he beat his wife and kids regularly, had seven mistresses, and cheated on his income tax. As for the professor, for all he knew, we were crooks, thieves, and liars — the way they'd talk at home, my momma and her sisters, about a lot of white folks they worked for! I mean, we could be giving him all the right answers, beautifully written, on his tests, then we'd leave the Morningside Heights campus to go be crooks, thieves, and liars!"

She turned to Alan, who was looking at the floor. "That guy who you told us about, who never even learned how to read or write, and he sure can't vote, and he sure isn't worried about it, the way he should be — but he doesn't sound like Satan to me. A lot of time, I hear my mind clicking away, and I think *I* sound like Satan! So I agree with you — the mirror first, before we start pounding the gavel!"

At that point Alan did look up, and he and Alice looked intently at each other. The others looked at one of them, then the other, and then, as if chastened and suddenly informed, down at the floor, perhaps to look inward. Both Alan and Alice had suggested bringing an end to the sidelong glances, the invidious comparisons, the assured assertions of what *is*, what *ought* to be, what *will* be. Most of all, they urged an end to the kind of self-preoccupation that prevents one from being able to look directly and openly at those who live across the street or across the railroad tracks or under some other flag or banner or mandate.

After a couple of minutes of stillness, a long time for those in that room, Alan turned to his friends and told them what he had concluded. "If I get a chance, I'll go back to him [the farmer] and tell him about my ideals — that I believe we should try to do the best we can for others, not only ourselves, and we should also remember the difference between others and ourselves, and we should try to live out what we believe in. And if we *half*-succeed, we should realize how lucky we are, and not spend a big part of our lives pointing our fingers at others while we shake our heads, and another big part patting ourselves on the back, and trying to make sure everyone in sight and within hearing distance knows why we're doing it!"

He smiled for the first time and mentioned an irony: "Listen to me lecturing, pointing *my* finger!" This brought smiles from the others, and his smile became broader. Suddenly he exclaimed, "How do we get out of this trap?" The others continued to smile for a moment, then all of them turned quite serious. No one supplied an answer. Each of them, perhaps, was aware of the vexing problem, the irony confronting them: if you started *propounding*, you might well become travelers in the very boat the two pro-pounders had just described. And then one of the other five, who up to that moment had said nothing, commented, "Moral: talk is cheap, action counts, but action has to be examined, and that takes words, whether you speak them or not."

Everyone nodded, and then the other black woman, Maggie, laughed vigorously and said, "Hey, we're getting ourselves in a trap worse than the ones the sheriffs set for us! We're the *Student Non-Violent Coordinating Committee*, and so naturally we do a lot of talking! Let's not stop being ourselves! We're not that tenant farmer. He may know better about *his* life than we do, but we know something too — and maybe he'll have some second thoughts about what *he* should be doing now, just the way you've had some second thoughts about what you should be doing or saying to him, or thinking to yourself.

"We've got to keep going, each of us; and the roads can be different, and you're right, we shouldn't be asking someone over in that road to come and walk with us on our road — forgetting his road. But he needs some pushing, too. He pushed all of us through you. He might need a push from us. Let's not romanticize him — 'the peasants,' the way Tolstoy did!"

She turned to Alan as she mentioned him and the tenant farmer. When she mentioned Tolstoy, his face lit up — as did the faces of all those tough, seasoned, battle-weary organizers in the front-line trenches of the civil rights movement at its most danger-ous time. They hadn't talked about Gandhi and Tolstoy and nonviolence (so central to their organization's title) for a long time. They had been putting aside books and professors and assignments. Yet all of these young men and women had been introduced to Tolstoy in college, through his stories or novels, through his social writing, or through Gandhi's writing, which connected so significantly with Tolstoy's.[7] Moreover, they had heard Dr. King, as well as other ministers and intellectuals who had joined the movement, talk of Tolstoy and Gandhi, of James Agee and Zora Neale Hurston, of Richard Wright and Ralph Ellison. And as students they had read those writers and storytellers who searched for truth.[8]

In no time a spirited discussion developed about Tolstoy's view of peasant life and about the aspects of the lives of peasants that may have been unknown to or undocumented by him. It was astonishing to witness the healthy intensity of those quite unashamedly intellectual exchanges. The full range of the words SNCC was meant to abbreviate was called into play. These were students talking about Tolstoyan and Gandhian philosophy and the connections between those two prophets and the humble folk whom each so earnestly sought to know and, at times, to celebrate, to hold up as thoughtful teachers.

Eventually, that prolonged and somewhat diffuse conversation came back to the initial topic of ideals — what they are or ought to be, what the more generic word "idealism" means, and how one tries to connect with it in life. Again they reminded one another, almost to a fault, of the matter of relativity, taking a big detour (I thought) on Hitler and the "idealism" he inspired in Germany's youth. After a while they agreed that the word "idealism" probably did apply to some of those Germans who were so passionately self-sacrificing in their embrace of Nazi ideology.

Yet they also agreed that they were not about to let *their* notion of "idealism" be constrained by an awareness of all the historical moments in which young people have embraced with fervor a social or political ideology that proved to be murderously evil. "Let's stay with the idealism we're trying to find here, right now, for ourselves," said Alice. "This is not a history class," she insisted, "or a class in human development, like the one I took in my senior year in college, when we discussed youth movements in Germany and the Soviet Union, and compared them to the Boy Scouts. Maybe one day they'll include us, the civil rights movement, in that class! But let's try to stick to what's facing us right here, and how we should behave, and not end up thinking of ourselves as 'late adolescents,' or 'people caught up in a political swirl.'"

She feared the embrace of the abstract, of history, psychology, political theory, even as she tried to discuss moral behavior without getting entangled in philosophy. They *were* students, all of them, the two white men, who said very little, but nodded, grimaced, and shook their heads, and the five blacks, three men and two women. They were warily trying to connect their day-to-day experiences with remembered lectures, texts, papers, examinations. They used their experiences to mock some teachers and celebrate others. But they were not loath to mock themselves and wonder out loud about some of their errant notions of what should or should not be done.

By the same token, they had stumbled upon some new examples of the good and the bad — new exemplars, if not heroes. Some of these were ordinary, even quite lowly, people; others were from their own ranks (including one youth who stood tall in the face of police threats and worse); and some — a white lawyer in Alabama, for instance — belonged to an older generation. That lawyer had dared to defend them, and they well knew the risks he took. He easily might have offered a dozen reasons for refusing to have anything to do with them. Would *they*, in fact, be like him down the road if they ever got to the point of being comfortably established in a leading law firm? "Idealism has many sources, and it must have its ups and downs in every life," one of the students pointed out — a function, they all agreed, of a person's commitments, state of mind, and family situation, not to mention all those accidental and incidental moments that influence and even give shape to the direction of one's moral energy.

Years later that remark about the ups and downs of idealism, the complexity of its origins, would echo in my mind as I listened to college students describe how they got involved in a particular community service project. Sometimes even cynical ambitiousness can be an unpredictable prelude to substantial and worthy service, as a rather bright and forceful law student, Carlton, indirectly indicated as he reflected upon what had happened to him in the previous two years.

He said, "I came here [to Harvard Law School] determined to be a corporate lawyer. I had no patience with the soft side of law, and when I was in college, I wasn't one of the do-gooders on campus. I don't want to overdo it — turn myself into some real cold-hearted moneygrubber. There *was* some of that in me; if I hadn't lost my [older] brother [in a car accident] I think there'd have been more. Ever since he died [when the soon-to-be-lawyer was a college sophomore] I've been a little more reflective. I stop myself a lot of times and think of him and all he meant to me. He was my big hero. He taught me how to play sports, and he was in law school when he died. He majored in economics and so did I. We used to talk of having a law office together. We'd clean up for fifteen years, then retire and become ski bums — that was the big fantasy! We'd, maybe, practice a little law in Aspen or some other place — Wyoming, maybe. But first, as we kept reminding each other, we'd have to be 'aggressive, really aggressive'!

"When he died, I didn't turn soft. If anything, I got tougher, harder. I was carrying the ball for both of us now. Our dad worked for a newspaper. He wasn't a writer, no; he was on the business side of things — circulation. He always wanted to be a lawyer, but he never had the dough to go to graduate school. That's when he started drinking a lot. That's when he began to become 'a mean drunk' [his mother's description] for a day or two. But he'd snap out of it. He went to night school — that's how he got a college degree. Then he worked his way up so he could pay for our education. But he had to sacrifice, and my brother and I realized, even when we were kids, that if you want to enjoy a comfortable life and be a generous husband and father — well, there's no substitute for a big yearly salary!

"I had plenty of drive during my first year there [at law school], and by now I'd be signing up for one of the really big-deal law firms. But I fell in love with a girl — she wasn't in law school, she had no interest in law, she was a schoolteacher. She worked in a ghetto school, and she told me these stories about all the kids she taught — it was something, listening to her! At first I listened because it was *her* talking. I'd even argue with her about crime and drugs and welfare: who's responsible, and what you *should* do, and what you *can* do. She was the softy, of course, and I was the tough, worldly-wise guy. She quoted her liberal heroes, and I quoted what I read in the *Wall Street Journal!* We had plenty of shared interests, so we weren't fighting all the time, but when we did get into a disagreement, there could be fireworks! Then she'd tell me these stories, and she wanted me to meet some of the kids and their families, so finally I agreed.

"It was just before the summer between my first and second year at law school, and I had a great job lined up in a law firm. I went with her to an after-school meeting. I heard all those mothers talking about their children. There weren't enough fathers there, but the ones who were, they were powerful speakers. I'd never seen anything like it; I'd never been in a room like that. I kept trying to push my feelings down. I didn't want to get carried away. I got angry with Sally — I wanted to get out of there. I became cynical: what's in this for me? The more I was moved by what those folks said, the more I talked to myself cynically! I hate to think back."

Carlton was no sudden convert to the liberal welfare state, but some of the comments and discussions got to him. Days, even weeks afterward, he began to think more and more about those people he'd met and their life, and also about himself, what he wanted to do, to be. He asked his girlfriend dozens of questions about her work, about the children she taught, about their families. She began to wonder what was happening — and, he noticed, she wasn't totally pleased with his new interest.

"It may sound strange to you, but at the beginning Sally looked at me as if I was trying to move in on her territory. When I get interested in something, I *really* get interested. I started reading and reading; I built up a clip file, and I went back and read the clips several times. I even bought books — expensive for someone buying fat law-school books and not loaded with money. In a couple of weeks' time we were fighting; she claimed I was being too cerebral, and I was trying to conquer all those people by turning them into a subject I could master! *Wait a minute*, I told her, give me a break! We fought, but she did have a point: I was trying to figure out what I thought, and then I was ready to go argue for it, and that's me, a lawyer by instinct!

"She was different. She didn't want to debate, and she had no statistics in her mind — just her desire to help those kids, and not only in school. She'd go on home visits; she met their families that way, and she says it made a huge difference in how the kids did at school. The more I heard of *that* — those visits to homes in the worst part of the ghetto — the more worried I became. I told her she was going *way* beyond the call of duty! No way; she felt that if she didn't go on those visits she'd be guilty of the worst kind of 'dereliction of duty.' When I heard her use that phrase, I kidded her: 'There's a little bit of the lawyer in you!' She bristled — she started arguing with me. She said I was seeing her through my eyes. You bet — how else could I! Anyway, we got through our troubles, and I asked if I could go with her on some of those home visits, and that did it."

He was surprised, touched, and appalled after meeting several families in their homes. He witnessed firsthand how some landlords refused to supply adequate services to tenants who were paying rent: he saw the inadequate heat, treacherous stairwells, plumbing that often didn't work and wasn't fixed for weeks after the initial complaints were made. His girlfriend was deeply sympathetic to the families she had come to know. She regularly filed complaints against landlords or tried to get help through city agencies. But Carlton wanted to fight even harder. He threw aside his proposed summer internship in a law firm, became involved with a community legal services group, and soon enough was a zealous, crusading lawyer, out to win one case after another. Some of his friends thought he was going through a "stage" and told him that he'd eventually be "back in corporate law." He didn't disagree. He knew he was "going through *something*," though only later did he realize how significant that summer had been to him.

When Carlton graduated from law school, he embarked on a three-year commitment to legal work on behalf of the poor. He was then able to look back to that summer between his first and second year at law school as a defining moment. "If I hadn't gone to those homes, I think I'd be getting ready for a six-figure-income life. I'm no ascetic. This is going to be hard — I'd best admit it to

myself! Maybe some people who do this kind of work are genuinely saints. Not me! But I'll tell you, I can't get some of those kids
out of my head, and their parents and grandparents. They have a
rotten time of it, and a lot of them, they're good, decent, hard-
working people. If I hadn't met them, talked with them, I could
move them out of my mind, call them welfare cheats, and lazy, and
all the other names. There are plenty of cheats in our ghettos, I
know — and there are plenty of them in our universities and on
Wall Street and in the government, the Congress, as we know from
reading the papers!

"To be honest with myself, I think my brother had a lot to do
with this. After he died, I wasn't the same person — ever. It isn't
only grief. I do still miss him, but when he died I had to stop and
realize that you can't just take life for granted. One minute you're
here; the next, you're gone. You might say, Yes, so what else is new!
Most of the time, though, people don't think like that. When
you're young, you think you'll be around forever, and you make
decisions on that basis. Since my brother has been gone, I think
differently. I live as if I might go at any moment — crazy, I know,
but that's how it is.

"He was really idealistic. I was always the practical guy, the
realist; he was the dreamer, and he had a big, big heart. Sure, he
liked money, too, and we both dreamed of making a lot of it. But
deep down, he was too gentle, I think, to be a tough corporate
lawyer. I don't mean to brag, but during the last few years, doing
this kind of work, I expected to wear down at some point, get the
'burnout syndrome' you hear people complain of. But I seem to be
as strong as ever, and I think I have an explanation: I have some of
my brother in me, his big heart and his goodness, and that's what
keeps me going. My friends say I've had a personality change, but
it's not really that. It took a few years, but my brother seems to
have found some resting place in my head! The Indians in the
Southwest would say something like that, I think: his soul wandered around, and then it decided to take a chance on me, and I'm
trying not to disappoint it — him!"

When I asked Carlton about his brother's idealism and his
own, he became unusually reticent. He didn't know how to describe or explain the idealism he had just mentioned. He described

his brother as "generous almost to a fault," as "self-sacrificing," even as "selfless." When I asked him about that last quality of mind (or soul), he told stories of his brother performing acts of kindness, but in a way that did not call attention to himself. "Idealists are people who really work to help others," he once said, thinking of his brother, "and they're willing to lose some things themselves, if it'll help the people who need help." After saying that, he wondered whether he wasn't being a bit too inclusive and glib. Who was *he* to define idealism or to characterize idealists? His brother was indeed an idealist, and he most certainly seemed ready to pay a price for being one. Yet perhaps it was all too easy to romanticize idealists or fit them with halos, when in truth they struggled with everything that the rest of us struggle with.

He listed his own disqualifications for the idealist label, mentioning his greedy, vain, ambitious side. But then he turned and wondered whether many idealistic people might be greedy and vain and ambitious in their own ways, even though they tamed those emotions or tailored them to supply energy to their idealism. He mentioned a friend of his, also a poverty lawyer, and another friend, a doctor who worked with the very poor and the homeless: "Those two guys — they are doing the Lord's work, my aunt would have said, but they both can be so full of themselves sometimes. They are conceited, each of them. They can be very tough fighters — I'd hate to be an opponent of theirs! They're not greedy for money, but they're greedy for the power to win the fights they get into. And they are tremendously ambitious — they love winning every struggle, and love letting the world know they've won.

"I'm overdoing things here, I'm making them into caricatures of themselves. But I'll tell you — it's foolish to think of them as naive or innocent men, full of humility and love and without a real mean, fighter's instinct in them. I know most people wouldn't even be surprised by what I'm saying — but *I'm* surprised. I used to look up to my brother as if he could do no wrong, absolutely none, and when he died, that totally sealed my ideas about him: he was as pure as a person can be in my mind. But the longer I live — and especially since I've been working as a poverty lawyer — the more I realize that he wasn't some saint or angel; he was a human being, with his good side and his not-so-good side, and maybe a few bad habits, like we all have, even the most idealistic person you'll ever meet."

One person who very much wanted to consider that young lawyer's remarks, his personal and professional experiences, was Anna Freud, who had a long-standing interest in the sources of idealism, its various aspects, and its history and fluctuations in individuals over time. In *The Ego and the Mechanisms of Defense* she considers "altruistic surrender" — the willingness to give up a number of one's own gratifications so that others might enjoy them — as a possibility for some individuals.[9] Her lifelong efforts on behalf of children certainly attested to idealism at work, but she could be skeptical about motives, about the denials and reaction-formations, the projections and identifications, that make mental life so topsy-turvy, and convert envies, rivalries, fears, rages, and lusts into what seem to be quite the opposite.

I have presented, in my writing about Anna Freud's work, our extended discussions about idealism; but her comments on many subjects were often most revealing and spirited when connected to a particular story, whether of a patient or of a friend or colleague. She was highly responsive to stories offered by others, as I once again realized when I told her, during a visit in New Haven, of my former student's surprising law career. She was especially interested in the relationship between Carlton's brother's death and his moral conversion of sorts. She commented at length upon that connection and upon the sources of what she once termed, intriguingly, "idealistic attachments."

She said, "The young lawyer has not relinquished his ties to his brother. Their father was not a very nice man, we gather from what you've learned, and the younger brother seems to have found a father in the older brother. We will never know the whole story here, obviously: only the younger brother survives this family — a psychological orphan, his parents and brother dead. He is not in analysis with you, so he tells you bits and pieces by indirection. Still, he has told you a lot — and even more, his actions tell us a lot as well. Let's not dismiss behavior as an indication of what is happening in the mind! Here is a lawyer who has turned from one kind of career to another. He is doing a very good job at this kind of idealistic law. He seems to be enjoying himself, and he is not becoming shrill or moody and humorless — signs of an idealism in serious psychological trouble! When he tells you about his satisfactions, his accomplishments, the *learning* he has done — that is evidence of someone who seems to be making a longer commitment to an idealistic life than some young people are prepared to make.

"The more he talks of his brother and what his brother intended to do with his life, the more he sounds like his brother; it is as if he has *become* his brother, who is 'alive,' in a way, by virtue of what has taken place. It is as if the lawyer has said: I cannot bear being alone in the world; I need to be reminded of the good in my family's life, and it was my brother who stood for so much of that, and I will hold on to it, to him, through the way I live my life. Yes, the mother's values may have been given to both brothers, but apparently this young lawyer can't quite take those values for granted in himself the way many others do with respect to their parents' ideas or preferences.

"For this man, the work he does [in the ghetto] is psychological work, too — he keeps his ties with his family: the brother's protection and his strength, so important to him as a child, stay alive as he lives out the kind of life the brother wanted for himself and for this man, too. I suspect he sees himself in many of those hurt, troubled ghetto children he defends with such ingenuity and conviction and success. He felt himself to be a victim of his father's alcoholic arbitrariness and his mother's seeming helplessness before it, which he might have regarded as a kind of indifference, or even collusion. Now he tells you he is taking on cruelty and injustice, but also indifference — he makes *much* of that last aspect of the work. He also tells you he feels as if he has been given 'a second life' by virtue of his decision to do this kind of law — and I wonder whether that phrase isn't his way of saying that he and his brother, the two of them, now have this exceptionally fulfilling shared existence: an idealism sustained by the healing of old wounds that takes place, symbolically, when this man rescues and fights for others the way his brother used to do for him."

She was eager to credit this young man's professional life with a major psychological accomplishment rather than use technical language reductively to cast a long shadow of doubt (if not smug scorn) on his motives or deeds. Mostly, however, she spoke in her wonderfully clear, direct, even earthy way about "the many different roads to idealism," as she once nicely put it. What mattered, she kept reminding me, was not so much the various motivations, per se, as the manner in which all the yearnings and vicissitudes and consequences of a person's childhood and experiences in a family are worked into a life. If a childhood of pain and hurt (even bitterness and resentment and envy and any number of misbegotten or unacknowledged lusts) can in adulthood result in a relaxed and effective idealism that exacts no harmful, self-defeating penalties, no strenuous punishment from others or from the idealist, then she was ready to clap her hands and say an enthusiastic, admiring hurrah.

On the other hand, if idealism has turned sour, has become brittle, driven, insolent, unforgiving, then she was prepared to sigh and shrug and point out yet again the irony: "How sad that in the name of goodness and kindness to others one can see plenty of mean-spirited behavior — a demanding, controlling, manipulative, condescending self-centered ruthlessness that masks itself as good will, as an effort at charity, as an attempt to change the world, reform a given society. Perhaps you have noticed that among those who set themselves up as 'agents of change,' as philanthropists, as people of ethical credibility and ethical vision, there can be no shortage of vanity and conceit, of cruelty and selfishness, of lies and deception. I am making such an unpleasant list of human attributes because I have been surprised once too often over the years by what seems to be a paradox. I have been privy, for example, through one patient or another, to the confessions of a person who tells me of rather nasty behavior carried out in the name of what can only be considered virtuous projects. I begin to be confused, until I remember that such inconsistencies go to the very essence of our nature: we feign, we cover up, we pretend, hoping to fool ourselves, above all, and if others should also be misled, then that is a big bonus!

"Just as I am ready to throw up my hands in regret, and sometimes, a degree of disapproval, even disgust, that tells me about my own life, and the demands I've learned to make of myself — it is just then, so often, that such a patient will break down, and soon I am hearing the sources of all those paradoxes, the reasons for what can turn out to have been a valiant, if unsuccessful, struggle to convert trouble, a lot of it, into a kind of triumph. It is at such moments that I lose my outrage, my condemnation, in favor of sorrow for the patient and, very important, sorrow for those meant to be the recipients of the patient's effort at good will or benevolence or idealism or whatever you choose to call it."

For herself, as Miss Freud made clear many times by example, as well as in her writings, idealism or altruism had to do with putting oneself in the shoes of others, absorbing their needs, their vulnerability, their weakness, and their suffering, and then setting to work.[10] We all contend with what psychoanalytic theorists refer to as our libidinal, aggressive, and narcissistic drives and requirements; and in varying degrees most of us contend with a conscience that sets limits on what ought (and ought not) to be done to satisfy those drives. We all try to figure out how we can indulge and satisfy our passions, live up to the demands of our consciences, and survive — and perhaps prosper — in the world.

For some people the "altruistic surrender" Anna Freud describes (with a touch of autobiographical knowledge, one suspects) serves to express their urges and appease their consciences. They derive a sense of affirmation and satisfaction and achievement; not least, from those whom they teach or attend or coach or befriend, they receive a sustained thank you or two, and maybe, on occasion, wildly grateful applause. "You ask me why I do this," a patient of Miss Freud's, a young English teacher and poet, once said to her. "To see the smiles of the children while I'm with them, and to know how much they mean those smiles."

After Miss Freud told me that, the then seventy-eight-year-old veteran of many an analytic hour said, "I was very moved by the way she spoke then — not her words, really, but the feeling the words were expressing. I had been knitting, as I almost always do as my patients talk, and at that moment I stopped. I think she heard the utter silence; knitting is not a noisy pastime, but at that moment you could have heard a pin drop — a knitting needle drop. I noticed the look on her face: she had a smile that was full of pleasure and self-respect, without being boastful or smug. I then noticed my own face: I had a smile on it, though she couldn't see it from the couch. I suspect she felt it, though. I am saying, I think, that a young idealist like her can bring gifts to children, as she did. She was a wonderfully gentle yet firm tutor, teacher. In return, she receives gifts from children — their respect and affection — and is warmed by all that, as I suspect I was in that consulting room of mine!"

Miss Freud went on to remind herself and me of the other side of the coin — of idealism that doesn't work for the intended recipient or for the donor. Many quite giving and able and thoughtful volunteers test themselves mightily by doing work that does not give them the satisfactions described by that young English teacher.

A student of mine, an imaginative fellow and an actor in a number of college productions, confessed to me how enraged he sometimes became at the response he received — stony silence and, worse, sometimes taunting, even heckling — in the class he taught at a correctional center for young men. He knew better than to condemn himself as responsible for it. He had been doing such work for three years and had been told by authorities at the institution that such a reception was all too characteristic of what took place in the broken-down, inadequate classrooms available to him and the other student volunteers. Indeed, he was considered by the prisoners and the staff to be among the very best of those who gave of their time, energy, and resourcefulness — all, apparently, in vain.

Yet every once in a while he would see, in a turn of the head or a momentarily sustained look in the eyes of one of his students, in a composition written, a passage recited, in a show of impatience toward some callousness expressed by a classmate, something that gave him hope. Such momentary responses worked miracles for this hard-working young man, whose own tough, stoic demeanor made him a perfect counterpart, one guessed, to those he was trying to teach. "I feel a little rewarded," he commented, then observed, "Maybe that's all the reward I want to see." He knew that he'd be embarrassed by a more openly responsive situation and had therefore found a volunteering assignment that fitted his nature, his gifts.

Once he remembered a prisoner who had been especially provocative all autumn. "Just before Christmas, though, he came up
to me and said one word: 'Thanks.' I almost keeled over; I actually
got choked up. It was a huge Christmas present to me!" He wasn't
aware of his own taciturnity, I remember thinking, and slowly,
maybe too slowly, I came to understand that his lack of awareness
was not a bad thing. At times self-consciousness, even self-aware-
ness, can make such work even more burdensome. As that young
man put it, "I wing it with those guys. I don't plan ahead — you
set yourself up for a disappointment that way. I try to be ready to
seize a good opportunity if one comes along. It's a state of readiness; but you don't do yourself any favors by trying to figure those
guys out, or yourself, either. You just ride with the class and try to
steer the flow toward something half worthwhile."

He was no mean pilot, but he did like his passengers to give him
a signal or two, and he was surprised (chagrined, actually) at how
needy he could sometimes be. A long stretch of working with
glum, testing, and testy prisoner-students made him morose back
in college. Once, writing a paper on (of all subjects!) the moral and
political justifications for the English welfare state in the early
decades of the twentieth century, he found himself doodling repeatedly: "Give-get-give." Later he realized that what some political leaders and theorists had argued — that the poor, having
received government generosity, would in time be able to give
it back as workers and taxpayers — also applied to himself. His
youthful idealism needed an occasional gesture of acknowledgment from these other young people who had, comparatively, so
little in life and yet had the power to affirm him in a significant,
telling (though discreetly shown) manner.

The reward, the big reward, indeed, is in those seemingly slight
gestures: a nod, a tentative smile, the offer of a hand at the end of
a teaching session, a good-bye spoken with feeling by someone
hitherto indifferent or hostile, a sidelong glance followed by a soft
"thanks," a question about when the next time will be, a lingering
look by someone who used to leave class right away, a letter of
appreciation written with obvious care and affection — all an affirmation of the hard work that goes into young idealism by those
of any age who have come to know it, experience it, firsthand over
time.

· SEVEN ·

Older Idealism

I N EARLY DECEMBER 1977, two years before she died, Dorothy Day agreed to speak with a group of nine Harvard freshmen at the Catholic Worker soup kitchen she had helped found at Saint Joseph's House on East First Street in Manhattan. The students in the freshman seminar I taught had been reading Agee's *Let Us Now Praise Famous Men* and Orwell's *Down and Out in Paris and London, The Road to Wigan Pier, Homage to Catalonia,* "How the Poor Die," and "Hop-Picking."[1] We had also read Dorothy Day's autobiography, *The Long Loneliness,* and a collection of her nonfiction pieces, *From Union Square to Rome.* We piled into a van and drove to New York City to talk with her and with those who worked alongside her.

Before heading downtown, we stopped in Harlem to meet with Ned O'Gorman and the people who worked with him at the Storefront Learning Center, a college preparatory school located right in the middle of abandoned buildings and all too evident despair.[2] O'Gorman, a poet and a marvelously vigorous and disciplined teacher, talked with us for three hours. We hoped to have time to come back and talk again, but we hastened on to see Dorothy, as all who knew her called her, in the early afternoon. At age eighty she suffered from coronary insufficiency and congestive disease, with occasional episodes of shortness of breath, tiredness, and "moodiness," as she told her friends. Still, there she was, standing up in the soup kitchen, cutting celery neatly and methodically, with several bunches of carrots waiting their turn. I could see how pale, weak, and thin she was. She was quite chipper, though — more so than she had been for several weeks, according to Frank Donovan, an old, stalwart member of the Catholic Worker family. "She loves working, when she can. She especially loves sitting with the guests and just gabbing with them," he told us.

We had to wait until she finished the cooking tasks she'd assigned herself. Then we went to the dining room, where all those Bowery bums had eaten for so many years, found ourselves a long, long table, and sat down to the coffee and bread that had been set aside for us. The students were in awe of Dorothy at first, but it didn't take long for her to help us get through that mix of admiration and secular idolatry. On our drive down to the big city, the students had spoken of her "saintly" nature and her "awesome altruism." That phrase was turned into a playful chant as we plowed through an early winter snow on the interstate highway: "Three cheers for the awesome altruist!"

That "awesome altruist" told us that she was lucky to be alive although she had been looking forward with increasing eagerness to meeting her Maker. She also told us that until that day came, she hoped she would be able to "be of some use, still, to our guests." We all nodded as if to give her a vigorous show of support. We also were telling ourselves that it was good for this elderly and ailing lady to keep busy, to have something to do during this last, prolonged illness.

But Dorothy had a different notion of what she was about then and what she had been about all those decades since the early 1930s, when the Catholic Worker was founded. "I pray that God will give me a chance to pray to Him the way I like to pray to Him," she told us at one point. As we tried to figure out what she meant and what strategies of prayer had worked for her, she elucidated: "If I pray by making soup and serving soup, I feel I'm praying by doing. If I pray by saying words, I can sometimes feel frustrated. Where's the action that follows the words or precedes them? I may be old and near the end, but in my mind, I'm the same old Dorothy, trying to show the good Lord that I'm working for Him to the best of my ability. The spirit wishes, even if the feet fail some days! When I'm in bed, and the doctor has told me firmly to stay there for a few days, I don't feel I've earned my right to pray for myself and others, to pray for these poor folks who come here for a square meal."

She stopped, and the students tried to understand her line of reasoning. One young man said, "You've done so much already for these people!" She smiled and slowly answered, "The Lord has done it all; we try to be adequate instruments of His." The young man was not at all pleased; he tried to be respectful, but he answered back, "Well, it's been *you folks* who have done all this."

She was quiet for a moment, then said, "Yes, at someone's behest." A strange way of putting it, I thought — and a clever way, too. She did not mention God this time around, in seeming deference to the sensibility of a Harvard science major, but she insisted upon making the point that the labor of all those who lived in that Lower East Side tenement building, which housed a soup kitchen, the offices of the *Catholic Worker*, and some dormitory rooms, was all being done in response to a larger will.

The student wouldn't retreat, either. Politely he asked, "How do you know?" Not in the least offended, she replied, "He has told us — in His way." The young man persisted: "How?" She patiently answered, "Oh, when we pray, we are told — we are given answers to our questions. They [the answers] come to us, and then we know He has sent us the thoughts, the ideas. They all don't just belong to us. He lives in our thoughts, the Lord does."

The student was silent for a few seconds. Several of us were made nervous by their exchange and wanted to steer the conversation in a less provocative direction. But the student resumed, "How do you know whether it's the Lord who's in you or just you yourself talking to yourself? And how do you avoid becoming pleased with yourselves — too pleased?" She wasn't set back by his outburst of analytic and phenomenological psychology. She smiled and told him, "I don't think it has to be either/or. I think that the Lord can speak to us through ourselves. He can inspire us to follow Him! He can persuade us to show our faith in Him by offering to

Him what we can. As for smugness and the sin of pride — thank God you mention it, because we *do* fall victim often, a great danger, and one we need to be reminded of all the time. By the way, have you ever read *The Imitation of Christ?* It's a fairly popular book."

A strong and confessional reply. She went on to explain her affection for the book, which recounts the author's struggle for an honorable but not saccharine piety. When she fell quiet, the student told her, "No, I haven't — I haven't really heard of that book. Who wrote it?"

"Thomas à Kempis; he was an obscure priest who wrote of his struggle to be a good person, a good Christian, centuries ago." The youth was ready to let the matter drop in a manner befitting an incipient intellectual: "I'll try to find the book in Cambridge and read it." In a playfully sardonic mood, she said, "I hope you can find it there."

We all laughed, she along with us. Then she turned to the young man, and much to his surprise, to the surprise of all of us, she apologized to him. "I'm sorry if I didn't make myself clear. I'm sorry if I'm getting sharp with you. I think you've put your finger on some of our weaknesses. I can see that you find it confusing — how we think about things here in this community. We're not all that sure ourselves of what we are doing! I don't want you to feel we're afraid to discuss our beliefs with you as fully as you wish. I was trying to tell you that for me, for us here — I think I can speak for many of us who live here — the work we do is not a sacrifice or something done because we are interested in doing good, or in finding an answer to the demands of our conscience. All that, yes — all that, true. But I think we are quite happy here a lot of the time, doing what we do, because we believe we feel the spirit of Christ at work — *in the work.* We are not so high on ourselves that we feel Christ is *in* us; no, we hope we are moving a bit closer to Him, to His spirit, through the work we do, and that gives us the strength, the desire, to keep working at it here. But, of course, we are human beings, and we can be hypocrites and phonies, no question about that!

"I know this — what I'm saying — is hard for some of you to understand. I wish I could be clearer. You know, we are groping in the dark here; it may be different for you people. When people ask me why I'm doing what I'm doing, in this last time left of my life, I try to tell them that I'm doing what I was put here to do by the Lord. But they think, so many I've talked with, that I'm an old lady who needs to keep active, and who feels better when she's busy, and who would go into a state of senility or depression if she didn't have something to do. It's very hard to tell people who think of you that way — it's hard to say, For the Lord, time isn't what it is for us. When I was twenty, or now [when I'm] over seventy-five, it's all the same *in this one respect:* I'm a person who's trying to find out how to live. At twenty I didn't know; now I *think* I do — so I *do*, I work. But the worst thing would be to try to tell others to do what I'm doing, and if they don't, to condemn them!"

The student who had engaged with her had no more to say. He had begun exploring with his eyes the dining area, noting the posters on the walls, the kitchen where people were both cleaning up and preparing for the next day's meal. In a sense, I began to realize, he was following her lead — paying attention not to what she was saying about her psychological and intellectual life, but to the world she inhabited, where she felt the daily desire to do the work we had glimpsed before she set it aside for this conversation.

The rest of us now asked our far less pointed questions — about routines, about the "guests" and their problems, about the more formal aspects of the community's beliefs and the values espoused by the newspaper and by the volunteers.

She let us know that by no means was she the only older person on the line, preparing and serving food and engaging with the people served. "We have people come and help us from the neighborhood, men and women in their forties and fifties and sixties and even seventies. They are poor, but they've got a roof over their heads, and food to eat, and families, and they'll see those men and women we feed lining up, and they feel sorry for them and they come to us and ask if they can help. You bet, I say.

"The other day a husband and wife — he was seventy-one and she was sixty-eight — came by, and they'd baked three cakes, and we cut them into small pieces eventually, but first we put candles on them and asked the folks to gather around, because a few had birthdays in November and December, so we called the cakes birthday cakes. There were plenty of tears. A lady came up to me and told me that the last birthday cake she saw was for her ten-year-old boy, and then he got killed in an automobile accident, and she never recovered. She took to the bottle, and then the streets. She was crying hard. I sat with her, and we ate cake together and washed it down with good, strong coffee. The woman who baked the cake came over, and the three of us had a wonderful time talking. Since then, the woman who lost her son has been on the wagon, and she comes to us now to volunteer her help. She gets down on her knees and scrubs our linoleum floor to the point that it's spotless. She helps set the table. She empties the wastepaper baskets. She takes out the garbage. She's a whirlwind!

"A lot of people think of our community as made up of college people, the well-educated, and the devoutly Catholic. It's true, we've had our intellectual side — Peter Maurin was strong on thought as well as action, and I guess I was, too.[3] But we've always been a *mixed* community, people of all backgrounds and ages. Our volunteers can be young people here for a few weeks from Georgetown or Fordham or Yale or Columbia. Young people who are living nearby see what we do and come and tell us they want to help — *and* their parents and their grandparents. A sixty-four-year-old woman comes here twice a week to serve food. She takes the subway from Brooklyn. She's an Irish lady who used to be a maid for some judge, I think it was, and his family. Her mother had been reading our paper when she was growing up, and she'd tell me that she loved coming here to help, because she's sure her mother is in heaven, watching over us, and when she sees her come to us and work, she must have a big smile on her face! I loved hearing her say that! She brought me a picture of her mother, and now I picture her up there, smiling, when her daughter walks into the kitchen.

"She always brings wonderful loaves of rye bread, light and dark, that she gets from a Jewish baker who's a friend of hers. He laughs and tells her he sets aside five or six loaves to hedge bets. He's her age and he has heart trouble, and he could die at any moment, and he said to her 'just in case your religion is God's favorite, I'll give you plenty of bread — but be sure to mention me in your prayers!' Well, we do include him in our prayers. We thank him and ask the good Lord to smile on him, just the way his friend's — *our* friend's! — mother must be smiling on all of us. One day he came with her, and the two of them helped feed our guests. He signed up to come back, and he's been here four or five times recently. When I see him, gabbing with our poor folks, and telling them to take care of themselves, I get a bit teary. That's a wonderful scene: a genuine goodness of heart in the Jewish baker and the old Irish cleaning lady, helping out our poor folks here!"

A month later I met those two people. Their friendship reminded me of the old story "Abie's Irish Rose." Not that they were anything but proper friends, but they were close spiritually — each willing to take the time to cook and serve so that others would get a hot, nutritious noonday meal. The baker sat and talked with me about how much it had come to mean to him to visit and work at Saint Joseph's House.

"I put aside bread as soon as it's out of the oven. I'd never sell those 'Catholic Worker ryes' — yes, that's what I call them. I have to hide them, because on lots of days they would disappear fast. We've got a good reputation! I love seeing the people here notice the bread and talk about it. 'Hey, this is *good*,' they'll say, and I want to go over to them and say, You can say that again — the best bread in all Brooklyn! But it wouldn't be the best idea — Pat [his Irish lady friend] says that would be boasting. I guess she's right. I'm a stranger to the Catholic way of thinking, so I follow her cues. With my people — we'd love to know who cooks our food or bakes our bread. But these folks, they're very sensitive in ways I don't understand. They talk about pride, and you mustn't lord it over the guests, or make them feel they're getting handouts and they're not your equal. To tell you the truth, I wonder who's kidding whom! Those poor people over there [in the next room] aren't fools. They may be in a lot of trouble; they might not have a cent to their names, but they're not fools. I've talked with them a lot. Some of them are as smart as can be. They know the situation they're in. They know we're not in the same trouble they're in. But look, it's not my business to start telling these folks how to run their charity. I don't think they'd like hearing me call it that!"

He made a point of telling me of his admiration for Dorothy Day and her coworkers. He complimented "the young people who come and help" and told me how much it means to him to help: "I don't have a lot of time left. I have bad angina. The doctor has told me to take each day as it comes. What he doesn't say out loud is that I should take each day as if it's my last one.

"Now I try to go there once a week. I forget myself and I listen to other people, and I do some cooking so they'll eat, not me! I feel I'm learning all the time. I hear the [college] kids talking, and I read their paper, and I feel that maybe I'm a quarter of an inch a better person. Even if I shouldn't say that because it's boasting, it's how I feel. I told my doctor [about his volunteer work], and he said it's good for me. I fired right back at him, It's good for those folks we feed, I hope — that's what counts. He gave me a look; he smiled. He asked me if I've had an angina 'over there.' I said no, not yet. Then I told him, 'Maybe it's their influence with the Big Guy.' The doctor really got a kick out of that. He said, 'Maybe.'"

While working at the soup kitchen, he made good friends with Maria, a Puerto Rican grandmother who had only recently moved to the mainland to be near her son and his family. She had no great command of English, but she was a willing worker. She would see the guests coming and going from Saint Joseph's House, and she would actually cry for them. The baker described her for me: "She's a very emotional woman! She'll see someone come in, and he's been in a fight or he's sick; or a woman, she's been beaten up. And Maria, she's rushing to be of help with the bandages and with food, and I've seen tears in her eyes as she's talking with the person. Pat said to me last week, 'God appears to us through Maria,' and you know, a year ago I wouldn't know what she was talking about, but now I do! I told my [grand]nephew: 'I'm getting an education, that's what I'm getting over there.'"

His relaxed, wry, earthy goodness of heart; Pat's earnest, devout, worriedly prayerful (will I get to heaven, go to hell?) goodness of heart; Maria's passionate, seemingly selfless goodness of heart — these are all instances of the older idealism Dorothy Day welcomed out of her own grandly determined, occasionally messianic goodness of heart. Once, as we talked about older people who gave themselves unstintingly in service programs, Dorothy told of a white friend of hers who worked in a Head Start center in Harlem, and of a friend of *hers*, a black woman, Mrs. Pratt, whom I ought to visit.

I said yes, I should visit her, but Dorothy picked up on my perfunctory tone loud and clear, for all the deafness she complained of. She went to the phone, made a call, and came back to tell me there was someone who wanted to talk with me! I claimed to be grateful, but I was really annoyed. The word "bossy" crossed my mind later, as I pretended to be pleased at the prospect of the Harlem interview she had just arranged. Only when I went uptown a day later and sat with Mrs. Pratt, whom I later, at her request, learned to call Alice-Mae, did I find that word "bossy" giving way to "helpful." What Dorothy managed to do and got others to do was a surprise, a revelation almost.

In her fifties, with "four children alive, three dead" and fourteen grandchildren, Alice-Mae had spent her life taking care of people, including a husband who had tuberculosis and then cancer, of which he died at the age of forty-one. She had nursed him while trying to instill what she called "spine" in her two daughters and two sons — meaning a moral backbone that wouldn't crumble in the face of what Harlem had to offer. She was haunted by the deaths of a son and a daughter: the boy killed by a drunk driver whose car went out of control, the girl by a pneumonia that proved resistant to antibiotics. Another daughter, born with a congenital heart defect, had died at the age of two.

"I think of my children who are gone every day," she told me. "I get up, and I have their pictures beside me on a table, and I look at them hard and long, hard and long. I tell them I love them, and I tell them I hope God is watching over them, and I'm sure He is. When people say to me they feel sorry for themselves, and they want others to feel sorry for them, I tell them they're so lucky, and they don't even know it! I tell them what happened to my three, and then I say, Here you are, given a chance by the good Lord, and all you're doing is crying over yourself, as if you were going to leave and be in the Devil's land for the rest of time! Usually they'll stop and do a minute's thinking!"

She was no great churchgoer, but she talked often of her dreams of God. She'd be sitting at the kitchen table, and He'd come and say hello, and she'd tell Him of her "good times and her bad times," and He'd tell her that He had a few of both Himself, and then He'd usually be gone, though every once in a while He'd stay longer, giving her a chance to go into the details of her troubles or the "nice things happening" — a school promotion, a graduation. It became a "blur," those longer visits with Him, yet they had a decided impact: the next day she'd be more awake to the difficulties of her friends and neighbors, and she'd offer to help.

Alice-Mae went to the market every day even though she had a refrigerator. This was a habit from old times in the South, dimly recalled, when her mother would take her and her sisters to the grocery store in a black neighborhood of Mobile. She often thought of her mother walking to the store, meeting people there, talking away, hearing about everyone, and going back home with food and with news, a food all its own. Her mother would feel buoyed by all she had heard.

Alice-Mae, too, loved to go shopping for a quart of milk one day, a loaf of bread or canned goods the next. "I'll learn of what's going on, and then I sit in my apartment and think about the people. There'll be sickness; there'll be people going out; there'll be babies born, and old folks saying the last good-bye — and I hear of the big troubles with the police and gangs and drugs. It's like checking in with my neighbors. I walk slowly, and I meet folks. At the store, I shop slowly, and I meet folks. On the way back, I'm carrying my bag, and so I go slow, and I meet folks!"

One late morning she heard that two Head Start teachers had departed after a squabble over funding of the center, located in the basement of a church, and now the whole program was threatened with collapse. She was upset because one of her grandsons had been a beneficiary of that program, and she knew that the grandchildren of some of her friends were enrolled in it. She got to thinking about whether she ought to try to be of help.

The next morning, as she was dressing and talking to her long-gone children, she remembered yet another nighttime visit by the Lord Jesus: "He told me I seemed fine, and I said, 'Thank you, sir.' He asked if all was going okay, and I said mostly. And then I told Him of our Head Start troubles, and He said He hoped everything came out fine. Then He was gone. When I woke up I recalled Him telling me He was praying for the center — I think He was. And so I thought, I should pray too! So I did — I said a prayer. Then I forgot all that, because I had to start with the pancake mix, and I don't use the store-bought kind; I start from scratch.

"It was while I was getting all that food ready that I thought, Those little kids could use me, just like my kids and my kids' kids had me there for them, and maybe I'll see if I can be of help there. I taught myself to read, and I taught my kids and their kids, so why not find some more kids to sit with and read to them, and give them a boost if I can. Now maybe it was the Lord Jesus putting that idea in my head, or maybe it was just me trying to get myself closer to Him — I'd be in His favor. Or maybe it was just my momma in me talking to me — she was the one who got me to go to school and learn to read. She couldn't [read] but she wanted me badly to learn."

She shunned talk of her motives for helping the Head Start center. She "just dropped by," and within a year she was the leader of ten women who gave their time to that program. "Others get paid money," she said, "but a few of us get paid by seeing the children grow up better than they would if we didn't have that center."

She was a bundle of energy there. She knew each child's name, and there were a lot of them. She deferred to the teachers, yet she had her own way of persuading them to be more inventive, more engaged with the children. She had a special eye out for sick or hurt or disabled children, boys and girls already in some trouble. She latched onto them and brought them food they liked and occasional toys — but also she asked something of them. She went to their homes, made an informal investigation, came back with news, some of it saddening, some of it horrifying. Then she returned and returned until that child knew that she knew a lot and until she found someone, if possible, in the Head Start program or in the neighborhood who could work with her to help that boy or girl.

She spoke of her home visits with great emotion. "Going to those folks, seeing what I see and hearing what I hear — oh, Lord! I've had it bad, real bad — but I've never lost my heart, and my head, and my soul. You know, that's what they've lost, a lot of people: all three. They'll be drinking or snorting; they'll be shooting that stuff into their veins. Lord Almighty! They'll be sitting, and they don't have much to say. They've taken a 'trip,' so they're gone, and I'm in their home, but they're gone. I'll look at the kids, and I want to scoop them all up and take them with me and never, ever bring them back, never, ever. I told a friend what I just said to you, and she said, 'They'll haul you into the police, and the judge will send *you* away, and you won't come back for so long, we'll all be on our way to the Lord by the time you're released.'

"I'd never do that [take the children from their parents]; but when we send those kids home after they've been with us, we're all down in the dumps, way down there, the kids and us, and I'll see kids crying and asking us why they can't stay longer, longer. And then a real smart one will push it more, and say, *sleep* here, *sleep* here, and that's when I have to turn my head and tell everyone I have this bad cold, and it makes me sneeze and get water in my eyes!"

She did not despair, though. She had a great deal of energy, which she was ready to impart to the children, and she had enough self-respect, as well as confidence in some of the children, to avoid prolonged bouts of pessimism. "I know some of those kids love coming here, and I know they hate leaving — so that's a whole lot." She stopped as if to decide exactly how much "a whole lot" would be. Then she went on, "A whole, whole lot — enough to get them going in school. Now I'll tell you, if I had another life or two, I'd start a program *there* — I'd have us helping the teachers, and going to get the kids who don't show up, and walking the kids home who are scared. There's a lot to do, a lot we could be doing. But there's only this one body I have, this one chance."

She tried to push herself even harder sometimes. At one point she was tempted to become a foster parent, to take in a child or two caught in the worst disasters, about which she has come to know more than she ever wanted to know. But she had to draw a line. "People said I was the one to save this kid and the next kid, and I knew I might be able to make a difference. But then I'd be in trouble with my own kids and with their kids. I help out a lot. My daughter has to work, and I give her a hand. Her kids aren't home much except for supper, but I get that supper going because she's home late. It means a lot that I'm there: it's no good when boys come home and the house is empty — that spells *trouble!* They're ten and twelve and fourteen, but they're little ones in their own way, and aren't we all, a part of us is! So you don't walk out on your own to save the world — but I've been tempted, I'll admit!

"I always was a soft one; that's what my momma told me. She'd say, 'Alice-Mae, watch out, because you're a soft one, and you trust people a lot, and you could have your heart broken and your bankbook gone, and you'll be with a child, and no one to care for you both!' Well, I married a good man, but the Lord didn't protect him too well. He must have had His reasons, but I can't figure them out. A long time ago I stopped going to church regularly. It's in me, though, to turn to God and to cry when I see someone hurting and try to do something if I can. Maybe I'll tire of this one day, but I doubt it'll be before I fall flat on my face! I'm hooked on all those kids, and they're not going to take advantage of you, like so many grownups. So there's protection there, if you see what I mean! I'll come home good and tired, and I'm ready to 'work in my own garden' [help with her own grandchildren] and then put myself to sleep, and it takes about five seconds at the most!"

She spoke of being kept alive by the work she did. She paid more attention to the news because she worried about the fate of children like those she had come to know. Head Start meant something concrete to her, and she talked about her experience of it with friends and relatives. Some asked why she gave so much of her time to volunteer work, when she might get a job in a store or office or in a private daycare center. If she loved working with children so much, her neighbor once pointed out, she should go find salaried work at a nursery that took in the sons and daughters of the working poor. But that neighbor immediately received an impassioned, irate sermon, with many references to Jesus and His activities during His ministry, none of them rewarded by a salary.

Alice-Mae reminded the neighbor that there were satisfactions that went with doing something out of the heart rather than in anticipation of a weekly check. She was profiting in her own way, and

that was that. This activity was a "second chance to be young" —
a chance to be with children and enjoy them without the worries
she had had as a mother. It was almost as if she was reliving her
life or redeeming it.

"I look at these children, and I remember my own. I remember
my mistakes, I have to say. I was so young, and my husband got
sick, and money ran out, and I'd take it out on the kids. Now I can
be as good as my heart will let me be with the kids, and it's done
me a lot of good, doing good at the center. There will be some days
when I'm sitting with some kids and teaching them the alphabet,
and I think I've finally found some peace for myself."

Older men and women involved in community service or in a
charity or in a social or cultural cause to which they give time and
money often speak with embarrassment (if at all) about their idealistic side, their generous instincts; rather, they try to proclaim a
kind of egoism at work, an enlightened self-interest. It is as if in
our present culture, youthful idealism is a laudable but passing
phenomenon. The young man or woman grows up and becomes
practical, or at least that is what is expected. No wonder, then, that
an older person won't directly acknowledge the passion of idealism: it is supposed to have given way to other passions — those of
the householder, the burgher, the person headed for success. Since
these days the self is so much discussed and held up as something
to be cultivated and "esteemed," why not summon it as an explanation for the good works one does?

Alice-Mae's remark that she did herself "a lot of good, [by]
doing good" stayed in my mind, echoing sentiments I had heard
expressed for years by people whose lives were much different
from hers. When I heard her use those words, my mind wandered
up and away from Harlem to Marblehead, a town on the coast
north of Boston. In a lovely oceanside home I met a woman, Betsy,
who was a bit older than Alice-Mae and no less active with children, no less passionate in her devotion to them. But she was quite
unnerved at being described as a wonderfully kindhearted, idealistic person. Betsy's idealism, like Alice-Mae's, emerged in late middle age when a son's moral convictions became an occasion for the
family to stop and take stock. Yet she found it hard to give herself

credit for the self-effacing labor she did so continually on behalf of others. She was a bit bored with her life, she explained, she was "looking for a hobby," and she just happened to find that there was a need for the kind of volunteering she did: not only driving boys and girls who needed physical rehabilitation from their ghetto homes to hospitals, but also teaching them and keeping them company while she was with them.

Betsy's involvement, she kept reminding others, really had its origins in her son Ted. She tried not to boast about him even as she tried to underplay the energy and enthusiasm she herself had contributed to the program of transportation and tutoring. Her son had initiated the driving and tutoring program as a college freshman, when he became a Big Brother to a ten-year-old boy, Eddie, who had sickle-cell anemia. He also had one leg enough shorter than the other to give him a noticeable limp. In a neighborhood where manliness counted greatly, Eddie felt painfully inadequate and constantly afraid of being beaten up. He spoke of death from illness as more desirable than death at the hands of a gang. He turned that preference into a reluctance to seek medical assistance on a reliable schedule.

In April of Ted's freshman year, Eddie had to be admitted to Children's Hospital in Boston. Ted visited him there, brought him toys and food, and walked with him down the corridors. He made an appointment to see Eddie at home two weeks later. When he arrived, Eddie told him he really should be at the hospital's clinic right then, but he had decided it was "too hard" to go, that it was "a real hassle," and besides, there was no good reason to keep going to see those doctors. "They can't cure my blood trouble, and they're talking of operations for my leg, but they're not sure when. It's all a big waiting game, and I don't trust them." Ted, worried, drove Eddie to the hospital, took him to the clinic, and ran interference to get him seen. (His appointment had been a morning one, and they arrived in the early afternoon.)

With that visit, Ted became Eddie's companion on hospital visits. He drove him there and back, making sure he missed only half a day of school and finding out what classes the boy would not be able to attend. While they sat waiting to be called at the clinic, they read, practiced spelling words, and did arithmetic problems.

During the summer Ted drove down from Marblehead to the ghetto neighborhood of Mattapan to sustain Eddie's contact with the pediatricians and orthopedic surgeons.

From those doctors he learned that Eddie was not alone, that other children all too often failed to show. These were boys and girls who had developed abnormalities of their bones or joints or were suffering from chronic disease. They needed regular outpatient checkups and treatment. They also needed as much school time as they could get. Often their parents would skip clinic appointments when they thought their child was doing all right, much to the chagrin or alarm of the doctors. Often, too, a trip to the hospital meant a whole day of school lost because of time spent taking the bus to the subway, and then another bus, and then waiting and waiting in the corridors of hospitals.

With the help of church and school officials, Ted got a list of such children and began working the telephone. He also consulted with Eddie, whom he designated his "cocaptain" in the proposed project. The boy would establish contact with families like his own, and his Big Brother would arrange transportation for the children to and from the hospital. Also — a really interesting idea — Ted arranged for some informal catch-up tutoring to be done before, during, and after the hospital visit. Soon, some ten children were ready to take advantage of this unlikely, even surprising offer, and the older Edward scurried around in search of drivers and tutors. At the suggestion of the younger Edward, the program was called the Free Taxi-to-Hospital Service.

Many of Ted's friends had no cars. Those who did were reluctant to drive them into dangerous neighborhoods. His mother offered to give her car to the service and then buy herself a new one. To her surprise, Ted told her that if she wanted to drive her car rather than give it, that would be wonderful. The need was not for "wheels," as he put it, but for "wheels and someone who would steer them — and tutor the children being driven." This challenge was a big breakthrough in the somewhat distant, even tense relationship between mother and son.

With a good deal of apprehension, this fifty-two-year-old woman began driving once a week to a part of Boston she'd never before seen. She became a regular, expected person in the lives of several children, and familiar to the nurses and doctors who cared for them and the teachers who taught them.

Looking back after a year of this effort, Betsy observed, "I've always done some volunteer work. I was brought up to do that. My mother did. But this is different. I have to admit, I'd never have gotten into anything like this if it hadn't been for my son. Now it's probably the biggest thing in my life, the work I do with those children. I never in a million years would have thought I could do this — that I had what it takes. I've lived such a sheltered life — that's one of the things I've learned from doing this work. I've also learned that you can't ever be totally sure of who you are and what you'll end up doing — and why! A year ago, if someone told me of this project I'm now so involved in and asked me if I ever could do it, I'd have said no, I'm sorry. Of course, when my son asked me — that was another matter! If I'd known more before I began, I would have panicked and pulled out. Ted was wise to be so laconic with me. He wasn't withholding, or if he *was*, he was *also* being very shrewd. He wanted me to learn gradually by going out there and feeling my way from situation to situation.

"Now, I practically *live* for those Wednesdays, when I leave this cozy world of mine and take up the challenges of that other world. I don't mean to be melodramatic, but it's an enormous transition for someone like me, and it gives me a lot to think about, not only when I'm there doing the work, but when I come back home. Those children, their life — they're on my mind a lot when I'm going about my chores in this lovely town. It's hard to say — and I sound like one more spoiled suburbanite saying it — but doing this work has given me more than I can possibly give back. I'm more aware of the good luck we have, living here in this town. And I have a real purpose in life each week — something a little more important than a tennis or golf game!"

She wished others in her town would do the kind of work she did, and she tried to enlist some of her friends, with occasional success. One friend who spoke fluent Spanish signed up and accompanied her sometimes, but she preferred to work as a translator at Children's Hospital, as a mediator between doctors or nurses and Spanish-speaking parents and children.

* * *

One such parent, Mrs. Sanchez, lived in Lawrence, Massachusetts, an old mill town struggling with high unemployment among a large population of Spanish-speaking people from Puerto Rico, the Dominican Republic, Mexico, and Central America. Although she spoke English quite well, she was grateful that she could be understood in Spanish as she poured out the story of her son's struggle with increasingly severe asthma. Mrs. Sanchez was a poor, single mother, whose husband (the father of their two children) had abandoned the family.

But her response to her child's illness was to become determined that others like him should get medical care and the educational assistance they needed because of the school days they missed. Against great odds, she managed to make a dent in an urban bureaucracy by persuading the schools to let her and several other parents go to the homes of sick children and, using bilingual texts, tutor them and keep them in touch with the schoolwork they would otherwise be missing. This strong-willed, intelligent, introspective mother of a severely asthmatic son converted a continuing source of anxiety into a significant volunteering initiative.

I was working in the Lawrence schools at the time, but I had not yet met Mrs. Sanchez.[4] When I did get to meet and talk with her through the help of her translator friend, I found myself in the presence of a woman nearing thirty who was herself surprised by this turn in her life in recent months. She was quick to tell me that she had never intended to do what she was now doing with such success — that she had never thought of herself as anything but an ordinary woman on welfare, who was quite ill with a congenital bone and joint disease and a cardiac problem.

She had a disarmingly self-critical and confessional manner of presenting herself: "I used to think of myself so much that the priest would warn me that the worst part of being sick is you forget the rest of the world and sit there listening to yourself breathe and feeling your pulse to see if it's strong or weak! Be glad your ears work and your eyes, he told me many times. I'd get angry. I said, 'I want my heart to work better, that's what counts! When the heart stops, the ears hear nothing and the eyes see nothing.' He gave it back to me; he said, 'When the ears stop hearing other people and the eyes stop seeing them, then the heart *already* has

died!' That shut me up — but only for a while. I'd be back complaining, and he'd be back giving me one of his short speeches. I've
heard them all!

"For a year or two I stopped going to church. I got headaches
hearing that we should do this and do that and not do this and not
do that — and I'd look around and say to myself, We're all poor
people, and we can barely get through the week with the food we
have the money to buy. And the buildings where we live are all
falling apart (today the plumbing, tomorrow the heat, or the rats
and the pipes of lead), and they are telling us we shouldn't use
condoms, and we should have as many children as possible. I agree,
they don't put it that way [I had asked], but they get the message
across.

"When Federico got sick, I thought it was the end of everything. My daughter has problems with her digestion. She needs to
go to specialists in Boston. My son's asthma is bad: he has almost
died twice during an attack — and here I am, with my troubles!
One day, when my children were both home and fighting with
each other as if they were enemies for life, I started losing my
mind. I threw a dish at my daughter, and I hit my son, and then I
started crying. My daughter calmed me down, then she said she
wished she had some schoolwork to do. I was cleaning the kitchen,
and I said, Yes, that would be great.

"Suddenly I had this thought: I would go to the school, and I
would find out what she is missing, and I would ask the teacher to
help me, so I could help my children. That wouldn't be easy, but I
would try and try. So I went there. I was so scared that I could hear
my heart beating, and I thought I'd die right in front of the school.
I put my finger on the bell, then I took it away. I couldn't press it,
so I just stood there. Then the door opened: a kid was leaving with
his mother. I wondered why, but it was none of my business. I just
walked in, but I didn't know what to do, so I walked and walked
until a woman came up to me and asked if she could help me. She
was a teacher, she said. I told her why I was there, and she said
I should go and see my children's teachers. I didn't know their
names, so she asked me my children's names, and she took me to
the office.

"That's how I met the principal, and I told her that I'd like to be able to bring some books home to my son and my daughter when they're sick and do the work with them, as much as I can. And I said I'll bet there are other mothers like me who would like to help, maybe even some dads, if they're not at work. I said, 'What if a few of us came to school and helped there, and then we'd learn what the children are learning — and then, if one of them got sick, or two, or a lot, when the flu goes around, then we could go to the homes and talk with the kids and bring them the books and teach them and give them homework, and then we could return to the homes if they're still sick, and go over the work, or we could be there in school when they return, and give them the special attention they'd be needing.'"

She had come up with an original idea and had offered to get it going informally on her own. She asked for not a single penny, not even the bus fare she would need to go back and forth from the various homes to the school. She wanted to come to school herself and learn what the first- and second-grade students were learning if their teachers felt she could be an adequate teacher's assistant. If she herself felt some reasonable confidence in that regard, she would begin her experiment as an outreach worker, an intermediary between homes and the school. The principal liked the idea, and with little delay Mrs. Sanchez started going to school to learn how to help teachers; in two months' time she had embarked on her first home visits. A year later, she had enlisted four other mothers to help her, along with one father who worked an evening shift and so had some daytime hours to offer.

When I asked her how all this came about so successfully, and why she had chosen to give so much of her time and energy to the project, she was initially at a loss to answer. She "just happened" to think of the idea, and of course, her children's illnesses constituted a rationale: "Because they were sick, I thought of the idea — probably so I could be of help to them." Yet her mind had rather quickly moved from her own children to others, and she had put a large amount of time into learning how to do what she now did so well.

Mrs. Sanchez had a kind of restless moral energy, best described by one of the teachers with whom she worked. "Maria is a devoted student. She doesn't realize what it means to the children to see her, a grown woman, a mother of children, paying such close attention to the same books they have in their hands and the same blackboard lessons and hand-out sheets. They know that if they get sick, she'll be there for them; she'll ask their parents if she can come and visit, and bring some assignments, and go over them one by one. She doesn't have any money to spare, but we've scraped up some bus money, and we give her some cookies to take to the kids. I found out she was buying cookies on her own, and I went to the principal to ask for a little help for her!

"She's done a wonderful job with those sick children. She's had sick children of her own, and she knows how to treat them — and I mean 'treat.' She's gentle and reassuring, but she's no softy. She comes there as a *teacher.* I know — the kids have told me. She gets them to do work, and she rewards them with praise and cookies if they do. If they don't, she has her sermons, and she knows how to ask and ask and ask. She's not pleased with the priests, but she can be a pretty stern minister — or nun! — herself! She warns children who are using their illnesses to escape school altogether that they are making a serious mistake. She tells them how important an education can be. 'A ladder of escape to a better world' — those are the words she uses.

"Since she has got this informal program going, our sick children have really kept up, even when they're out for several weeks. She keeps after them, and of course, she's got *her* volunteers now — those friends who have joined her. Just think: there's not one ounce of bureaucratic fat in all this — no red tape, no regulations, and no money to be allocated and justified! Here are really poor parents and a couple of young grandmothers, helping us out as if they were society matrons with a lot of time on their hands and not wanting or needing money for what they do. I've sometimes thought to myself that if we had every mother of our children as involved with them as much as this one mother is with so many children, then we'd sure be doing a better job of teaching. When Maria Sanchez gets to know a child, that child has begun to understand what school is all about, what it means to get an education: what's at stake, is the way I should put it."

I asked the teacher whether she had any clues to Mrs. Sanchez's motives for such a full-fledged commitment of time, energy, and intelligence. She was at a loss for an explanation. She mentioned the illnesses of both Sanchez children. We both knew that Lawrence had a substantial population of quite poor families in which many children and parents were chronically ill.[5] As I listened to Mrs. Sanchez talk, I occasionally wondered whether the priest who lectured her had not prompted in her, first, anger, then an effort to follow his urging. Yet I remembered that lots of people are counseled and admonished by ministers, priests, rabbis — to no apparent effect. Mrs. Sanchez herself once spoke of the sense of achievement she had begun to feel — but by then her program was well on its way, and she had recruited others to it.

Her only other idea with respect to her motivation was the memory she had of a teaching nun when she was a child in the Dominican Republic. She was seven or eight when she began helping the nun by sweeping the floor of her classroom and dusting its furniture. The nun had offered to take her into her class, but soon thereafter the family had emigrated to Florida.

The nun lived in her memory, though. "She was a very tough person. She demanded that everything be kept neat. She would ask us to hold out our hands, and she would slap them with her hand, or she'd get a ruler and come after us. Once she was coming after me because I'd knocked something from her desk while dusting it, a glass, and it broke. I swept it up — but she came into the room just as I was finishing. She asked me what happened. I told her. She went and got her ruler; she came to me, and I put out both my hands, but suddenly she put the ruler down, and she took my hands and held them, and she told me I should try to be a teacher one of these days, even if my classroom was my home, and my class my children! I wasn't sure what she meant — why I should be a teacher and what I should do with my children that would make me a teacher. I sure wasn't going to ask her any questions, though. I just nodded my head up and down a few times. She told me I could go, but I remember her eyes staring into mine. I've been thinking of her lately."

Memories of the nun and the priest became images that Maria Sanchez could call upon as she gave rein to her conscience. Her mother had implored her to try to get an education, to try to break out of the poverty that seemed to be the family's destiny. Her own illness interfered with any efforts she might have made to get an education, as did her early marriage and motherhood and her husband's abrupt departure. Still, she kept certain voices in mind, and at a certain moment, she became a most idealistic citizen who figured out what was needed and devised a way to accomplish for others something that would make a difference for her and her own children. The harder she worked at this project, the stronger she felt, and the more she began to call upon her two children for help. In time they took note of who was sick in their classes and of what lessons the ailing children needed at home. No wonder each of her children talked of becoming teachers when they grew up.

Older idealism, like its younger counterpart, may have many sources in one life. At times it seems to appear out of nowhere or to take root in soil that does not strike an observer as very hospitable. A year after her program was well under way, Mrs. Sanchez was amazed that she was its founder and amazed that the program had grown so steadily. In this she was like Betsy, the well-to-do suburban mother, who "couldn't quite understand" how she had become so involved in an effort that would have struck her, a few years earlier, as way beyond either her desire or reach. So, too, with Alice-Mae, who stood up for so many children and pointed out the obvious problems that ought to be addressed by "someone" — hence her definition of her work as "doing what obviously needs doing, doing common sense work."

Such "common sense," however, is not altogether common. So many of the older people who give of themselves generously to others tend to downplay the gift of their time, their moral and intellectual and physical energy. Nor are they as readily acknowledged and admired (by some, at least) as younger people, whose idealism is frequently applauded by social observers or critics. The everyday efforts of older men and women may not be so apparent.

One sixty-five-year-old man, who had retired from his job at a factory in Lynn, Massachusetts, began a new life visiting a neighborhood nursing home, playing checkers with patients, bringing them magazines, sitting and talking with them, helping those who were quite incapacitated write letters or make phone calls. This man pointed out during a discussion of his "hobby," as he called it (his older idealism constantly mobilized, I might say), that he wasn't part of a movement or trend. He didn't even like to tell some of his relatives what he was doing, so it was even less likely that the news of his work, and of similar work that a few of his friends were doing, would come out.

He added a moment of sourness to the comparison he was making, prompted evidently by a newspaper story he'd read. "You hear about all that our young are doing, and I think it's wonderful! I sure don't want any reporters coming around to talk to me and my buddies, to find out what we do with our spare time now that we're retired. But I'll tell you, we *are* doing things. No one's going to call us 'the idealistic old,' 'the idealistic elderly,' the way the reporter talked about 'idealistic young people.' I'm grateful more and more of our young people *are* idealistic, but we're out there, too! I have an older brother, ten years older; he's seventy-five, and he goes once a week to read to a blind guy who lives down the street from him. It's only an hour or so a week, but to me that's a sign of someone thinking of more than his aches and pains, and you sure get plenty of them at his age. But you know, if they did start going after us with a lot of stories and praise, a lot of us might go in hiding! Who wants to think you're some big-shot do-gooder! I'd slip by them and take a dive into the nearest pool parlor!"

Modesty, like idealism, wears many faces, responds to life's circumstances in ways that tell a lot about the person in question. This man was suggesting that his kind of older idealism had a pastoral rather than a prophetic quality, in contrast to the idealism found among many young people. Yet he was quick to remind himself and me of young people he knew who very quietly went about their appointed tasks of teaching or visiting people in hospitals, prisons, or nursing homes. He knew quite well that the ordinary gestures of good will he found so inviting and congenial fitted into a long life during which he had had many occasions to sort out what he wanted to do with his time.

I suppose many idealistic young people are just starting to do that, and, of course, their lives are subject to interruptions and

What They Mean to Us

I N THE MIDDLE 1970s I spent some time in the Catholic
Worker community studying the intellectual tradition that had
inspired Dorothy Day and Peter Maurin, cofounders of a social and religious movement that was still very much alive. I was
especially interested in Dorothy Day herself, in the books and
articles she had written and in the ways her life connected so
intimately with various forms of service. I spent a considerable
amount of time talking with her and with others who had known
her well or worked with her at Saint Joseph's House. I talked with
priests and nuns, writers and intellectuals, students and older people, who came from all over the world to do service at one of her
"hospitality houses," and who usually went home to further such
efforts.

Dorothy was very patient and forthcoming as we talked, and
after some months I began to feel I was arriving at some sense of
how she did her work as an activist ever ready to put body and soul
on the line for one or another struggle. (I well remember her in
the civil rights struggle of the early 1960s, taking buses to places
where dangerous confrontations were taking place.)

One day, after a fairly long interview in her room in which we discussed her literary preferences, her religious interests, her writing life, and her contributions to the Worker family, I began to say good-bye. I thanked her profusely for all her help, told her I was getting ready to do the writing I'd hoped to do for years on the Catholic Worker and on her work. I promised to send her my efforts fairly soon. As I stood up and prepared to turn off the tape recorder and gather my notebook and a copy of her book *The Long Loneliness*, which I'd brought for an autograph, along with a letter to her from my mother (which I kept forgetting to hand over), and my winter coat (thrown on the floor not far from *her* coat and hat, for want of any other place to put them), she got up as well. The serious, intent look on her face indicated that she had something important to tell me; by then I'd come to know that look fairly well. Suddenly she said, "I'm not sure you're as close to the end of this as you hope."

I stood in silence. I had always been deferential to her, maybe too much so at times. I asked her for further suggestions and told her I hoped I'd contacted most of the people who were important in her life but that I'd be glad to seek out others. She replied that she much appreciated my interest in the Worker, but that I had not, so far as she knew, connected with the "most important people" in her life and in the lives of others there at 36 East First Street: "our guests."

I stood without saying a word, so she started talking, half out of conviction but also out of a desire to rescue me from what seemed to be a fit of wordlessness. "Our guests *are* the Catholic Worker. Without them, we'd not be here as we are. They come for lunch, and we have come to know how much they mean to us, how much they *give* us. If you talked with them, you'd get to know more about us than if you talk with professors about the 'worker-priest movement,' with all due respect to that subject — and it's always been one close to my heart."

That afternoon we had been talking about priests who allied themselves with the labor unions, and I wished I could return us to that time, for she had been far less stern, less forbidding than she seemed now. Finally, again trying to rescue me, she said, "If you want, I'd be glad to ask some of our guests if they'd mind having a word or two with you." I was jolted out of my muteness to say, "That would be great." She could see, I later realized, that my facial muscles were not quite in agreement with my larynx. I felt reprimanded, and I also felt a rising annoyance, silently expressed by one of those quickly passing thoughts we are wont to call "associations."

I still remember the words that crossed my mind: "Many of them are drunk when they arrive and still drunk when they leave — Bowery bums." So much for one researcher's methodology: an eager interest in intellectuals, in writers and theologians, in the "interesting" array of volunteers who came to give their time and energy; in the ideas and actions and hopes and disappointments of a well-known essayist and moralist who had a complex relationship to a host of eminently recognizable people, from Eugene O'Neill and Mike Gold to W. H. Auden and Hannah Arendt. But, alas, I had no apparent desire to "expand the sample," as they say in the social sciences, by talking to the folks she sat with every noon after preparing and serving them food and asking them to pray with her, pray *for* her.

Not that I then had hugely interesting or informative meetings with her guests. I certainly did sit and ask all sorts of questions of three men and three women whom she suggested. I found them at times rather incoherent — as wordless with me as I had been with Dorothy when she mentioned them as a "subject." But one woman, who was about fifty, I'd been told, though she looked to be in her seventies — her face heavily lined, her skin broken out in a rash, hair unkempt, clothes loose-fitting, dirty, wrinkled — told me something I've tried never to forget. I'd been asking this woman what she thought of Dorothy Day and the Catholic Worker people, and of the food served and the general attitude of those who worked in their hospitality house. She told me how grateful she felt for "a good hot meal" every day. I was pressing her for distinctions between the Catholic Worker approach and that of any other soup kitchen or city relief effort she had encountered.

Glaring at me, she asked *why* I was interested and why I didn't just forget my questions, throw away my tape recorder, and go help the people who were serving food or cleaning up. I mobilized my mind's interpretive faculties: she was snide and hostile, yet another alcoholic with the kind of paranoia one often finds in such people as one presses a conversation and thereby threatens them, for they are sensitive about any halfway trusting acquaintance. That kind of psychological interpretation was a mode of self-protection, if not self-enhancement, on my part, even as I began to note *her* self-protectiveness, which was gradually gathering expressive momentum. After I heard her out, I told her I was sorry if I was in any way upsetting her. She bellowed back, "I'm only upset because you seem upset yourself, mister!"

I *was* upset, and I wanted out — back to books on the nineteenth-century papal encyclicals or workers' rights, back to interviews with old Greenwich Village bohemians who remembered Dorothy Day from earlier times. While I mentally prepared my psychiatrically saturated broadside (more associations!) to match her outburst, she gave me something else to consider, now in a much lowered voice, her face softened by a thin smile. "Dorothy is always afraid that she and her friends might not be doing right by us. I keep telling her that she's creating problems for herself that don't exist. We're doing fine here! We *love* coming here! They're great to us! But I'll tell you something: I don't think she'll let herself know what she and her friends mean to us, what they mean to us every single noon, and what they mean the rest of the time, when we hold on to them for dear life. I think of them first thing when I wake up and last thing when I go to sleep." She stopped and stared right at me for the first time. She repeated the phrase "what they mean to us," then drifted off, her eyes with her thoughts, to another part of the world. I tried to continue our exchange, but she was no longer paying attention to my words.

Hours afterward, mulling over the remarks I'd heard from various guests, that phrase "what they mean to us" kept returning to me — a pointed psychological observation by someone who was not normally given to pointed comments of any kind. "I don't think they know," she had observed, implying that the Catholic Worker volunteers didn't understand how very much they meant to those they assisted so fervently. Was she speaking a truth, I wondered, and if so, what would account for this lapse in awareness by men and women who were surely more self-conscious, more self-aware and responsive to others than the rest of us?

I brought up that lady's comment in my next discussion with Dorothy Day, and I mentioned it to several of her colleagues, including Frank Donovan, one of her closest associates, a long-time resident at Saint Joseph's House, and a good friend of mine. For Dorothy the comment came as no surprise. "Maybe she is right. Maybe we spend so much time trying to be of help to them, we end up not thinking of the consequences — what we come to mean to them, as the lady said. But I'm not sure we should go around giving much thought to what we've become for our guests; that is their business. They mean a lot to *us*. They are our fellow human beings, and if we are to call ourselves Christians, they are the people Jesus would have us think about and try to be with."

Later, as Frank Donovan and I talked, I realized that he was willing to be a bit more psychological. He pointed out that Dorothy's remarks told of her "essential modesty." He explained, "Dorothy wouldn't want to think like that, what she means to others, for fear she'd be in grave sin: the pride of the giver, the benefactor. She spends a lot of time these days denying the importance of her role in this movement. She gets especially angry when people talk of her as a saint; or she just laughs and laughs! She knows, somewhere inside her head, that this place is important for the people who come here, and not only because we feed them. More than anything, our guests need to be treated as the human beings they are, 'children of Christ,' as we say here, and worth everyone's respect.

"Sometimes people come here to volunteer, to help us for a few days or weeks, or months, and they have a hard time when they're provoked by some of our more colorful and desperate and troubled guests. After a few bruising encounters — psychologically bruising: we've rarely had a physical disturbance, and that tells you something! — our volunteers aren't so ready to think of the guests in the way Dorothy does! She's used to all the shouting, the hysteria, the outbursts, the bickering and squabbling: harsh words from people who have lived harsh lives. These new people — you can understand their feelings, the confusion and the irritation, the anger sometimes. If you were to ask them what *they* think many of our guests think of us, you might hear, 'Very little'!

"These new people — some of us call them — have heard too many rude remarks made; have heard all too few thank you's spoken; have felt ignored, even abused by the salty if not obscene talk that is so much a part of street people around here. Yet I have seen those same street people cry when told that one of us regulars in the Worker community is ill or, God forbid, has died. Often the ones who cry and want to go and say prayers for the sick or departed person are the very ones who have been most difficult in the dining room or out in the street waiting in line for us to open and begin serving.

"There may be more to all of this — it may be that we protect ourselves from a lot of anguish by not seeing, not acknowledging what our guests think of us. If we had on the top of our heads a sense of what has developed between them and us, we sure might feel a bit overwhelmed at times. I had an experience a year ago: a man was dying; he had come here for years, three or four times a week for lunch. I knew him well, and vice versa — at least in that formal sense of immediate recognition by name and friendly talk. Then he'd disappear into the arms of those cold, callous streets — those murderous streets sometimes.

"Well, one day last winter he came here as usual, early, and we got to talking, and he told me he knew he was going to die soon. I asked him how he knew. He said he had bad chest pain off and on, and he was getting short of breath. I got worried, and I told him I'd take him to the hospital, to Bellevue. He said no. I insisted. I said that we do it all the time, and I knew a good doctor there, and right after lunch, we were going, and that was that! He started crying, right then and there. I comforted him, and we fed him a good, nutritious meal of soup and bread and more soup, and some meat and vegetables. He still had his appetite, I noticed.

"Then we set out. One of our community had a car, and she drove us. I was worried about public transportation. He seemed frail, even with his good appetite. When we got to the hospital, the doctor I knew was busy, so we had to sit and wait. It was then that he started crying again, and once more I tried to comfort him. I was sure that he was afraid that he was dying and that the doctor would tell him he had to come into the hospital right away. But I was wrong! Finally he started talking. He told me how much he

loved us, each and every one of us, and he said we are his only
family, and we're all he's got, and all he's had for years. And he told
me that every day he goes into a church and says a long prayer for
us. He sits in a pew and thanks God for us, for all who work in our
hospitality house.

"I was amazed, listening to him. I'd never before thought that
carefully about what our guests think about us! I just assumed that
they were grateful; and of course, Dorothy always talks about the
gratitude *we* feel for the opportunity to be of service to others. But
this was about something more than being grateful — the way we
all feel when we're in deep trouble and someone holds out a hand
to us. Remember, many of these people, they are alcoholics and
they're in pretty bad shape emotionally. They tend to be disorga-
nized, and it can be hard for them to follow their thoughts, to think
in the traditional way we do. I'm not putting them down; I'm being
honest about what I see every day. Suddenly, one of the men I'd
always considered about as agitated and disturbed as anyone who
came to us, a really heavy drinker and a guy with a violent side to
him, we'd heard, though everyone commented on how he was a
lamb with us — suddenly, that fellow turns out to be a daily sup-
plicant at church for all of us. A half hour and more, he told me.
I almost started crying myself. I just sat there with him, and I
said, 'Thank you,' and I repeated it, 'Thank you'; and I said, 'Bless
you,' and then he did start crying again, and so did I. Very emotional!

"Then he told me he had some money hidden away, and he
wanted us to have it. I said no; I asked him if he had any relatives.
He said probably, but he'd lost touch with them a long, long time
ago. He looked at me, and then he jolted me again: 'It's been "the
long loneliness" for me, too.' He knew of that book! I looked him
in the eyes. I asked him if he'd ever read Dorothy's book. Yes, he
had. He would sometimes go on the wagon, completely and suddenly. He'd stay that way for maybe a couple of weeks. He thirsted
all the while for beer and for whiskey and for a mix of the two,
until he couldn't stand it any longer, and he'd go crashing down, a
heavy binge, as if he was getting himself back in good standing!
Apparently, when he was sober, he read a lot, and had read her
autobiography and a couple other books of hers; and he'd read

some of the novels she mentions — Dostoyevsky and Dickens, I think. He'd gone to college, he told me, to the University of Pennsylvania, and had dropped out in his junior year. He said he knew he was an alcoholic when he was as young as eleven or twelve!

"All this while we sat waiting for the doctor! It was then that I thought about the others, too. I said to myself, How many stories like this one are there among those regular guests of ours? I'll tell you, I felt as if the whole world had fallen upon me! I felt I'd been thoughtless: I hadn't appreciated what we mean to them. You see, we spend a lot of time trying *not* to think like that — we/them. We think of ourselves as brothers and sisters in Christ, or as God's children, all of us, or as plain, ordinary people, each one of us, maybe some luckier than others, but each of us worthy of the respect one human being owes another. But I was suddenly thinking that 'we' didn't really give some of 'those people' their due; I mean to say, we thought of them as hurt, as wounded, as fighting terrible demons, but I hadn't thought any of them was doing what he'd been doing, praying for us so hard and regularly.

"I guess I'd assumed *we* were the ones who were doing the praying! Talk about arrogance! Talk about being wrapped up in your own world! That's what I saw in a flash — that in this work, you can get quite isolated from the very people you're trying to serve. 'We' are the servers; 'they' are the people served. This man was trying to serve us in the highest way possible: he was asking the Lord's blessing on us every day, and now he was preparing to bestow an inheritance on us, I was finding out, not a huge one, but a few thousand dollars, a fortune to him, and a big sum to us, also. I used to think he was out of control a lot, but he was in more control than I ever dreamed! He could have had access to that money. His father had left it to him, and he had refused to touch it. He sat there, telling me all about it — the beatings his father gave him. He was a lawyer, the father; he went to Princeton. He was a manic-depressive and an alcoholic. He'd go berserk and beat his wife, and then he'd turn on his kids. Our friend decided one day he'd never lay eyes on his father again after hearing about a bad beating he gave everyone at home, the wife, the other son.

"I didn't hear the full story. The doctor came, and he listened to my friend's heart and took an EKG and told him he'd had a serious coronary, and he had to come in right away if he wanted to live. You know what he said to the doctor? He said, 'Doc, I've wanted to die for years, for decades; I've never had the guts to take my life, but if my heart can do it, just like that, end things, then I'll be happy!' The doctor didn't know what to say. He looked at me. I decided that I had to be strong; I had to get this wonderful friend of ours into the hospital. So I put my arm around him, and I didn't say a single word. I just nudged him alongside me. I walked, and he walked with me — and the next thing we both knew we were following the doctor into a room that was called the Cardiac Intensive Care Unit, I think. That was where the doctor and the nurses took over. I said good-bye, and I left, and there I was, crying again!

"I didn't go right back to Saint Joseph's House, though. I stopped at a church and just sat there, and let all I'd heard and learned wash over me! Then I prayed; I prayed real hard for that fine man, and his life — such as it was. When I got back, I was going to tell my friends — tell Dorothy — but I was still 'under a spell,' that's how I thought of it, a spell that the good Lord had put on me, with the help of this guest and friend of ours!

"The next day I went right to Bellevue, and it was clear he was worse. He smiled when I approached the bed, but he was having trouble breathing, a lot of trouble. He told me he had some business to talk about. He told me he'd asked the nurse to call a lawyer, and he was going to make sure that money got sent to us. I asked him who 'us' was, and he said 'Saint Joseph's House — the Catholic Worker community.' I didn't say anything, and that's when he spoke — he told me, 'You people mean everything to us; you treat us as though we're part of your family. I guess we are. That's what you mean to us — we're part of your life. It's not "we" and "you" or "we" and "them," it's all of us, together.'"

Less than a day later the long-time guest died, and shortly after his funeral (arranged by the Catholic Worker community) his modest estate went to the only "family" he had known all through his adult life. But for Frank Donovan and others at the Catholic Worker community, I think it fair to say, this man's greatest legacy was his insistence on making clear with words what he had felt for so long. Indeed, the outbursts he inflicted on others and on himself were a measure of trust. Here was a place where the accumulated suffering of a life was offered a safe moment's expression. He was not given indulgence or interpretation, but the firm, rallying attention of volunteers who had no interest in being police or psychotherapists. They were companions in the literal meaning of the word: people who sat with others and shared bread with them.

Frank Donovan once remembered with me how Dorothy Day responded to that man's seemingly unpredictable explosions of anger or moody mutterings: "She'd see him glaring and glowering and hear him cussing away, and she'd go right to him and ask him how the soup was that day, how it tasted. He'd be taken by surprise: there he was with all those attitudes and feelings that he was trying to express — a mixture of political raving and intense rage directed at individuals (most of them weren't in sight, but some might be, giving us plenty of worry that he'd 'let go') — and there *she* was, asking for a critique of the soup or the bread or the coffee.

"Once, I remember, he waved her question aside, but she persisted, and she joined ranks with him a little. She said she thought the soup that day wasn't so good, and she said it was her fault, she hadn't given her cooking the care and thought it properly deserved. He was undone in a way, I began to realize. He shut up, and he just stared at her. Meanwhile, she gave him one of her talks. She explained that sometimes people like her make mistakes — that they want to do a good job as volunteers, but they have things on their minds, or it's just not the best morning or afternoon or evening in their lives, and so they 'stumble and fall' — that phrase was sure Dorothy! She asked him for his forgiveness! She promised she'd do better the next day. She said there'd be more vegetables in the soup, and it would be richer and have more flavor. She hoped the bread would be a bit fresher, too!

"There he was, fuming and ranting, but the more she talked, the more she went into the small details of *our* life as volunteers at the Worker, and our missteps, and the more she asked for a little charity of feeling from him toward us, the more he seemed to calm down. We thought at first that she'd done an end run around him: he was griping and griping about things and people, and she had come over and said, 'Hey, listen to *my* gripes!' But we began to understand (we were eavesdropping) that she was up to something else. She wanted to show him that for her it wasn't a matter of *him*, the noisy, disturbed bum and wino, the homeless man, the beggar, being taken in and given a meal by *her*, the person congratulated by everyone — and so in constant danger of congratulating herself, she well knew! — because she was ready to give her time and strength for such people, feed them and get clothes for them, and take them to doctors, and try to find a place for them to live, and if they were up to it, some work. Instead, she was telling him, quietly and by indirection, I guess you'd say, that she and he were in the same boat, this fragile canoe, rowing upstream, maybe, and both slipping up a lot.

"I'm not doing a good job, even now, of explaining what was happening, but I understood after he died that he had done a very good job of figuring out what she was trying to do. She'd let him know what *he* meant to her — there she was hearing him out and being self-critical about herself! She wanted him to know that, even so, she was ready to go on: there would be tomorrow's soup. As he quieted down, he must have been realizing what he told me before he died — that she was the only one in the world he knew who was out there for him, but who wasn't taking advantage of him by lording it over him: you poor fella — let me help you, let me treat you, let me feed you, and then I'll feel just great, and others will tell me I'm great! She was saying, Maybe we *are* the only ones ready to feed you and listen to you, but we're in this mess called life *with* you. It's the *community*, we keep calling it, the *family*, all of us who break bread together, the way Jesus and His friends did.

"I guess that message got to him without Dorothy saying a word of it explicitly. Maybe she never said a word of it to herself, explicitly! She had a lot to say about a lot of subjects, but she never really talked or wrote about how she did the most important thing in her life by her own standards: serve others, give herself to their needs. She just did what needed doing, but she did it in a certain way, and that's what we were getting to understand as we watched her and her guest that day, and that's what he was getting to understand. By quieting down and listening to her, he was telling her more than a mountain of words could tell her: I *do* know what I mean to you — me and the rest of us here. And now I'm showing you (not telling you) what you mean to me, what all of you here mean to all of us here. I guess that was a big moment in my own life: I began to understand a little better how to *be* with our guests, not talk, talk with them, using all those strategies and techniques you read about, and I began to understand that the food we offer isn't the be-all and end-all of what we can offer."

As I sit and talk with college students or men and women in professional schools who are engaged in community service, I often think of that parable of sorts. These young people are quite naturally trying to understand how to work with various "others" in a manner that is useful and productive and reasonably free of rancor and suspicion and misunderstandings (though, Lord knows, everyone "stumbles and falls" again and again). So often the emphasis is on how "we" ought to comprehend "them" (all those orientations and on-site training programs!) and then how we ought to "work with them." The imagery is often a mix of the psychological (if not psychiatric) and the technological — as if a kind of human engineering would carry the volunteer safely through the threats posed by the barriers known as class, race, ethnicity, culture, language, mental illness, alcoholism, addiction, deafness, blindness, old age, imprisonment, hospitalization, and homelessness as they become concrete: one person talking with, being with, another in particular situations.

Again and again I hear individuals who are giving a good deal of themselves worry that they may not be doing enough, or not doing what they are doing in the "correct" way, the most "effective" way. Their concerns are inward, with what they are doing, how they are doing it, and what they should do. Always they themselves are the subject of the scrutiny. Not that anyone else is taking them to task. Those students are by and large enormously and generously interested in the people they are trying to assist, and they show that interest in their readiness to study the habits and values of the men, women, and children with whom they work, in their readiness to read books and articles with great concentration and zeal, discuss them long and hard.[1]

Still, much less attention is paid to what they, as volunteers, come to mean to those with whom they work, probably for the same reason my Catholic Worker friends were loath to bring up that matter. The last thing in the world volunteers need (as Dorothy Day and Frank Donovan surely knew in their bones) is a kind of consciousness that turns into *self*-consciousness, a constant (sometimes paralyzing) awareness of what others are thinking of them and why. Indeed, when a person being fed or tutored or assisted talks from the heart about what a volunteer has come to mean, the result can be embarrassing. And that is no help in the everyday rhythms of volunteering.

A black college junior, Fred, talked to me once about a group of seven tutees he was teaching in an after-school program in a ghetto neighborhood. He said, "I've been having a mostly good time." I thought I'd now hear a description of his experiences, but he suddenly stopped, seeming both introspective and uncomfortable. The word "mostly" was a tipoff, and I sat there, trying to figure out how to learn about the stories that must have prompted that word. My silence prompted him to reverse course in an interesting manner: "I guess I haven't been having all that good a time." Then, as we seemed at another impasse, a shared, wordless nervousness, he came up with another qualification, this one quite provocative: "But maybe it doesn't make any difference. . . ." After a pause, he continued: "I guess I'm not sure about what I'm trying to say. I thought I had some ideas, but they don't seem to be very clear — or maybe I don't know how to say them!"

We talked around and around the subject Fred had in mind. At my request, he gave me a more or less factual description of what he'd been doing, then offered an account of which students were taking well to the reading tutorial, and which were doing not so well. I asked him whether any of them were doing very poorly, were "out of it" for all practical purposes. He said quite quickly, and with some annoyance, "No, none."

I pressed, asked whether this was an especially able group of youngsters, or whether he'd discovered some magic that enabled him to do so very well with *everyone*. He caught my not so covert sarcasm, but rather than take offense, he decided to help educate this poor older fellow: "You see, they are really glad to come and be in the class. We have juice and cookies. I bring candy. They have been told by their minister and their parents that I'm some whiz because I go to Harvard, and besides I'm on the football team, and besides, I'll end up being some big-shot lawyer or businessman! The first time we met, they were looking up to me as though I'd be walking on the water, not swimming in it if we'd have been near a lake or the ocean. They wanted to know all this stuff about me, and finally I said, 'Come on, you guys, I'm here to find out about *you*, so I can work with you on your school lessons, and we can accomplish something.'

"They heard me, but they weren't really listening too carefully. I got more questions, a barrage, and then, I just decided to answer them all. I figured they were testing me. But they never did stop testing me! Sure, we got down to business. We worked pretty well. Two of the guys were fairly well motivated. Two were real goof-offs and wise guys and headed for a lot of real trouble one of these days, that's what I decided right off. The other three, they wanted to talk football and track and basketball with me all night, and they wanted to know how many roommates I had, and what food I like, and where I'd traveled, and if I had a girlfriend, and what she's like. They never did tire of asking! Finally I said, 'No more questions about me; and no more questions from me about you!' I had to insist!

"Things went a little better then, but I really had to fight them on talk about me — and I was embarrassed by it. A lot of the time, I felt that I didn't deserve any damn credit for what was going on! I was trying to be a good teacher, but they weren't reacting to me the teacher. It's hard to put into words what I felt was going on there. I was a 'big guy' — someone in a fancy college and with all the luck going his way, even if I was one of their own, a brother; but I wanted most of all to get their minds going, and they were going all right, but I had the feeling it wasn't because I was using my *brains* with them, it was because of what I *meant* to them."

Fred stopped with that distinction, almost as if he now had to think about what he'd just said. I was struck by the importance of what I'd heard. At first my mind fell back on my psychoanalytic knowledge and experience, and I thought of transference. But these youngsters weren't in treatment, and their reaction began even before they met their teacher. They were "all excited," he'd been told by a minister. Call it a cultural transference of sorts, something akin to the phenomenon of the celebrity in late twentieth-century American life.[2] True — but there was more to it than that. He was *their* celebrity, who came weekly to teach them and brought lessons, books, recommendations, stories, ideas to pursue, and, not least, a willingness to say no as well as yes. He was not the silent or reticent psychoanalyst, watching the slow development, in the office's privacy, of reactions that tell of a childhood, a family's one-time life.

Nor was he a "star," an athlete or actor or politician or social reformer, waving and smiling — here today, gone tomorrow (or, more likely, in five minutes). He would be with them for the school year, and that summer he worked with them in a two-month intensive enrichment program. To be sure, teachers commonly elicit so-called transference responses, becoming a kind of parent in the student's life. But Fred wasn't one of their regular teachers, and he brought to them special qualities: he was much younger, and he was a volunteer, as they were, albeit prodded by parents, relatives, a minister, or school authorities. Moreover, he had no set agenda for a long while. He tried to be prepared for them to bring him their various school problems, and he did his best to work with them so that they might do better in school.

Fred and I kept trying to put in perspective his distinction between himself as the intelligent auxiliary teacher of sorts and himself as a person with a different significance for his young charges. The summer Fred worked full-time with children in public housing (he lived there too, with other students in an apartment provided by Boston's Redevelopment Authority) I decided to talk with those children and ask them what they thought of Fred and the other volunteers. I also talked with the residents in a nursing home about the students who came and read or helped in other ways.

When I talked with Jake, a member of a July day-camp contingent and one of Fred's year-long tutees, he told me this (condensed from several conversations): "He's a great guy. He comes here to do what will help us, but he doesn't force himself on us. If we want to sit and talk basketball and football, he'll go along. But he tells us, You guys are losing. He says *he* is, too: he really likes to see us improve in school. When we do, he says it's as if *he* did, too! That's cool, man! *He's* cool! He wears these great sneakers and sweatshirts sometimes. He borrows someone's car sometimes — a nice one. Mostly, he comes on the bus. He's the kind of person you might want to be if you thought you had a chance of being him! He's someone you can look up to, and you know he won't let you down. That's what we think."

When pressed for concrete and specific details, other children whom Fred worked with obliged readily, and I began to realize that they were not at all glorifying this college student. They were enthusiastic about him, as he was while with them — his enthusiasm was one of the qualities they most admired and for which they expressed gratitude. He was patient and interested in them and quite attentive to their work, and they offered examples of these attitudes. I realized that he had earned their thankful affection. I took a plunge and told them I wasn't sure their teacher was fully aware of how they felt about him and why. They didn't seem at all surprised! Suddenly I felt tentative, uncertain of what to say, but these "culturally disadvantaged" youngsters were thoroughly savvy and knowing.

Don't you see, dude, they told me in various ways, this guy is a real big help to us and has been for a long time now. One of the reasons we like him so, and one of the reasons he works so well with us, is that he doesn't bask in the very warm feeling we generate, doesn't even seem to understand it. Sure, he knows we look up to him as an athlete and a guy who goes to Harvard and a guy who's headed someplace — and all of that explains our tremendous *anticipation* with respect to him. Hell, we need all the hope we can get, and like anyone else, we don't mind a little glamour, too. But after a few weeks, we settled in with him, and he with us; and he was so interested in trying to be there for us and work well with us, and get on the same wavelength we're on — well, he had no time to stop and think about what we thought of him. The guys who have come here this summer — they knock themselves out for us, and they're not sitting around, waiting for us to toss them compliments or asking us what we think of them. We wouldn't tell them that kind of stuff, anyway, but it's there, and if you need an explanation, then you might have to wait a little, mister. You might have to wait a long, long time, because we're not into thinking about what happens among us, and between us and our tutor.

From elderly recipients of youthful service I heard much more explicit and extended comments. The men and women were ever so glad to have "such nice visitors" and were pleased to call them "friends." But there was a divide of sorts between the students determined to work with others and those "others" harboring a largely unexpressed appreciation.

"The young people come here," an eighty-eight-year-old woman I'd interviewed fairly closely for a year told me, "and they try very hard to do anything they can for us, and they seem to know more about us than we'd ever dreamed anyone would. So we thank them and thank them, but they don't let it go to their heads, and to tell the truth, I'm not even sure they know what they mean to us." The phrase stopped me in my tracks. I told her I'd heard others say that exactly. Please explain, I said — let me know why you think these young people, whom you have just described as so observant and astute about getting along with people, are unaware of "what they mean" to you. She didn't have to ponder the question for long. She told me, "Well, they've got better things to think about than their reputation! They're not running for office, you know — and we're not voters!"

I began to feel reprimanded, and maybe a bit insensitive and thoughtless to have brought up the matter. But abruptly she changed tack. "Once in a while I've noticed some of those students seem to be worried that they're not getting through to us — not doing all they might, or they feel that they should. I guess they are looking to us for some guidance, and we're not supplying it! What do you call it — 'feedback'? I'd tell them that they're doing fine, just fine! I'm tempted to tell them that they're a real lifeline to some of us. We wait for them to come, and we're full of joy when they visit. They read to us, sit and talk with us, help us do things like sew and knit, and they do errands for us — a wonderful break in these last, boring months and years of life! But I've begun to understand why we don't lavish praise on them. It would make them feel uncomfortable — it would make too much of all this. When you say what we would say, what's in our hearts, you are making it awkward to go on about your business. Do you see what I mean? In a family, there are times to express love, but a lot of times, you assume that the love is there, and that way you just relax and get through the day!"

She seemed ready to let the matter drop, but all of a sudden she added, "Besides, I think it can be very hard for people like us to say out loud, or even to ourselves, how it feels to be in need of help, and waiting for it — and then it arrives! I feel ashamed of myself: I never did for others what those young people are doing for us. I never even gave 'the elderly' a thought until I joined their ranks myself. So you see, when I see them — well, they remind me of how inadequate I am now, *and* of how inadequate I used to be!

"I'm making too much of all this, maybe — but you were asking me those questions, and the next thing I knew, I was remembering how I'd feel sometimes when those volunteers came and when they left. They remind me of my past youth, gone forever. They remind me of the mistakes I made, and what I didn't do but might have — and so I'm ashamed a little, frankly, that I never volunteered my time, as they do now. It isn't all 'thank you, thank you' that crosses my mind — and I'll bet I speak for a few of us, at least! It's our failures of the past that come to mind. And then you say to yourself, I don't deserve this; I haven't earned it! That's a terrible feeling: to be helpless and in need, to like people so much and enjoy their company, to look forward to them with such pleasure and eagerness, to have a good time with them and feel so much better — stronger and more hopeful — after they've left; and then to remember your own young days, when you never gave so much as a second thought to people like us who are staying in places like this. It's shame I feel — I'm sorry to keep repeating myself. I wouldn't ever want to tell those young people this — that they make me realize the sins of my past! (I'm being a bit melodramatic, I know!) It would be awful, wouldn't it, if we said *everything* to one another in this life! Even with my husband, we didn't talk about everything that crossed our minds, and we were happily married for over fifty years! No, I think it's best that I smile at those young people and thank them with all my heart, and hope to be alive for their next visit!"

She had managed to say a lot about attitudes and feelings usually not mentioned. Even Frank Donovan and Dorothy Day, for all their years of work as volunteers, had not brought up what she dared discuss — that the volunteer may be an accuser of sorts in the mind of the person being helped, who is ashamed, suddenly made to feel guilty because of another's earnestly tendered assistance.

The more I thought of that elderly lady's confessional remarks (she died six months after we talked), the more I began to wonder about the children my student volunteers had told me about and even about the man Frank Donovan had described to me. What *else* did those ghetto youngsters feel, as they met weekly with their teachers, apart from the obvious pleasure of a sometimes quite special human connection? Volunteers can bring hope, but they also can remind children of who *they* are in contrast to the volunteers. That is, every visit can remind those children of a volunteer's virtues — and quite possibly, of their own limited prospects and even their vices, the mischief and worse they may have done.

I asked one of the nine-year-olds in the urban summer camp run by my student, Fred, to sit with me and talk about his life and about his two summers of that combination of fun and learning. I was well acquainted with this child.[3] Mark was not the most voluble of the children I had come to know and was certainly not the best at schoolwork. Fred had tried hard to help this somewhat fearful child be more comfortable with books and with the classroom give-and-take that can inspire a child to study harder, prepare better for school.

As we talked about that tutorial program, Mark was unwilling to depart from the obviously conventional — the "great time" he'd had and the "great person" the teacher was. Yet he did venture to ask, "I was wondering how you get to be like him?" I told him I didn't really know. I didn't want to throw the question right back at him in the psychiatric mode. He replied, "Me neither." I said, "I've wondered, though." He answered, "Me too." I asked him if he'd come up with any answers: "No." When he asked me about my own search, what I had come to believe, I said, "Well, I think some people are born lucky, and others work very hard, and some find themselves fairly quickly, and some find themselves gradually."

As I heard my conclusion, I decided I had been both evasive and trite. Mark, however, picked up on my categories in a startling manner, saying, "Maybe a guy like Fred, he gets help from people and that's how he can become someone everyone looks up to." I nodded, and he smiled tentatively. It took me a few seconds to guess what he might be getting at — and I later realized he had been able to tell by the look in my eyes that I'd been slow on the draw. Finally, I said, "Oh, right! You mean that for every teacher, there's a student to help him out!" He smiled and said, "Yup." I asked him if he was one of those who had helped some teachers. He laughed. "Plenty of them." Then he reminded me of our subject: "But most of them I didn't like; I was just there because I had to be."

We went back to discussing his tutorial, which was quite a powerful experience. He had really prospered in the after-school class, although he had never felt, there or in any similar situation, that he could be an able student. Fred had been patient and kind and very likable, and he had responded. But all the while, Mark let me know, he had felt inadequate — "dumb" was his frank word. To be told that one is "making great progress" — the comment written on one report — is not to be convinced of a newfound brilliance. "He'd come into class, and he was really ready for us," this boy said about Fred. "He'd come here, and he seemed to know everyone, and he got along with everyone, and he was a great pal to us, and he got us to study. I don't know how he did it! I wish I could be good with people the way he is! I get into trouble here a lot!"

Envy and gloom were the underside of Mark's declared admiration and affection for his teacher. He didn't directly say all of what Fred had caused him to feel, because those emotions hung around in shadows and corners, every once in a while springing forth, but wearing the disguise of worry, self-arraignment, a yearning lamentation, a *cri de coeur* — an "I wish," or an "if only," or a "maybe, someday."

In his open declaration of respect, even veneration for Fred, the boy was furtively reminding me of what his mind had glimmered:

"what they mean to us" can have to do with what we believe we have come to mean, as judged by ourselves and by others around us. The volunteer can be a moral provocateur on occasion, as well as a wonderfully helpful and lovable friend and instructor. No wonder Fred, so sensitive to all the undercurrents in his class, and in his out-of-class involvements, knew that he should be apprehensive about what he meant to those youngsters and about the ease and fullness of their admiration, even awe of him.

· EIGHT ·

Consequences

A T THE BEGINNING of the last chapter of *Middlemarch*, George Eliot reminds her readers of life's never-ending complexities and paradoxes, offering in a brief paragraph a point of view more spacious than so many evoked for us today in the name of social science and developmental psychology.

She begins, "Every limit is a beginning as well as an ending." So much for those confidently categorical formulations of stages and phases, through which so many of us march like sheep or allow others to march as they talk about who we are and where we are going.

Then Eliot asks a question presumably addressed to all of us who are interested in a perspective that extends over a life's time: "Who can quit young lives after being long in company with them, and not desire to know what befell them in their after years?" Finally she takes off her gloves and becomes very much the teacher who is impatient with those who have figured out others through various reductive generalizations: "For the fragment of a life, how-ever typical, is not the sample of an even web: promises may not be kept, and an ardent outset may be followed by declension; latent powers may find their long-waited opportunity; a past error may urge a grand retrieval."

Such a recitation of ironic possibility should not be necessary for the reader who has faithfully attended *Middlemarch* up to that concluding moment. Yet the author knows full well how hungrily, how desperately, we crave clear-cut definitions and assured pathways. Even as she prepares to head us toward the future of the lives we have been watching unfold in their immediacy and particularity, she admonishes us to keep in mind the important distinction between an authorial tidying up and the defiant unpredictability of our own lives, so influenced by luck, accident, and incident.

Her novelistic authority challenged, she asks for the reader's open-mindedness at just the moment when she prepares to close up shop and tie up the loose threads inevitably generated by an ambitious novel. The narrator will supply a final factuality — but only provided that we readers don't forget the rules of life, as opposed to those that apply in the writing of a novel's last pages. The narrator leaps into the future and speaks retrospectively — something impossible for even the most prescient person attempting to chronicle real lives. We who live in the present, even the present of a study, or research project, had best understand what is *beyond*, in two senses of that word: what is yet to happen and what is not within our province of definitive clarification, never mind prophecy.

The Longer Run

With the above caveat self-addressed, I nevertheless ought to mention some of the consequences a "call of service" can set in motion for those who have heeded it. If one keeps in touch with people through letters and occasional meetings or through more conscientious efforts, such as taped interviews, one can discern certain consequences of earlier decisions made, actions taken. But by no means, as George Eliot reminds us, should a narrator such as I call those consequences a last word: the "finale" of *Middlemarch* was meant to be a leap into the future of a kind denied us mere mortals who give accounts of people we have met, rather than fictive stories. Still, if we are lucky enough, as I have been, to remain in touch with people over the years (it is now more than three decades since I began work in the South with children going through school desegregation and with young and older people taking on segregationist laws and customs, and I am still in touch with a number of these people), then we can at least tell some of what happened when an idealism exerted at one moment in life sets in motion certain forces, crises, choices, that allow for new possibilities.[1]

People who have been involved in the civil rights movement and "graduates" of the Peace Corps or VISTA often speak earnestly of those past times in their lives. As happens with memories, the tough and difficult times, the petty or rancorous moments, the experiences of disappointment or outrage, the occasional sense of betrayal by people on one's own side, can give way to the hyperbole of a glorious past: courage affirmed, a moral life lived to the fullest, compromises shunned and utterly unassailable principles constantly upheld.

Many veterans of those social and racial and economic struggles attribute the nature of their current lives to what happened "back then" — to friendships and activities that decades later continue to exert a strong and decisive influence. Once they were college students on leave or unsure of what they wanted to do and how they wanted to live their lives. But they were sure of certain social convictions and ready to work to realize them. Now they are lawyers, doctors, journalists, teachers, businessmen, nurses, architects, politicians, even political organizers, and some are working in the rural South or Appalachia or the Rio Grande Valley, where they started out in the 1960s and 1970s. The more of those men and women I pursue with my tape recorder and questions, the more resistant to inclusive summary their lives and stories turn out to be. Many of them continue to observe their own kind through friendships that have survived, often sustained by informal reunions and letters that periodically renew memories and connect them to contemporary events.[2]

"What I *am* today started with what I *did* in Mississippi in 1964," Nick, a middle-aged lawyer, told me, consciously and unashamedly emphasizing those verbs: *being* as a consequence of *doing*. He worried about a possible misinterpretation of his remark and quietly corrected himself: "I'm not trying to boast. I'm not saying, 'Here I *am*, buddy, and you take yourself one long look!' I was a small-town kid from Tennessee. My folks weren't political and weren't out to change the world. They went along with things as they were. Dad owned a hardware store. He wasn't 'for' segregation or integration; I mean he treated blacks with respect, and he detested racist slurs, but he also felt, deep down, that 'the races are different' — I remember him saying that. My mom was a gentle, kind person — she, too, was a friend to many black people, but she was also a white, middle-class person, so there were sure limits to what that word 'friend' could mean.

"Anyway, it wasn't a huge surprise to them when I got involved with the civil rights movement — but it did bother them. I think, frankly, Dad worried about his business. What would white people think if word got out that his son was down there in Mississippi, agitating with a lot of Yankees! My mom said she prayed all the time for me, because she was afraid I'd get hurt. She told me she was basically on my side. I can still remember her pausing as she used that adverb. Then — you know what? — she used it again, at the end of the sentence: 'Son, I'm basically with you on this — basically.' She lowered her eyes, probably so she wouldn't have to face my quizzical stare! I never pushed her, though. They were your ordinary family, trying to get by, and without much money put away, and so having to be out there, making every dollar they could, and being nice to all kinds of people, and not being controversial.

" 'You have to respect the differences in people,' my dad used to tell me. But he didn't mean it the way some of us, struggling for racial equality in the 1960s, meant it. He was telling me something else: that he had a whole lot of customers with a whole lot of different views, and while they bought seed and fertilizers and rakes and shovels and pots and pans and gadgets big and little, they spouted off — what they thought about this, that, and the other — and Dad, he had to respect what each of them said, if he was to balance those books of his and have the money to put food on our plates and keep that nice roof over our heads."

Nick stopped, feeling once more the anguish he had felt a quarter of a century ago — his love for his dad and his understanding of his dad's situation, but also their disagreements, which became more serious as Nick became increasingly involved with civil rights activity. He was not only standing up for the rights of black people, he began to understand; he was leaving the safety of his parents' world for quite another kind of life: "People used to say to me that you never can repeat the life of your dad, because times change, so you're different. But my dad used to tell me he was very much like his dad, and there was a period when I wanted with all my might to be just like my father. He was a warm, kind man — and our minister used to tell me I was the luckiest kid in the world to be his son. Since I was the only son, and my older sister had gotten polio, and was lucky to be out of a wheelchair for a few hours a day — well, the pressure was on me to take over that store, though Dad sure wanted me to go to college first. I guess if I hadn't gone to college, I'd not have gotten involved in civil rights — that's where I heard Bob Zellner [of SNCC, a white Alabamian] give that talk, and it really got to us, not only what he said, but the way he was: a soft-spoken, sensitive guy, and strong, too, you could see.³ Then our sociology teacher [at Vanderbilt] got us going — I don't think he realized how much. Next thing, some students from the law school came over to our frat, and we all got to talking and to arguing, plenty of that.

"A few of us got more and more interested in what was happening, and we decided to try to do something. I recall speaking up — the first words I ever spoke on the subject at a meeting. I said, 'I'd sure as hell like to see us solve all this *ourselves*. We shouldn't have to see lots of Yankees come down here to get us to do what's only fair and just.' I can hear myself talking right now; my voice was a little shaky as I spoke, and I was holding on to the back of this chair in front of me for fear I'd collapse on the spot! That was a divide I crossed. When I got home and told my folks what I'd done — what I'd gotten up and said — my dad wanted to know who was there, and did the police have someone there, an informer, listening; and my mom didn't like it, that I'd *sworn* — used the word 'hell' — and she said I was 'talking a bit like a Yankee myself.' There I was, proud of taking a stand, and there they were, pretty scared, and not impressed at all. I didn't argue with them, though. We never argued in our family! I just clammed up totally, and they made light talk, and I'd nod or look away and be thinking of how many hours until I got out of there."

He paused, remembering what would become a fateful moment. After that he came home only rarely, and for a time his parents had to endure the suspicion, even animus, of their neighbors and customers as news of their son's activities spread. "Dad once wrote me a brief letter, telling me how lucky he was to own the only hardware store in town — but he was getting lots of 'snide remarks and furrowed brows and glares,' and he even heard that some people were driving ten miles and more so as not to buy from him. And he drove to Nashville — would you believe it? — to mail the letter to me, because in the small post office we had at that time, well, as Mom would put it, 'there are wandering eyes.'

"When it [the Mississippi Summer Project] was all over I felt as though I'd helped in a big struggle, and here were all these black people feeling they were finally becoming part of America, but meanwhile I'd lost my own bearings. I didn't feel I belonged to the world I'd grown up in. I know lots of people go through that when they're growing up, but this was different. I came home and found myself a source of embarrassment to my own parents. It's true, in a couple of years all that changed, as the South became used to the effects of the civil rights laws Johnson got through the Congress. But by then I had really made a break: I moved to Chicago, and I've never gone back but for a few days here and there — the longest [time] to bury my dad three years ago. He'd retired and sold the store, and his hobby was reading Civil War history, especially the battles. He was always rooting for the Confederacy!"

Nick went to law school at the University of Chicago and became interested in the North's civil rights problems, which he had plenty of occasion to witness in his new hometown. Eventually he became a self-described "poverty lawyer," working in a federally sponsored legal services organization. "I've spent my life fighting landlords," he once told me, and he reminded me that he had married the daughter of a well-to-do landlord, who happened to be Jewish. She was as estranged from her parents as he was from his. She had been involved in the civil rights movement up North, picketing national chain stores in order to get their southern branches to desegregate lunch counters. Her parents, rich and politically conservative, were shocked when she told them whom she intended to marry.

Nick remembered that time: "My folks had about given up on me. For them it made no difference that I wasn't marrying a Protestant. They never really knew any Jewish people, but they weren't anti-Semitic. Her family went crazy for a while. They threatened to disown her — disinherit her. She said, 'Wonderful.' They said they wouldn't give her away; she said, 'Wonderful' — she wasn't *anyone's* to 'give away'! Finally, they came around. We were married in a Unitarian church with a Methodist minister and a rabbi there 'making noises over us,' as one of my college roommates said. It's been a good marriage."

Their children have continued the tradition of working for political and social rights. One son as a teenager helped found a soup kitchen for the homeless. A daughter, two years younger, worked in that soup kitchen. A second son, at ten, talked of working in Africa for an international relief organization that fed hungry people.

When the maternal grandfather of those three children died, he left each one a half-million dollars, and each wanted to give much of it (the younger son wanted to give all of it) to the poor in America or abroad. Their mother also inherited a half-million dollars, which she told the children would be set aside for their education. All right, they responded — all the more reason for them to tithe heavily. (No nominal ten percent for them!) Finally there was a long family discussion, an entire Saturday afternoon. As Nick reported it, "We talked and talked and came near arguing. My wife was furious at all three of them — they were quite moralistic with us! It came to us defending our credentials as do-gooders against them, and them telling us we'd stopped putting ourselves on the line a long time ago.

"That evening I sat and stared out the window, and my whole life went marching before me. I thought to myself, This is a long way from where I began, a *long* way! Even my old college friends, who agreed with me back then on civil rights, haven't ended up where I am. They went back to their middle-class southern towns, and now they're businessmen or professional men, and they're mostly, still, moderate Democrats, though some are Republicans

— you're talking about a sample, maybe, of seven or eight! My explanation for the difference? I don't truly know. But if I was pinned down and I had to answer something, I'd say I went and got myself into the thick of things. I lived in that Freedom House, and I got to know all these people from California and New York and Massachusetts, and after that I couldn't come home again, like Thomas Wolfe said. I was changed in ways I didn't even know about; it took me years to find out, and when our kids had that Saturday confrontation with us over their grandpa's money, I began to see that I'm *still* finding out about the effects of the civil rights movement."

He went into a long reminiscence, describing the various turns in his life after he left Canton, Mississippi, in September 1964. It was as if one summer had become, with respect to the tree of his life, the trunk. The branches that grew from it had to do with his professional and personal life, his values and beliefs, his everyday activities. He had been working for many years as a tutor in an evening program for ghetto youths, and often, as he talked with those young men and women, his mind went back to the South.

The students liked him because of that aspect of his life: "We're both from down there," one early adolescent boy had reminded him. "You and I speak alike," the boy had also remarked, and Nick was greatly pleased. At times, with certain children, he felt a surge of warmth as he shared memories, compared favorite foods, bemoaned the cold, snowy winters of northern Illinois. "I worked on math with this boy who came from Memphis. He'd only been up here four or five years, and he felt homesick. I told him I do, too. We became known as 'fellow Tennesseans,' and I made sure he could spell each of those two words exactly right. I also got him to spell Mississippi right, and Talladega, Alabama, where his mom was born. We got on so well, he started taking me seriously, *very* seriously. He studied hard and came to me with all sorts of subjects — he wanted to do better in *everything*. And he did — he jumped to the front of his class. Both ways: his grades became outstanding, and the teacher moved him to the first row, so he could be near her, a sign of recognition! When I went to a school party, she asked me what my secret was. I told her we're kin. She looked at me a little strange. She raised her eyebrows. I said, 'Southern kin.' Then she got it! Some of these Yankee liberals don't know how to talk to us and don't understand us."

Nick was being serious as well as teasingly humorous. He had tried to hold on to his southern tastes in food and music. He loved jazz, gospel music, the blues; he had "tons" of Elvis records and Ray Charles records — his all-time heroes. In politics, his heroes were Dr. King, Robert Kennedy, and some of the southern federal judges, both Republican and Democratic appointees, who implemented the Supreme Court's 1954 school desegregation decision: Frank Johnson, Elbert Tuttle, Skelly Wright, John Minor Wisdom. He waxed euphoric over their willingness to turn their backs on the old, privileged habits in favor of a nation's new imperatives. He corresponded with each of them and told them of his high regard for them. He also realized that those white southern men, several of quite aristocratic background, were not heroes to some of his old SNCC friends or his contemporary activist friends, even those who were lawyers.

"There's so far you can go," he declared — talking not generically but about himself. Indeed, he made that very clear. "Some people can go much farther than others. Some people seem to be ready to bend with any wind; I start resisting at certain points. I won't turn my back on the South, with all its warts, and I won't become so political that I lose sight of some other things in life. I guess I *am* a liberal, despite the fact that in the old days, back home in Tennessee, they all considered me a radical, even my poor folks, who didn't know what to make of me, or do with me, for a time there.

"To me, the biggest challenge has been not to forget what it once felt like to be young and idealistic. You can't stay young forever, that's for sure; and you can't be the kind of young and idealistic people a lot of us were back then in 1964 in rural Mississippi. I mean, we're not in a political movement, and no one writes stories about us in newspapers and magazines, the way they used to when everything we did was being covered — but we're here, going strong in middle age!"

He looked at his arm, noted some white hairs amid the brown, joked about his "swing to the right": he couldn't stand a lot of hard rock music, and he wore a necktie even on Saturdays, out of force of habit. He even worried sometimes about the younger generation! But after expressing that last thought, he laughed, mocked his newfound worries, and extolled the idealism of his children. He mused about a gene for idealism, the "do-good gene," and pointed out that for him and his wife there seemed to be "an almost genetic basis" for the continuity of their concerns. (She put in a lot of time in a volunteer program at Cook County's municipal hospital, and also tutored eighth- and ninth-grade students in an urban school.) He was trying to convey the lastingness of their commitment to service, a commitment he and his wife cherished and had handed on to their three children.

Perhaps, I thought to myself, the intensity of the 1964 Mississippi Summer Project accounted for the long run of his idealism, though I certainly know some graduates of that effort who are now indistinguishable from those who have other things on their minds than community service. Another lawyer, Walter, who spent that summer in Canton didn't at all apologize for his contemporary life.

"Look, I'm older, I'm living a different life — and the country has changed. I'd do it again if I had a chance to go back in time. But you can't do that, reverse your life and reverse history and become at this moment the person you were when you were a twenty-one-year-old college senior who was appalled when he learned that Negroes can't register to vote in the United States of America, and decided that he was going to do something about that, even if it was a little dangerous. That was then, and now is now.

"I'm worried now for black people — not about their voting habits but their educational problems, the high number of teenage pregnancies in our ghettos, the soaring single-parent families in our ghettos, problems like that. You can't address all of those issues by joining with other volunteers to go to Mississippi — or any ghetto, either. A friend of mine tried to do some mentoring in a ghetto school, and he wanted to give up after six months; he couldn't take it. He said he felt overwhelmed. He poured out his heart and soul with those kids, and he honestly believed he was getting nowhere, absolutely nowhere. I told him to stop and think and come to his senses: he was blaming *himself* for being ineffective and for not having the time the kids need. Hey — the problem is social pathology and family pathology."

Walter stopped and picked up his cold cup of coffee, pushed it away, and shook his head twice to convey his sadness and impatience and perplexity and anger all at once. Then he spoke at length of his sense of utter remove from what once was so much a part of his life. "I used to think I'd end up as a civil rights lawyer, or even working for the NAACP Legal Defense Fund. To tell you the truth I just don't think of race much these days. I'm working hard on my [tax law] cases, and I'm with my family whenever I can be. I'm interested in our foreign policy. I give as much time as I can to the Council on Foreign Relations, and I travel abroad a lot. I have a number of overseas clients."

We engaged in an extended discussion of our relationship with China, and he gave a strong critique of that country's attitude toward its young people, who ache for democracy. As I listened to him speak of China's embattled students, I saw a touch of his old idealism appear. He was more open with his emotions, more willing to show the compassionate side of his personality. He was afraid, he told me, to travel to China, for fear he'd lose control of himself. "If I ever met some of those students, I'd be tempted to join them. I probably wouldn't, if push came to shove, but I know how I'd feel!" He opened his mouth to say more, but nothing came out. I waited, prepared to change the subject, when he abruptly said, "There's still a little of 1964 in me, I guess." That was all — soon we were talking about Gorbachev and what he might do.

The friend he had mentioned, Ray, who struggled as a mentor and volunteered at a soup kitchen for the elderly, was ten years his junior, too young to have joined the social struggles of the 1960s. He had, however, done volunteer tutoring as an undergraduate, and he tried to continue doing that kind of work. A hard-working, quite successful lawyer, he nevertheless talked of his "soft side." His mother, who taught English in high school while he was growing up, had died of ovarian cancer when he was in law school. He made a point of saying that his recent work as a tutor was a "memorial" to her. Ray thought of her as he set out to help young children, wondered what she'd say or do in various circumstances. She was his link to people and places he'd otherwise keep at a great distance, as he quite willingly admitted. His father was the kind of tough, demanding businessman he had always held as an ideal of how to succeed in a world of "dog eat dog," the expression he often heard his parents use, the mother disputing the father's assertion. She was an exemplar of the self-sacrificing person who cared for her family and yet somehow found a good deal of energy left over for the children she taught.

After his mother's death, her idealism prompted his extended volunteering, but he constantly struggled within himself in the same way his parents had struggled with each other. "There are times when I think I'm nuts to be doing this. I get worn down and often wonder if the kids get anything out of it. They love the junk food I bring — they gobble up the candy and the potato chips and popcorn and Cokes, but they're not so hungry for the books and the math puzzles! I know most kids are like that, but these kids, unlike a lot of kids, don't study at all, and they're headed nowhere, absolutely nowhere. *They* say so; they tell me that unless they get some deal for themselves, they're going to be in real bad shape. The word 'deal' means 'drug deal' — selling. A few want to learn, but they're scared. They're even scared of being known as school kids: the others will go after them.

"I suppose it's interesting for me to learn about all this, but I have my own life. I have a wife and two children. My dad thinks I should see a shrink for doing this — and so does a friend of mine who is seeing a shrink. He says I'm a masochist. When I told him why I was doing it, he said I'm guilty about something connected to my mother. The one who's in favor of it is my wife: she says it helps put our life in perspective. Besides, she'd like to become a teacher when our kids are grown up.

"I can't stop what I'm doing here with these kids, even if I do get down. I made a vow, and I'll live up to it. My mother was a wonderful person, and I know she'd be proud of what I'm doing, even if success isn't around every corner. This is my way of staying in touch with her and all she stands for — the good neighbor or golden rule side of life: try to help out the next person, and do unto others as you'd like them to do unto you. That's what she preached, and I'll try to carry on her ministry until I'm ready to go meet my maker. And I suspect, even with the good work I do with those kids, He'll flunk me and send me to the fires below when he looks over the whole case, the story!"

For all his self-deprecatory comments, Ray was quite proud of what he was doing. As I look over the records I've kept of individuals who have made a sustained, long-term commitment to service, he stands out: not someone who began volunteering in his teens or at college out of a youthful idealism or curiosity, but someone who began taking his *mother's* idealism quite seriously only after she died, when he was twenty-five.[4] The psychological complexity and tensions of his life say less about masochism and guilt than he and his friends may think, and more about the many varieties of moral experience and their sources in the ordinary events of our daily lives. If there was a "masochism" in him that found expression in mentoring, a "guilt" that found expression in the guidance he offered youngsters badly adrift, then he deserves the substantial respect of us clinicians, some of whom may have been less resourceful in finding expressive outlets for our own conflicts and passions.[5]

For three decades now, as I have talked with individuals about the kinds of service they perform, I have tried to learn what psychological and moral energies motivate people to get involved for a relatively brief time and what forces lead individuals to give themselves over to a project for years and years. The experiences of the two men mentioned above, Walter and Ray, provide an obvious contrast: one college student participates in an historically important and dramatic struggle, then decidedly turns away from service; the other man makes a conscious decision, well after he is out of school and into a professional life and marriage, to find a way to give his remembrance of his mother a place of honor and influence in his daily affairs. The satisfactions and challenges of doing community service work may take hold amid less historical or psychological drama than was the case with those two men. Nonetheless, I have heard men and women express plenty of reasons to keep at the volunteering they do.

"I started community service in junior high," said Doris, a

woman in her middle thirties, describing the evolution of a life that brought her, as a physician, to work in a clinic in a dangerous ghetto neighborhood. Her first encounter with people whose lives were different from her own was at a nursing home, on a visit with her junior high school class, when she was twelve.

"I can still remember the first visit to the home: all the people just sitting there, some of them staring into space, and some staring at the television as if it was on, when it actually was off! I don't remember anyone saying hello to us. I remember our teacher clearing her throat and raising her voice *loud* to get their attention. We'd done this skit, and we were going to perform for them and sing for them. We knew our parts cold, and the songs, too, but those people were scary to us at first. It was as if we'd gone to another planet! We got nervous, and we didn't do too well. I remember this man sitting right up front — he was shaking and drooling. Today I know he had Parkinson's disease. Back then, I believed the man was weird, dangerous, out of his mind: that was the direction of my thinking.

"The teacher took us aside when we got back to school and asked us what we felt about the trip there. We were all totally silent. She knew! Then she gave us a talk, and she apologized for not speaking with us *before* we went there. To tell the truth, *that* impressed us more than anything — a teacher apologizing for a mistake. We didn't hear *that* all the time! We started telling her it was okay, and we'd like to go back. We were feeling sorry for her — she was upset — instead of feeling sorry for ourselves. That was a big first step in getting out of ourselves and into someone else's shoes, first that teacher's, then the old folks'."

Doris continued with an account of the work she did in high school, bringing food to shelters for the homeless, and in college, tutoring children and working on a psychological crisis hot line. In her senior year she decided that she wanted to be a physician. She took premed courses for two years after she graduated, while working intensively at the crisis hot line and a follow-up counseling center. She also volunteered at a shelter for battered women, where she encountered a most impressive husband-and-wife team of doctors who combined a career in academic medicine with a major commitment of time to a free clinic for the poor.

"I began to see what was possible by watching how others [those two doctors especially] spent their time," she explained, though she did do more than merely observe. "From the beginning [of medical school] I was impatient with the usual routine of grinding away in the lab and with the books. I had learned to work with people — that's why I'd decided to go to medical school — but during the first two years there's very little of that kind of contact. So, I kept doing the [volunteer] work I'd been doing in college. When I did start seeing patients, I still wanted to be in touch with the kind of people we otherwise wouldn't see. Remember, in a teaching hospital you get to see the more exotic patients, or those brought in by the staff. What about the people on the streets or in shelters? They didn't come to our hospital. I guess it was in my blood by then — to reach out. I'd been doing it so long, I had a 'reach out' reflex!"

So even during the extremely demanding and exhausting years of her residency in internal medicine Doris found a few hours each week to work with those two doctors, whom she described as her inspiration, her mentors, and her guides. She encouraged other medical students to find ways of working with the hurt and ailing people who live at the edges of society. Under her direction those students, and some college students headed for medicine, connected themselves to shelters and soup kitchens and emergency wards and neighborhood clinics to assist people whose lives had fallen apart.

When her residency was over and she was married to a high school teacher with similar concerns, she created her own version of a public service medical career. She worked in a women's shelter and in the ghetto clinic. Even though the neighborhood was dangerous, her white skin and white jacket never seemed to put her in harm's way: "I stop and talk with the kids. Some of them, boys under ten, are [drug] runners, I know. Others (teenagers) belong to gangs and are hustling drugs — and girls. I hear it all from my patients inside the clinic and sometimes outside. Look, these may be my famous last words, but those guys know my car, and they know me and what I'm doing there, and they leave me alone. They even come up to me and ask me if there's anything I need! You know what I said to one guy, a real powerhouse character, who drives a Mercedes-Benz and doesn't have any job so far as anyone knows? I said, 'I need for more and more of the children around here to grow up and go to school and graduate and go to college and make something of their lives.' You know what he said? He said, 'What's it to you, doc? Why are you so worried about all our kids here?' I looked right at him, and I said, 'We're all Americans. This is my country, and it's yours, and theirs, and we're in it together, all of us.'

"He kept looking at me, and I got nervous. I figured I hadn't, to my way of thinking, said anything really bad or wrong, but there was plenty of tension coming across, and maybe from his viewpoint I was being an outsider delivering a sermon I hadn't the right to deliver. But I also thought to myself, This is my life that I spend here, and dammit, it's *my* neighborhood, too, in a certain way, so I'd better keep talking with him, and anyone else, or I'm through here! Once fear makes me bite my tongue and not say what obviously needs to be said, then I might as well pack up my stethoscope and hammer and go someplace else."

In fact, that confrontation cleared the air, and Doris began to have rap sessions with some of the gang members who were keeping residents of the streets near the clinic in constant terror. They offered her "tons of money" for whatever equipment she wanted to buy, but she said no. They asked her once what *she* thought they should do with the money they were making. She said they should stop making it that way and try other ways of living. They asked her whether she minded not making more money when surely she could do so. She told them that she wanted to have enough money to live a comfortable life and satisfy some of her hobbies and interests — but she had to sleep at night and have some respect for herself during the day, *and* she did have certain values that meant a lot to her.

Such talks didn't by any means rid the neighborhood of violence, drugs, or prostitution, nor did they lower the high crime rate, and soaring school dropout rate. But two members of a gang and their girlfriends did come to see her one afternoon and asked for her help lest they become addicts, lest they die. She was able to arrange for them to live elsewhere in the city, enroll in an educational program, and find work.

That moment brought both fulfillment and gloom, and prompted her to look inward at the purposes she cherished and tried to uphold from day to day: "When they came to see me I wasn't as happy as you might think. I knew they were already in danger; they were being watched because they'd started objecting to certain deals the guys did, and to the use of little kids as runners. It was a matter of time, they knew, before they had their heads blown off. It was also a matter of time before I got into trouble — that's what crossed my mind as I sat there hearing those terrible, terrible stories.

"I talked with my husband. I talked with my mother — she was putting in a lot of time with my little daughter while I worried about these other children, whose mothers somehow hadn't been able to bring them up to say no to self-destruction. I told her, 'Mom, there are days when I want out — *out*. I want to walk away from that whole ghetto world, from my place in it, from that clinic, and never come back, never. I want to stay in our nice home and be with my husband and daughter, and with you, and maybe have a small private practice, or work in a suburban hospital and teach medical students. I get tired of the big odds against the people there — and that means the big odds against me and the work I do amounting to anything. But then I'll think of the kids I get to know, and the progress some of them are making. They come and see me for their colds and stomachaches, and they tell me they're doing better in school, and they try to remember what I told them — and I sure remember what they tell me. I think to myself, They're only a little older than my daughter. They're all part of the same generation. They'll all soon be Americans living in the twenty-first century. I owe it to my daughter and my country — to myself — to stay there. If I wasn't there, I wouldn't be able to sleep at night; and thank God, my husband is one hundred percent for me to be doing this work; and Mother, you and Dad *both* got me into this, you really did, and I thank you.'"

She was embarrassed by the emotional and sentimental tone of her remarks, which she characterized as an "outburst" — a consequence of the high anxiety (and no small amount of fear) she had been experiencing. Yet, she told herself that if she allowed that apprehension to curb her activities, she might as well quit. "I have to whistle in the dark as loud and clear as I can! I have to smile and walk rather than hurry — and *never* run! They get the message that way: this one isn't going to be scared off, so we'd better keep our cool, since she's, so far, keeping hers! I talk to myself the way I know they'd talk to me. Survival! I'm going to stay here for the long haul, so I have to know what to say to myself as much as to other people!"

Doris's conversations with herself (often a dialogue in which she constructed replies to her opponents' threats, taunting, and teasing) were the very heartbeat of the "survival" she mentioned; her mind was quite actively engineering a strategy (and a rationale) for the long run. As I listened to her, I thought of others like her: lawyers on the line who sometimes worked with her on behalf of a particular family; teachers who stayed in difficult schools for years and years, even resisting offers of rotation or transfer; clergymen who worked hard in urban ministries or connected their suburban parishes with inner-city ones.

I thought of the Big Brothers and Big Sisters who work hard over the years to try to mean something morally, educationally, and psychologically to children badly in need of friendship, advice and guidance, of a boost for the mind, the heart, the soul, and of a little help with their homework. For such men and women service is not defined by a college calendar or a minister's season-connected sermon, or by a drive launched with the help of a politician or newspaper; it is, rather, a life's struggle with respect to what to do with the hours allotted by fate or chance, or by the Lord, depending upon one's beliefs. As Doris once said when she was reflecting upon her working life, "It may sound strange, but the bottom line for me is that I was brought up to be here, so I'll stay: it's all a part of my life."

The Larger Realm

Although Doris made a personal statement about her commitment to others, she was quick to use words such as "context" and "society"; she wanted her work regarded as part of what the nation required and what in fact was being done by many, if not enough, other people. She and others wonder not only about the particular effort they are making (what will it accomplish? does it make a difference? how long will I last as a volunteer, given the trying aspects of the work?) but about the overall significance of their work for the nation as a whole. Vividly, and with an achingly candid inwardness of reflection, those men and women move from their personal struggles as volunteers to questions and worries about their own region, as well as the nation that is theirs.

A college student of mine, Owen, spent a summer working in Appalachia (West Virginia) with a Catholic Worker farm community and as a tutor to children who lived up a nearby hollow. Back in Cambridge he was a Big Brother for two years to a young black boy. When he worked at a brokerage house and then a bank in Manhattan, he went weekly to the Bedford-Stuyvesant area of Brooklyn to do individual tutoring and small-group teaching with ghetto children. At Harvard Business School in his late twenties, he tutored at a Boston school and worked in a church-sponsored soup kitchen for two winters. When he returned to New York City to take up a new bank position, Owen helped initiate an important link between bankers and business executives, on the one hand, and children from ghetto neighborhoods on the other. He spent one weekday afternoon at a school as a teaching volunteer, and every other Saturday morning doing extra neighborhood work (arranging birthday parties, outings to the zoo or a museum or the Statue of Liberty). He was planning to get married, and his mother was gravely ill, so he visited her often.

All of those obligations weighed on him, and in their totality, they prompted not only personal but social reflection: "I'm almost overwhelmed at times — too much to do! It sounds as if I'm spoiled rotten, I know. Here I am, making a salary that's over six figures, and I'm just over thirty, and with a job that interests me, and I'm bellyaching, and crying ouch, ouch, when millions of people here in America, and hundreds of millions of people abroad, would give their right arms — their *lives* — to be in my situation! I say that to myself a lot, and sometimes it works, but a lot of times it just doesn't. I'm me, and I have *my* strains and stresses to face, and to tell myself that I should remember the misery and desperation of others just doesn't solve the problems that are bearing down on me. Sometimes, the worst problem is trying to figure out whether it's even smart for me to do all that I do in that tutoring-teaching project. We're supposed to turn those kids on, inspire them, advise them, as well as teach them how to use computers and some math, and tell them how important school is *practically* — how it helps them land good jobs and keep them, and how it helps them in other ways, too: you know more about the world, and you can read the papers with more savvy, and you can just plain *live* better, because you're more informed and you understand how the system works.

"The trouble is, I'm not so convinced myself all the time! On certain days I let myself become aware of the enormity of the problem — how much needs to be done in this country. It's not just a ghetto problem, you know. It's our nation's problem: what do we think really matters, and what do our leaders believe in, and what are they trying to do (if anything!) to make changes take place? There are days when I look at the *New York Times* or I read one of the magazines I get, and I wish I wasn't literate — I think I'm a fool for telling those kids about the glories of being able to peruse newspapers and periodicals and books. For what — so you can feel really down, because you know why you should feel down, and because you've been reading about twenty problems facing America that we haven't really decided to tackle the way we should and the way we could, and the way we *do* when there's a war facing us, or some disaster strikes, and everyone says let's fight back!

"I'm *not* working off something personal here! I should know better than to say that. Now, you'll decide I'm definitely doing that! I'm just stopping in my tracks for a few minutes and look-ing around and trying to see where we're all headed. Hell, the century is ending, this one, and we've beaten our big enemy abroad, but we're not in the best shape here. I don't just mean the perennial subject of the economy; I don't even mean the racial problem, in and of itself. I mean something bigger: what kind of country do we want — what kind of land and air and climate and trees and plants and animals, and what kind of people do we want to be?

"I go to church every Sunday, and I listen to that minister

talking about Jesus and what He said and how He lived, and I look around in the church, and I look around on the street, and, well, wonder what Jesus must be thinking about all of us down here, sitting in those comfortable pews, living our comfortable lives. I wonder what He *does* make of Bed-Stuy, and I wonder what He makes of us fat cats peeling out one-hundred-dollar bills to have lunch or dinner in Manhattan. Hey, I'm not becoming a leftie or a socialist; I read my [*Wall Street*] *Journal* every day, and I agree with a lot of what I read — not all, but a lot. It's not so much that the capitalist system is so good; it's that it's better than the other systems — better for a lot of us, but not so good for a lot of us, and pretty awful for some of us, who just can't seem to get into this whole system and get a decent living out of it.

"I'm not saying anything that thousands and thousands of people haven't said before. The trouble is, if you keep going to Bed-Stuy, you end up not being able to shrug off those folks, the millions of them, as surplus labor, or as the underclass while reminding yourself how great this system is compared with what they had in the Soviet Union, or how great it is for a lot of us. In that Bed-Stuy school, or in the homes I go visit, you seem to be on a different continent — maybe even planet — and you wonder whether that slogan in Latin, *E pluribus unum*, really means anything, at least to the people who seem to be out there, not voting and not earning a halfway decent living and not feeling that the schools and the police and the banks and the political system have any real meaning for them, any connection to them that strikes home, hits them where they can feel it and say, 'Yeah, man, I get it!'"

Owen began to pull back, apologizing for the melancholy drift of his presentation of America in 1990, "ten years short of the second millennium," as he put it dramatically. He wanted to bring the Bed-Stuy kids he knew into the system — so he kept reminding himself and telling me. There was "their turf" and then there was the "realm," "the great U.S. of A." Our realm was the envy of the world — but their turf was another story. If we only knew how to bring that turf into our realm, it would be much larger morally, culturally, economically, and politically. The country would be stronger, sounder, he declared, adding, "It's so obvious, what I'm saying. Why should I even bother to say it?" He pondered the answer, then decided that what mattered, actually, was his asking: "I think part of doing community service is this — to be stopped in your tracks sometimes because you've seen so much you ordinarily wouldn't, and you take time out and try to look at that big picture you usually don't even want to see.

"My boss at the bank, he'll say to me, 'Let's get through today, that's all I ask.' He means get through successfully of course! Usually we do. For most Americans, that's what they feel about their lives. I guess when part of your day is to leave that bank and go to them, over the bridge to Bed-Stuy, then you're not going to be able to think all the time the way my boss wants; you're going to wonder about this attitude of his, actually — the attitude of concentrating only on getting through the day.

"Instead, your mind will be crossing that bridge you travel on, back and forth, back and forth; and you'll even let your mind try to figure out what should be done, not only by the folks in Bed-Stuy, but by us here in the bank. You'll ask what we should do — America, the whole nation. It isn't just those kids who are going to change, if things work out well between you and them; it's you who might be having some new ideas and worries! A lot of people talk about what we're doing to try to change the people we work with — but what about the other direction? Our heads get turned every once in a while, too!"

His comments are echoed by many who leave their dormitories, comfortable homes, or office buildings and go to schools very much in need of repair, understaffed, and dangerous for those attending them as well as visitors, or to apartment houses that similarly contrast with what the visitors have known in their comparatively privileged lives. Even students who have come from poor neighborhoods are given pause by the travel back and forth, by the contrasts seen and heard, by their reflective responses to what others say and do in the teaching sessions, the casual talk and play in the gym and schoolyard or while getting an ice cream at a variety store.

One young lawyer who spent her childhood in Harlem, then attended Phillips Exeter Academy, Harvard College, and Harvard

Law School, gave up hundreds of thousands of dollars in salary by choosing to do legal services work rather than join a well-known Boston law firm. She continued to tutor children in one of the most dangerous parts of Roxbury, and she spoke in a distinctly confessional mode about the impact of those years of service on her life: "There are days when I wonder whether it's made much difference for a lot of those kids, my work with them. I know I've taught them reasonably well, but there's such a pull — it's like gravity — downward, toward the anger and the violence and the drug scene and the welfare life. Some can resist it all and escape. I was one. There are others, and I'm in Roxbury to try to find them! But most don't, and when I go there, I sure go back in my life, and I do a lot of thinking, not about myself, no, but about life, and what it all means, and about this country, and what *it* means, what it stands for."

Her reflections were not a consequence of moodiness or the first evidence of burnout. She knew what she was doing and why.[6] She had not overestimated what she could do, nor had she wanted to underestimate the possible impact one person can have on another. She herself had been tutored by a white Columbia College undergraduate, a young man who was a most improbable agent of her survival — her triumph, actually.

"He was a frail-looking Jewish kid with thick glasses, and at first I didn't know what we'd even talk about. But I'll tell you, he saved me, that's the word, *saved.* He was kind and thoughtful, and he loved reading and he taught me to love reading. He was the one who said to me, You can get out of all this, you can, and you don't need a lot of money to do it, the way the drug dealers and the pimps con people into believing. All you need is to reach for a good book: it's your passage out. Boy, do I remember that phrase, 'your passage out.' I just wonder how many others will take the passage; I wonder how to reach them and persuade them. At the time, I wasn't all that interested in leaving, making the passage, but he sure turned me on. Of course, you hear those voices calling you every bad name — traitor! — for making the passage."

For her the service she was doing as a tutor, as a Big Sister, and as a lawyer whose clients were poor or working-class people, often caught in endlessly frustrating bureaucratic tangles, had become a life's passion, rewarded repeatedly by successes with tutees and Little Sisters, and in courtrooms, too. To be sure, there were failures as well: students who didn't learn as much as she had hoped; Little Sisters who chose the "fast and easy" road to ruin, not heeding their Big Sister's voice; cases argued and lost before judges and jurors, much to her great anguish as a conscientious lawyer. Yet she worried not about those losses, but about the enormous needs of millions of people that still went unaddressed. Service for her, then, was a constant stimulus to social and political reflection. She wanted to connect what she was doing to what others were and were not doing, what the nation as a whole was or was not doing.

She made an interesting distinction between the psychiatric, the intellectual, and the sociopolitical: "When I try to figure out whether all of us volunteers and all of us poverty lawyers are getting anyplace, it's not that I'm having some doubts about the value of what I'm doing; and it's not that I have any doubt at all that it's good for the law as a profession that my kind of practice is appealing to a lot of us younger lawyers, and would be more appealing if you could make a half-decent living (no more, but no less, either!).

"It's that you see clearly what can be done, what you're doing, even with the disappointments, and you wish that more were being done, that more and more of us were 'sisters' and 'brothers' to each other and taught each other (I learn so much when I teach!). And so you look and look at the politics of the city, the state, the country, hoping that your service will get to be part of a nation that is interested in being of service to its people: a nation that serves those in need of housing, food, and work, rather than lobbyists in need of favors by the millions, and worth billions."

She apologized for ranting. I perked up at her use of that word, and she apologized for using it, saying it was an exaggeration. I explained that I had a friend who used the word as she did, in a self-deprecating way, and then, often, apologized for using it at all. His apology told me of the strength of his passions. I suggested that a similar explanation might well apply in her case. She accepted that comparison, but she wanted to remind me of an honorable aspect of "ranting." She was worried that I might think she was losing control.

She went further and reconsidered her apology. "*That* is the problem — I'm apologizing for the intensity of my convictions and feelings, which are stimulated by what I'm doing every day in Roxbury with my clients, my students, my two Little Sisters. It is as if I'm trying to change a political and social morality, but it has its claws inside me, deep inside me; it has control of my conscience no less. So at a certain point I stop denouncing the wrongdoing I see, the slumlords and the crooked politicians, and I turn on myself and accuse myself of ranting. Here I am, hoping for a different kind of morality in the nation, a morality informed by service — we take responsibility for each other in certain ways. But the old morality informs my conscience, and the result is that I give myself a kick, call myself a bad name. The next step will be a bad *psychiatric* name! Apology withdrawn!"

We laughed, but without disrespect for the important clarification she was making. She wanted with all her heart to see community service become a more widespread cultural and educational movement, a public ethic with solid national support that was worked into our daily lives as citizens. She knew that already millions of Americans volunteered on behalf of thousands of causes, but she wanted all that activity to be given a social coherence. She did not want the matter politicized — a football to be kicked around every four years. She was looking, I suppose, for a kind of political leadership in the country worthy of Tocqueville, but inspired by the moral vision of Dorothy Day or of Harlem's Mother Hale, who cared for so many troubled children and whom she knew and admired enormously.[7] All very fatuous, she hastened to say, given the enormous diversity of the nation and its inability to agree on so very much that comes under the rubric of "moral."

She tried one final time to explain the connection between her life of service and her wish to find a philosophical home for people like herself; she wanted to understand what they are about, what their efforts mean to those "served" and to themselves as "servers" (a distinction she at times shunned, while knowing its phenomenological usefulness), and also to the country all of us call our own: "The most troubling part of my work is not the actual time I spend with the kids or with my clients, and not my reaction, later, to the obstacles, the difficulties, the disappointments, the defeats. What gets to me and wears me down is the suspicion (at times, the worry) that volunteerism may be on the rise, and we may even get a national service program one of these days, a much bigger version of the Peace Corps and VISTA, and maybe, God help us, a truly effective program — *but*. And the 'but' is that we still won't be responding to that side of ourselves when it comes to the way the country works, the way it's run.

"Let me give you an example. I'm a lawyer. I was offered huge deals to join the biggest law firms in the country. I told them why I wouldn't sign up. They immediately offered me some more big deals: to do pro bono law, to be a public service lawyer for *them* — not all the time, of course, but enough time to get me plenty interested. I could have my cake and eat it too. All right so far! The problem is, I'd be doing my flings of pro bono law for firms doing work with people and institutions I really abhor. You might say that's the way the law works, and we all have to put up with evil in this world, in *our* world. My answer is, yes, I can agree, but I don't have to completely surrender to that kind of *realpolitik!* I can recognize plenty of evil in myself. I can recognize my need to make compromises in the course of my working life — and personal life, too. But I sure don't have to hoist up the white flag in my late twenties and say all right, it's not even a struggle, it's not a tough battle, it's plain *give up*, lock, stock, and barrel! That's when I say no way!

"That's when I sit and wonder what all this volunteerism means: is it a tranquilizer, an aphrodisiac, a sop to our conscience while we go and play footsie with the Devil? If volunteerism is part of an ethic — and lots of people say that, an utterly *un*controversial thing to say! — then what influence does that ethic have on our lives, our country's life? I'm not ranting, I hope, but I *am* getting rhetorical, and I *mean* to. I'm trying to address something I think is very important — how we live as a people. But when I get this far, I usually decide to stop — to stop thinking, to say good-bye to words, arguments, and ideas, and try *doing* something. There's a kid I can go sit and read with, and when I'm with her I don't have to try to connect what I'm doing to anything but her and her schoolwork."

She readily conceded that she had "surrendered," a word she had hitherto used with scorn and fought to keep at a distance from her own life. She had momentarily given up looking for that "larger realm" mentioned by another volunteer. Her search, though, was a consequence of her investment of time and energy, of "soul," in a particular kind of human activity. Over the years she had espoused a communitarianism not by words but through forms of human relatedness: sister to sister, teacher to student, lawyer to client. This pastoral life, she freely admitted, might make her uncomfortable with a prophetic posture — hence the deterioration into rage, the "ranting" she felt she had offered.

She ached for a home of sorts, wherein she and others who labored in those vineyards would all be together — a "larger realm," maybe, a late-twentieth-century version of civic humanism, of the "beloved community."[8] Several times she told me that if she weren't doing tutoring, if she didn't have those one-on-one relationships and Big Sister commitments, she'd surely have joined a major law firm, and she'd surely not now be tormenting herself with the moral and political inquiry that, every once in a while, became a preoccupation. She knew she was not alone in that regard, though — knew full well how often she and other volunteers would sit for hours trying to find in their work something bigger and more compelling: a way to live, a sign of what matters, a clue as to what this life means.

A major consequence of community service for many, young and old alike, is an inclination to think about those words "community" and "service," to seek in them some larger vision that might hold the attention of that community known as a nation and that institution dedicated to serving the people, known as government. Such moral and political inquiry (and meditation, with all the implications of spiritual reflection) need not be gloomy — may, indeed, generate a good deal of moral energy, hence this young lawyer's abrupt "surrender," her quickened departure for the immediate concrete challenges and frustrations, but also satisfactions, of tutoring.

Discussions with others or with oneself can have a transformative influence on one's life. As I write these words I see on my desk two letters, examples of ethical introspection expressed and shared. One is from a successful stockbroker who decided to volunteer in a working-class community of Latino immigrants. He is not leaving his paid work; he "merely" is tithing himself fifty percent. He will work hard to make money half of the week and work hard to teach the community's children the other half. The other letter is from a doctor, who tells me that with all due respect to the private practice of pediatric surgery he has enjoyed, there is another road now to be traveled: "I'd like to see if I can work with individuals who can't afford the kind of medical care my colleagues and I are now supplying to our very privileged patients. This is a small step, I know, given the seriousness of the problems so many people face, but a person like me at least has *that* power: the authority to decide what he'll do with his time."

We live in a culture that responds to such affirmations of intellect and spirit in a strongly psychological (if not psychiatric) mode. We call it a midlife crisis, or a career shift, connected, no doubt, to those "emotional factors" that are such a matter of widespread attention in newspaper reports (stories in the Living Section) or television discussions (talk shows galore). The surgeon who wrote to me, an old friend, has been told that he is doing something drastic and that he should "go talk with someone." The stockbroker, a former student, has received the same advice. I rather suspect that those who made the no doubt well-meant suggestions did not have a priest, a minister, or a rabbi in mind — unless they had had experience in pastoral counseling.

When Dorothy Day was asked by my admiring, awestruck, but also genuinely curious and honest students how she lived as she did year after year (no regrets? no desire to leave and check into the Plaza and live it up, or forget all the world's pain and travel around the world?) she was delighted by their candor. She was not at all surprised by the alternatives they posed, half in jest, but half to make the obvious point that her situation struck them as more than a little depressing.

She replied, "This is my way; I try not to urge it on anyone else. Sometimes I *do* have doubts about it for myself. But sometimes, as

I pick up the magazines or the papers, or watch television or listen to the radio, I think to myself that it isn't only here that you can get to feel down. Sometimes when I *do* feel down I take a long walk. I guess I do what you suggest I might want to do in a more extended fashion: I leave. I'll end up in a very nice part of Manhattan, and I look around and go into a drugstore or stop at a newsstand and look at what people see — and read! — all the time, and look at all the doctors' offices and lawyers' offices they visit: psychiatrists and psychologists and group therapists and Alcoholics Anonymous groups and Narcotics Anonymous groups and hospitals and halfway houses, and lawyers to handle separations and divorces and battles for custody and fights over alimony and over disposition of estates.

"I decide that it's not heaven on the Upper East Side and hell down here on the Lower East Side; it's all of us trying to get through this life, and here we've found one way of doing that. And I pray for us that we be kind to each other as we do that, and I pray for the folks up there, wherever they live. They have more comforts than we do, but they haven't escaped from or lost their humanity, that is for sure, and so they need as many prayers as we do."

She seemed to have more to say, we felt. A bit of a flush came to her cheeks, and her eyebrows were raised. Perhaps her mind was being challenged, provoked by itself rather than us — provoked by recognition of the obvious pleasures and temptations of an upper bourgeois life only sixty blocks away. Maybe she felt the seduction of rant, in spite of having warned herself that a life of service that depends for its psychological and moral sustenance on a constant animus toward others who do not choose to keep one's company *or* on an animus toward oneself will flounder badly both psychologically and morally. So she welcomed the students' questions, with all their implied reservations about her humanity — about anyone's. And indeed, best to take those questions as seriously as possible — hence her imaginary trip uptown, a reminder that if she was to be questioned, so were those characters in her great friend Eugene O'Neill's *The Great God Brown* — those people who stepped out of grand buildings on grand streets rather than out of Saint Joseph's House on East First Street.[9]

When she had finished we sat quite still. We were informed and provoked and, I was sure, ready to qualify, disagree, argue — and why not? She told the students that she was grateful that they had enough interest to be there and to be as open with her as they had been. She added, "Here on this one small island in the universe God has put so many of us to live. I think we at the Worker believe it would be better for all of us on the island — the earth is an island! — if we got to know each other, took an interest in one another. That is our ideal — what we try to do when we serve our meals. You know, to some who come here to eat, I *am* living in the Plaza. After all, I've traveled the world and lived a wonderful life — a wonderful life they've never had, a wonderful life they were fated never to have. So right here it's a challenge for us to try to get to know each other, to learn of each other, to be part of a community over a meal, to serve and be served. We serve, and they serve us by coming here — giving us the chance to serve, and so offering a service to us." She hesitated a second, and then added a very brief concluding remark: "I think Isaiah and Jesus explained all this to us some time ago."

I often think of that time spent with Dorothy Day as I sit with students and older people and hear of their tutoring, befriending, feeding, their efforts to heal others, to argue on their behalf in court, to enable them to start businesses. I listen to their accounts of linking arms with people who are handicapped, exceedingly vulnerable, down and out, or homeless; those who are dying alone and forgotten or born with terrible odds against them; those who are lost in mind, endangered or adrift morally, headed nowhere all too fast; those who are trying to become part of a nation new and strange to them; those who are deaf or blind; those who have done wrong and are paying for their crimes with imprisonment, and hoping against hope (some of them) that through courses and training a new life will be possible; those children who are without fathers, those mothers without husbands, the elderly without families. I also think of Dorothy Day as I hear the people who do community service talk of their own worries and fears, their moral anxieties and apprehensions, the drifts and drives that cause them to hesitate, to plunge ahead, to search hard for reasons, to shun everything save *this* practicality, *that* urgently felt requirement. I

· EPILOGUE ·

I SPEND MUCH OF MY TIME now teaching, talking, and working with students who have committed themselves to community service projects. I tutor some children and have taught fourth-grade English and eleventh-grade English in ghetto classrooms.[1] As I listen to those students, I learn much about people with scant hope of living in a manner I have long taken for granted. I also learn about the students, their hopes, their aspirations, their values, as they get worked into their lives. Not least, I am given some moral pause. How should I be living my life? That is the question I keep hearing my students put to themselves — and much more is at stake for them, obviously, than for me. When I wonder about the nature and worth of the various commitments I have made — wonder what the point of it all is — I hear not self-accusation, really, and not the criticism of my young friends, who have no interest in hectoring a teacher to boost their own opinion of themselves. Rather, I move back in time. I shed for a brief moment decades of accumulated thoughts, involvements, and entanglements; I hear a youth's voice wondering, asking, asserting, hesitating, insisting — and the ideas and ideals I once held to be so essential, so urgently worth advancing, are suddenly back in full force, in spite of the distractions always waiting.

At such moments I remember certain children I tutored long ago; I remember how they addressed pieces of their minds to me, the proverbial full-of-himself teacher who had no idea how very much he had to learn from these "troubled" children in need of lots of "help." Not that those of us who extend a hand to others ought to deny the usefulness of our efforts or condescend by setting up those we help as secret seers who offer anyone and everyone a moment of revelation. Those are the sad uses of sentiment. Back then, actually, I was too naive to know how to romanticize others or to imagine doing so or to feel such a momentum gathering force within me. Rather, I was teaching and teaching, but I was also exploring worlds I knew little about and gradually knowing more about certain people. I was more inclined to hear them out and to feel grateful for what they told me rather than recite with assurance how much they needed to keep hearing me.

As I was finishing this book, I was coming to the end of a long spell of trying to figure out how to connect the life of service to the life of the mind. I found myself one late afternoon yet again reading Tolstoy, my mother's beloved "friend," as she called him, whose wisdom she eagerly sought and cherished all her long life. She took Tolstoy with her to the hospital when she knew she was going there for the last time; I well remember her hand on her beloved *Anna Karenina* as she lay dying. In that novel Levin, out of his own neediness, seeks the company of vulnerable peasants, asking big questions of himself in response to the intimacy he shares with people who are apparently far less lucky than he. In response, my mom's moral imagination was always stirred and, I suppose, through her, mine was stirred as well.

As I turned the pages of this present book in its earlier form, an edited manuscript, and remembered days long past of tutoring — thinking of particular faces, remarks, events — I remembered my parents and the books that mattered to them, the ideals they espoused. I left my study and headed for a bookcase in the living room. I didn't know what I was looking for or why; I was just browsing, glad to be done with a task, a felt obligation, to have finished yet another effort. But in no time I was standing with my mother's worn, marked copy of *Anna Karenina*, and in it I encountered her familiar handwriting addressed to me, her twenty-year-old college son. There were a couple of paragraphs of pleasantries and of politics (how she loved Harry Truman at a time when so many others, including her own husband, had no use for him!), and then an abrupt shift, a response to a course she knew I was taking titled "Dostoyevsky and Tolstoy."

What she wrote was a plea, really, a cry of the heart out of her midwestern girlhood:

> Treasure your time with Tolstoy's characters, Bobby. He has much to tell us through them. He himself had much to learn from them! They drove him hard, I think, from all I've read of his painful life. Let them have a life in you, too, and let them teach you how to live your life. Let them teach you to avoid some of their mistakes, Tolstoy's mistakes. We all make them, blunder our way along. But we can step out of ourselves, now and then; we can take the hands of others and walk with them. That is what Tolstoy gives us in his characters; through them he approaches us and tries to be of help to us. We can return the favor with others.

There was more, and I remembered how I once chafed at her pieties, her sometimes preachy pronouncements. Later, when I was enough free of her and my equally strong-minded dad (*his* great love was George Eliot's novels) I was able to realize how much moral passion went into messages such as that one, sent to me on April 21, 1950. Still later, as I watched her taking leave of life and of her children and grandchildren, and of Tolstoy too, I understood the size of the debt she owed that Russian storyteller and moralist: he had helped shape her life as a woman, a daughter, a sister, a wife, a mother, a grandmother, an American citizen, an earnest, interested, lively, giving teacher, ever ready to forget herself and pay heed to a long line of people who connected in various ways with her life. I found myself taking that letter back to my desk, sitting down, and reading one more time her words written with the clarity of the old-fashioned Palmer method, then writing some of them, copying her hand in my own hand, so that I might hand her and her teacher Tolstoy along to others. So doing, I suddenly decided — was moved — to bring this witness to an end.

· NOTES ·

Introduction

1. I have tried to do documentary justice to that tradition in *A Spectacle unto the World: The Catholic Worker Movement* (New York: Viking, 1973) and in the biography *Dorothy Day: A Radical Devotion* (Reading, Mass.: Addison Wesley, 1987). The latter effort resulted from a stint as a volunteer in a Catholic Worker hospitality house and from my long acquaintance with Dorothy Day and many of her colleagues.

2. I have described this work in volume 1 of *Children of Crisis: A Study of Courage and Fear* (Boston: Atlantic–Little, Brown, 1967) and volume 2, *Migrants, Sharecroppers, Mountaineers* (Boston: Atlantic–Little, Brown, 1971). See also "Serpents and Doves: Nonviolent Youth in the South," an essay I wrote at the request of Erik H. Erikson for his *Youth: Change and Challenge* (New York: Basic Books, 1963).

3. I give an account of this work in *Chicanos, Indians, Eskimos*, volume 4 of *Children of Crisis* (Boston: Atlantic–Little, Brown, 1977), and also in *The Old Ones of New Mexico* (Albuquerque: University of New Mexico Press, 1974).

4. See *The Political Life of Children* (Boston: Little, Brown, 1986) and *The Moral Life of Children* (Boston: Little, Brown, 1986).

5. See *Simone Weil: A Modern Pilgrimage* (Reading, Mass.: Addison Wesley, 1987). Weil was a modern, secular (yet oddly religious) patron saint of ascetic, intense, and idiosyncratic idealism — a moral leader of

sorts, with no real army of followers, though plenty of students and admirers.

6. See Erikson's *Gandhi's Truth: The Origins of Militant Nonviolence* (New York: Norton, 1969).

1. Method

1. See volume 1 of *Children of Crisis*, for example, and *The Moral Life of Children*, as well as poems in *A Festering Sweetness* (Pittsburgh: University of Pittsburgh Press, 1978) and in *Rumors of Separate Worlds* (Iowa City: University of Iowa Press, 1989).

2. As I look back at my struggles to comprehend these children and their lives, I remember presentations made at psychiatric and psychoanalytic meetings and essays written for my colleagues. Inevitably on those occasions, the psychopathological (an aspect of all our lives, though in differing degrees) would occupy my speaking and writing mind. See, for example, "Southern Children Under School Desegregation," *American Journal of Psychiatry* (Oct. 1963), and "On Courage," *Contemporary Psychoanalysis* (Spring 1965).

3. See volume 1 of *Children of Crisis* and "Separate but Equal Lives," *New South* (Sept. 1962).

4. I described my initial involvement in the civil rights movement in "Serpents and Doves: Nonviolent Youth in the South." Later essays include "A Psychiatrist Looks at Young Civil Rights Workers," *New York Herald Tribune*, June 21, 1964; "Youth: Opportunity to Be What?" *New Republic*, Sept. 5, 1964; and "What Motivates Rights Students?" *Boston Globe*, July 31, 1964.

5. See "Bussing in Boston," *New Republic*, Oct. 2, 1965. In *The South Goes North*, volume 3 of *Children of Crisis* (Boston: Atlantic–Little, Brown, 1972), I describe studies done in a number of cities outside the South where school desegregation efforts were initiated.

6. See *The South Goes North*.

7. Many times in those trouble spots I was told by sheriffs to go home, to look for injustice in my own back yard, and now I had found it, all right — in company with millions of my fellow Yankees!

8. I know I would not have done any of the work I've tried to accomplish if I had not gotten to know Dr. Williams — the influence a person can have on the entire shape of a working life! See my *William Carlos Williams: The Knack of Survival in America* (New Brunswick, N.J.: Rutgers University Press, 1975) and my introduction to *The Doctor Stories of William Carlos Williams* (New York: New Directions, 1984), which I edited. (Dr. Williams's son, William Eric Williams, also a physician,

wrote the Afterword.) See also "William Carlos Williams," *Journal of the American Medical Association*, Jan. 2, 1981; and "Literature and Medicine," *Journal of the American Medical Association*, Oct. 17, 1986.

9. These are the opening lines of Book Two, "Sunday in the Park," of Williams's *Paterson* (New York: New Directions, 1963) — a memorable moment.

2. Kinds of Service

1. In early 1964, Bob Moses, who was a principal leader of the Mississippi Summer Project, told a group of us meeting in Atlanta that he assumed there would be "at least a ten-year struggle" for desegregation of the schools, restaurants, movie houses, and motels in the various Delta towns.

2. Those sermons, more intimate than the ones he delivered in churches, could be utterly overwhelming. Dr. King himself choked up, and the rest of us were busy with handkerchiefs from the start to the finish of his talk.

3. See "In the South These Children Prophesy," *Atlantic Monthly*, Mar. 1963, and "The Desegregation of Southern Schools: A Psychiatric Study," Southern Regional Council, July 1963.

4. See "Invaders and the Invaded — We Shall Overcome," *New Republic*, July 26, 1964; Nicholas von Hoffman has described that event in his *Mississippi Notebook* (New York: D. White, 1964).

5. I quote some of those students at length in *The Call of Stories: Teaching and the Moral Imagination* (Boston: Houghton Mifflin, 1989), with respect not so much to their service work as to their academic struggles, their moments of ethical reflection as they do their course work.

6. See *The Middle Americans* (Boston: Atlantic–Little, Brown, 1971). See also *The South Goes North*.

7. See *Privileged Ones*, volume 5 of *Children of Crisis* (Boston: Atlantic–Little, Brown, 1977). This was probably the most difficult work I've done, because many well-to-do families have learned to be exceedingly wary of strangers who arrive with questions and more questions, whereas more vulnerable families often have had to suffer inquiries (and fools) as a matter of course. In each of the books in the *Children of Crisis* series I discuss "methodological" matters at considerable length.

8. See *Migrants, Sharecroppers, Mountaineers* and "The Lives of Migrant Farmers," *American Journal of Psychiatry* 122: 3 (Sept. 1965), and "What Migrant Children Learn," *Saturday Review*, Aug. 15, 1965.

9. My work in those countries is presented in *The Political Life of Children* and *The Spiritual Life of Children* (Boston: Houghton Mifflin, 1991).

10. I have written of the struggle to understand the range of motivations in "Young Americans in a Social Crisis: The Mississippi Summer Project,"

American Journal of Orthopsychiatry 35: 5 (1965); "Comments on Youth in Social Action," *Science and Psychoanalysis* 9 (1966); "Psychiatric Observations of Students Demonstrating for Peace," *American Journal of Orthopsychiatry* 37: 1 (Jan. 1967); and "American Youth in a Social Struggle II: The Appalachian Volunteers," *American Journal of Orthopsychiatry* (Dec. 1967).

11. See "American Youth in a Social Struggle II: The Appalachian Volunteers" and the chapter "Method" in *Migrants, Sharecroppers, Mountaineers.*

3. Satisfactions

1. This episode is described at length in "Serpents and Doves: Nonviolent Youth in the South."
2. I have discussed the documentary tradition of research as it edges toward activism (with attendant psychological shifts) in "Observation or Participation: The Problem of Psychiatric Research in Social Issues," *Journal of Nervous and Mental Diseases* 141: 3 (Sept. 1965).
3. Ibid.
4. I report on this "moral call," as students give voice to it, in *The Call of Stories.* Of course, the person being called does not always take the step from having a sense of what ought be done to making a commitment of time and effort.
5. He had been reading and taking to heart Christopher Lasch's *The Culture of Narcissism* (New York: Norton, 1978).
6. I remember well Reinhold Niebuhr's frequent and unapologetic use of the word "guile" in a course I audited at Union Theological Seminary in 1952, and in sermons at Harvard when he was a visiting teacher there in the 1960s. I recall my work as a student of his in "Reinhold Niebuhr's Nature and Destiny of Man," *Daedalus,* Winter 1974.
7. I allude to the matters discussed in this section in a children's book of fiction based on the Boston school desegregation struggle: *Dead End School* (Boston: Atlantic–Little, Brown, 1968).
8. My work, done in conjunction with college volunteers, will eventually be described in a study on resiliency in the elderly.

Interlude: Mentoring

1. I discuss children's drawings in *Their Eyes Meeting the World* (Boston: Houghton Mifflin, 1992).
2. This mentoring program was initiated at Phillips Brooks House, the center at Harvard for student volunteer programs.

4. Hazards

1. See Erikson's introduction to *Youth: Change and Challenge*.
2. The article was eventually published in *Psychiatry*, Nov. 1964. By that time, much had happened to confirm some of the intuitive impressions I'd somewhat nervously set down. I discuss some of the doubts and hesitations I felt as I tried to understand the young people with whom I worked in "A Psychiatrist Joins the Movement," *Trans-Action* 3: 2 (Feb. 1966), and "Comments on Youth in Social Action," *Science and Psychoanalysis* 9 (1966).
3. I have been a faculty adviser to Phillips Brooks House for more than ten years. I have worked alongside my students in a variety of projects and sat with them through many an evening as we have tried to figure out what, if anything, we have accomplished.
4. See "Serpents and Doves: Nonviolent Youth in the South."
5. I have heard it so commonly, in fact, that I have despaired of seeing the word "despair." Many young men and women have told me that "despair comes, but it also goes — and then it returns"; it is a major demon, to be acknowledged and confronted.
6. The ubiquitous burnout is another demon whose presence may become a matter of routine discussion. Not rarely, what one expects to happen does happen — and then can be overcome. "I wish I'd experience burnout and then get beyond it," one young woman told me, as if she wanted to encounter and then be rid of a necessary stage or phase in her career!
7. As if to humor herself and obtain some larger frame of reference, she had bought Graham Greene's novel of that name and read it with great pleasure as a distraction from her own "case."
8. See "The Protestors," *New South* 22: 2 (Spring 1967).
9. I think of Cheever's melancholy evocations of suburban privilege in "The Housebreaker of Shady Hill," "The Sorrows of Gin," and "The Enormous Radio" — all in his *Stories* (New York: Knopf, 1980); and I think of Walker Percy's essays and all six of his novels, which I've discussed at some length in *Walker Percy: An American Search* (Boston: Atlantic–Little, Brown, 1978).

5. Doing and Learning

1. I've many times tried to evoke my father's great interest in Orwell. See, for instance, "Orwell's Decency" in *Harvard Diary* (New York: Crossroad, 1988) and "Dad's Walks with Orwell" in *Rumors of Separate Worlds*. See also "George Orwell's Sensibility" in *Reflections on America, 1984: An*

Orwell Symposium, edited by Robert Mulvihill (Athens, Ga.: University of Georgia Press, 1986).

2. This was a constant theme in conversations I had with him. I well recall his making sure I understood him by saying something once, twice, thrice, and more, in different ways!

3. Here is the course syllabus for "The Literature of Social Reflection."

I. DIRECT SOCIAL DOCUMENTATION: THE LITERARY AND JOURNALISTIC TRADITION

Week 1: James Agee and Walker Evans, *Let Us Now Praise Famous Men* (Ballantine paperback edition), first section up to "Shelter," and sections entitled "Education" and "Work"; Robert Coles and Ross Spears, *Agee* (Holt, Rinehart and Winston); Charles Baxter, "Gryphon"; Richard Yates, "Dr. Jack O'Lantern"; Tobias Wolff, "In the Garden of the North American Martyrs."

Recommended Reading: Walker Evans, interview, *New Republic*, Nov. 13, 1976.

Week 2: George Orwell, *The Road to Wigan Pier* (Harcourt Brace paperback); Robert Coles, *Migrants, Sharecroppers, Mountaineers* and *The Old Ones of New Mexico* (University of New Mexico Press).

Recommended Reading: Clancy Sigal, *Weekend in Dinlock* (Houghton Mifflin); Emile Zola, *Germinal* (Penguin); James Hurley, *Portrait of a Decade* (Louisiana State University); William Stott, *Documentary Expression and Thirties America* (Oxford University Press); Dorothea Lange and Paul Taylor, *An American Exodus* (Arno Press hardback); Robert Coles, *Dorothea Lange: Photographs of a Lifetime* (Aperture); Davis Pratt, *The Photographic Eye of Ben Shahn* (Harvard University Press).

II. ORDINARY AMERICAN, SO-CALLED WORKING-CLASS MEN AND WOMEN: SEVERAL ANGLES OF VISION

Week 3: William Carlos Williams, *Paterson*, parts one and two; *White Mule*, the first novel in the Stecher trilogy; and *The Doctor Stories of William Carlos Williams*, edited by Robert Coles (all New Directions).

Week 4: Raymond Carver, *Where I'm Calling From* (Vintage); *Fires* (Vintage); and *A New Path to the Waterfall* (Atlantic Monthly Press); Tobias Wolff, *Back in the World* (Bantam Books).

Week 5: Tillie Olsen's short stories in *Tell Me a Riddle* (Dell paperback); Robert Coles, "Next Door but Across an Ocean" (*Harvard Magazine*, June 1974).

Recommended Reading: America and Lewis Hine (Aperture); Robert

Frank, *The Americans* (Grove Press); Eliot Wigginton, ed., *The Foxfire Book* (Doubleday paperback); Robert Coles, *William Carlos Williams: The Knack of Survival in America* (Rutgers paperback).

III. WAYS OF SEEING RACE

Week 6: Ralph Ellison, *Invisible Man* (Random House); Robert Coles, *The Moral Life of Children* (Houghton Mifflin), chapters to be assigned.

Week 7: Flannery O'Connor, "The Displaced Person," "The Artificial Nigger," "Good Country People," "Everything That Rises Must Converge," "The Enduring Chill," "The Lame Shall Enter First," "Revelation," and "Parker's Back" — all in *The Complete Stories* (Noonday).

Recommended Reading: James Agee and Helen Levitt, *A Way of Seeing* (Viking); Robert Penn Warren, *Who Speaks for the Negro* (Vintage); Robert Coles, *Flannery O'Connor's South* (Louisiana State University Press); Alice Walker, "Beyond the Peacock: The Reconstruction of Flannery O'Connor," in *In Search of Our Mothers' Gardens* (Harcourt Brace Jovanovich); Ralph Ellison, *Shadow and Act* (Random House); Elliot Liebow, *Tally's Corner* (Atlantic–Little, Brown).

IV. INTELLECTUALS AND THE RELIGIOUS SEARCH

Week 8: Dorothy Day, *The Long Loneliness* (Harper and Row); Georges Bernanos, *The Diary of a Country Priest* (Carroll and Graf); Ignazio Silone, *Bread and Wine* (Signet); Leo Tolstoy, *Confession* (Norton); Robert Coles, *Dorothy Day: A Radical Devotion* (Addison Wesley); Elie Wiesel, *Night* (Bantam) and "Why Christians Can't Forget the Holocaust."

Recommended Reading: Robert Ellsberg, *By Little and By Little*; Dorothy Day, *Loaves and Fishes.*

Week 9: Zora Neale Hurston, *Their Eyes Were Watching God* (University of Illinois Press); Jane and Robert Coles, *Women of Crisis* (Addison Wesley); Simone Weil, *Waiting for God* (Harper and Row).

Recommended Reading: Simone Petrement, *Simone Weil* (Pantheon Press); Robert Speaight, *Georges Bernanos* (Harville Press); Robert Coles and Daniel Berrigan, *The Geography of Faith: Conversations Between Daniel Berrigan, When Underground, and Robert Coles* (Beacon Press); Alice Walker, "Zora Neale Hurston: A Cautionary Tale and Partisan View" and "Looking for Zora," both in *In Search of Our Mothers' Gardens.*

V. AN AMERICAN KIND OF EXISTENTIALISM

Week 10: Walker Percy, *The Moviegoer* (Noonday Press); John Cheever, *The Collected Short Stories* (Ballantine Books); Leo Tolstoy, title story and "Master and Man" in *The Death of Ivan Ilyich and Other Stories*; Robert Coles, *Privileged Ones* (Atlantic–Little, Brown).

Recommended Reading: Walker Percy, *The Message in the Bottle* (Noonday); William Alexander Percy, *Lanterns on the Levee*, introduction by Walker Percy (Louisiana State University Press); Walker Percy, *The Last Gentleman* (Noonday), *Love in the Ruins* (Noonday), *Lancelot* (Farrar, Straus & Giroux), and *The Second Coming* (Farrar, Straus & Giroux); Robert Coles, *Walker Percy: An American Search* (Atlantic–Little, Brown).

VI. HISTORICAL CHANGE: MORAL, PSYCHOLOGICAL, AND SOCIAL COMPLEXITIES

Weeks 11 and 12: George Eliot, *Middlemarch* (Harper and Row); Thomas Hardy, *Jude the Obscure* (Signet/New American Library); Charles Dickens, *Great Expectations* (Bantam Books).

Recommended Reading: Middlemarch: Critical Approaches to the Novel, edited by Barbara Hardy (Oxford University Press); Isabel Armstrong, "Middlemarch: A Note on George Eliot's Wisdom," in *Critical Essays on George Eliot*, edited by Barbara Hardy (Routledge Press); L. W. Berle, *George Eliot and Thomas Hardy* (Folcroft Library edition); Robert Coles, *Irony in the Mind's Life* (New Directions).

4. See the essay I wrote for *Agee* (New York: Holt, Rinehart and Winston, 1985).
5. See my essay on Tillie Olsen in *The New Republic*, Dec. 6, 1975. I have described the inspiration provided by Raymond Carver's stories and poems in "Teaching Raymond Carver," *American Poetry Review*, Jan. 1993.
6. I've tried to connect Flannery O'Connor, Dorothy Day, and Walker Percy to the matters discussed in the course in *Flannery O'Connor's South* (Baton Rouge: Louisiana State University Press, 1980); *Dorothy Day: A Radical Devotion* (Reading, Mass.: Addison Wesley, 1987); and *Walker Percy: An American Search* (Boston: Atlantic–Little, Brown, 1978).
7. I have written about George Eliot's *Middlemarch* in *Irony in the Mind's Life* (Charlottesville: University of Virginia Press, 1973), and about Dickens in "Dickens and the Law," *Virginia Quarterly Review* (Autumn 1983). My parents constantly read to each other from those writers, and when I go back to one of the books I hear my mother's or dad's voice as I read the printed page.

8. Olsen's four stories work wonders with those who have done very little reading or who don't read at all. I read the stories aloud one year to a group of adults who had been declared functionally illiterate, and I was stunned at the intensity of their response.

9. See *Spunk: The Selected Short Stories of Zora Neale Hurston* (Berkeley, Calif.: Turtle Island Foundation, 1985).

10. The medical humanities seminar is discussed in *The Call of Stories*. The course is an effort to understand what makes us distinctly human, as discussed by the physician-writer Walker Percy in *The Message in the Bottle, The Moviegoer, The Last Gentleman, Love in the Ruins,* and *Lancelot;* by William Carlos Williams in *White Mule, Paterson,* and his short stories; and by Flannery O'Connor, James Agee, and George Eliot. The course looks at contemporary views of human nature and the nature of social inquiry, including ethical issues. The emphasis is on novels, stories, and poems as bearers of a tradition important to physicians.

11. See my essays on Dickens in *That Red Wheelbarrow* (Iowa City: University of Iowa Press, 1988).

12. The course explores, through sociological, anthropological, and literary texts, the nature of community service and the possibilities, cultural obstacles, and psychological challenges it offers. The emphasis is on the volunteer's response to a particular world and that world's response to the volunteer's presence, as well as on the characteristics of certain neighborhoods, the medical problems of poor or homeless people, the asserted values of working-class communities, and the relationship between race, class, and occupational aspiration or achievement. Each member of the seminar is expected to engage in a public service project. The books read include John Gwaltney, *Dry Longso* (Random House); Jonathon Kozol, *Death at an Early Age* (Houghton Mifflin); Gloria Naylor, *The Women of Brewster Place* (Viking); Richard Sennett and Jonathan Cobb, *Hidden Injuries of Class* (Knopf); Jack London, *Martin Eden* (Penguin); Cherrie Moraga, ed., *This Bridge Called My Back* (Persephone Press; Manuel Maldonado-Denis, *Puerto Rico: A Socio-Historic Interpretation* (Vintage); Nicholasa Mohr, *In Nueva York* (Edicione Huracan); Piri Thomas, *Down These Mean Streets* (Knopf); David W. Haines, ed., *Refugees in the United States: A Reference Handbook* (Greenwood Press); George Orwell, *The Road to Wigan Pier* (Secker and Warburg); J. Anthony Lukas, *Common Ground* (Knopf); Robert Coles, *Children of Crisis;* Tillie Olsen, *Tell Me a Riddle* (Dell); Raymond Carver, *Where I'm Calling From* (Atlantic Monthly Press); Leo Tolstoy, *The Raid and Other Stories* (Oxford University Press); Jay MacLeod, *Ain't No Makin' It* (Westview Press); William Junius Wilson, *The Truly Disadvantaged (University of Chicago Press);* Elliot Liebow, *Tally's Corner* (Little, Brown); Alex Haley, *The Autobiography of Malcolm X* (Ballantine); Richard Rodriguez,

Hunger of Memory (David Godine); Hubert Selby, *Last Exit to Brooklyn* (Grove Press); William F. Whyte, *Street Corner Society* (University of Chicago Press); and Toni Morrison, *The Bluest Eye* (Holt, Rinehart and Winston).

13. Of course, most idealistic students express misgivings about the practical, the empirical, even as they embrace such a vision at other moments. The writing of William James on idealism (*Essays on Faith and Morals*, New York: Longmans, Green, 1943) can be inspiring to these young men and women — a welcome contrast to the more reductive psychology of recent years. Anna Freud's effort to understand altruism in *The Ego and Mechanisms of Defense* (New York: International Universities Press, 1946) is an exception to that kind of relentless interest in psychopathology. See also the chapter on idealism in *Anna Freud: The Dream of Psychoanalysis* (Reading, Mass.: Addison Wesley, 1992).

14. See "Silone's Religious Humanism" in my *Harvard Diary*.

15. I teach a seminar on political fiction at Harvard's Kennedy School of Government. The course is an effort to think about politics, social issues, and ethical matters with the help of seven novels: Robert Penn Warren's *All the King's Men*, Henry Adams's *Democracy*, Dostoyevsky's *The Possessed*, Ignazio Silone's *Bread and Wine*, Nathaniel Hawthorne's *The Blithedale Romance*, Joseph Conrad's *Under Western Eyes*, and Nadine Gordimer's *My Son's Story*. Each student is asked to do three hours of community service per week during the course, and that experience is discussed in connection with the novels read.

6. Young Idealism

1. Miller graciously made himself easily available to us tutees and, memorably, served us coffee and cookies. He was a patient listener and, on occasion, an emphatic, impassioned speaker.

2. It was Perry Miller who introduced most of us to Niebuhr and to Kierkegaard, whose work was then (1950) being translated from the Danish. Now I teach a course called "The Literature of Christian Reflection" with Robert Kiely, a professor of English, which draws heavily on Miller's reading list. Many students involved in community service and inspired by an idealism that has biblical connections take the course. The approach is literary, interior, and biographical rather than theological or historical. Authors studied include Augustine, Juliana of Norwich, Teresa of Avila, Luther, Calvin, Donne, Hopkins, Kierkegaard, Weil, O'Connor, and Bonhoffer. The reading list includes Saint Augustine, *Confessions* (Penguin); Teresa of Avila, *Autobiography* (Doubleday Image); Thomas Merton, *The Seven Story Mountain* (Harvest); Simone

Weil, *Waiting for God* (Harper paperback); Blaise Pascal, *Pensées* (Penguin); John of the Cross, *Dark Night of the Soul* (Doubleday Image); poems of George Herbert, Emily Dickinson, Gerard Manley Hopkins, and Robert Frost; *Little Flowers of St. Francis* (Doubleday Image); John Bunyan, *Pilgrim's Progress* (Spire paperback); Flannery O'Connor, *Letters* (Farrar, Straus & Giroux paperback); Ignazio Silone, *Bread and Wine* (Signet); Saint Benedict, *Rule* (Doubleday Image); Juliana of Norwich, *Revelations* (Doubleday Image); *The Cloud of Unknowing* (Penguin); Thomas à Kempis, *The Imitation of Christ* (Penguin); Martin Luther, *The Freedom of a Christian, Biblical Prefaces,* ed. John Dillenberger (Doubleday Anchor); Albert Outler, ed., *John Wesley* (Oxford); Søren Kierkegaard, *The Present Age*; Carlo Carretto, *Letters from the Desert* (Orbis); and Dietrich Bonhoffer, *Letters and Papers from Prison* (Macmillan).

The recommended reading includes John Calvin, *The Author's Preface to the Commentary on the Book of Psalms,* ed. John Dillenberger, and *Calvin's Will* (Doubleday Anchor); Ignatius of Loyola, *Autobiography* (Harper and Row); Jonathan Edwards, *Personal Narrative* (Basic Writings, Meridian); and John Henry Newman, *Apologia Pro Vita Sua* (Doubleday Image).

3. Not that Weil didn't make huge demands on others! See my effort to contend (the right verb, I fear) with her in *Simone Weil: A Modern Pilgrimage.*

4. The subtitle of Kierkegaard's *Fear and Trembling — A Dialectical Lyric* (Princeton: Princeton University Press, 1945) — more than earns its significance.

5. My journal, started in 1950, consisted of long descriptions of our talks. I watched him write down what he'd heard from patients on a clipboard he kept in his car. When I left him, I would use a notebook to record his words and the scenes, questions, answers, and exchanges he participated in. By 1958 I was a physician, and though Williams was ill off and on, he let me spend time with him, and he let me bring along the tape-recording equipment, then very cumbersome, that enabled his voice to have a long life indeed.

6. See my *Dorothy Day: A Radical Devotion.*

7. I remember Dr. Martin Luther King, Jr., telling a group of Southerners (members of the Southern Regional Council) that Tolstoy had inspired Gandhi, who in turn had inspired him, along with many others. This was, as he put it, "Tolstoy's historical side," as opposed to his literary influence.

8. Their reading was not always in connection with course work. At that time Zora Neale Hurston, especially, was little known, even among many civil rights workers. And Richard Wright and Ralph Ellison were better known, by far, outside the academy than within it.

9. I have tried to do some justice to her work in *Anna Freud: The Dream of Psychoanalysis*.

10. The many aspects of Anna Freud's work with children involved what she once described as "psychoanalytic curiosity" and, she added quickly, "another variable — an attempt to be compassionate." I was struck by the becoming modesty of that phrase, but she was more interested in psychological candor and accuracy: "It is not always easy for me to give full expression to some of the sympathy I feel for others. The detached observer has to give way to the person who is moved, concerned, ready to place herself in someone else's life!" When I read a wonderfully suggestive, informative book by Robert Wuthnow titled *Acts of Compassion: Caring for Others and Helping Ourselves* (Princeton: Princeton University Press, 1991), I thought of her comments. In his own way Wuthnow, a sociologist, is quite as helpful psychologically as Miss Freud. He may be even more helpful because he is less hesitant and reticent than she — more willing to examine at length what happens when we try to extend ourselves to others. Much of what I hear from students fits well with Wuthnow's sociological and philosophical observations.

7. Older Idealism

1. The seminar examines the ethical issues confronted by two writers of the literary-documentary tradition, James Agee and George Orwell. Readings include Agee's *Let Us Now Praise Famous Men* and some of his journalism, and Orwell's *Down and Out in Paris and London, The Road to Wigan Pier, Homage to Catalonia*, and several of his essays. Each participant writes a series of comparative papers analyzing the way in which each author deals with issues such as poverty, class, and education.

2. I have served on the school's Professional Advisory Board and have seen firsthand how that despair gets worked into the lives of even the youngest schoolchildren, the five- and six-year-olds starting out educationally.

3. Dorothy Day's complex relationship with Peter Maurin deserves long consideration. I attempted to do this in *A Spectacle unto the World: The Catholic Worker Movement* (New York: Viking, 1973).

4. I discuss my work in Lawrence in *The Spiritual Life of Children* (Boston: Houghton Mifflin, 1990).

5. This population is described in *The Spiritual Life of Children* and in a report I sent to Tom Joe at the Center for the Study of Social Policy, Washington, D.C., 1990.

Interlude: What They Mean to Us

1. Many of the books listed in the courses I have mentioned are read again and again by these students, carried in cars, kept on bedside tables, and sometimes brought to class meetings so that marked pages can be read aloud to the others.
2. I have described that version of transference in the *Children of Crisis* series, especially volumes 2 and 4.
3. See *The Moral Life of Children*.

8. Consequences

1. See *A Farewell to the South* (Boston: Atlantic–Little, Brown, 1972) and *The Moral Life of Children*.
2. *The Moral Life of Children* gives follow-up reports on some of those children.
3. See thinly veiled descriptions of him in volume 1 of *Children of Crisis* and in "Serpents and Doves: Nonviolent Youth in the South."
4. I began keeping records in 1982 and extended them in depth and breadth in conjunction with the "Community Service" seminar, begun in 1988.
5. I discuss these matters in *The Mind's Fate: Ways of Seeing Psychiatry and Psychoanalysis* (Boston: Atlantic–Little, Brown, 1975).
6. Nowhere are the dangers of reductive psychiatric thinking more dangerous than in such instances. See *The Mind's Fate*.
7. Tocqueville's *Democracy in America* was a great favorite of hers; she had read it twice and as an undergraduate had examined it at length in a major essay.
8. This was a phrase Dr. King used often, especially when he addressed church audiences. This young lady found helpful the work of Robert Bellah and his colleagues, described in *Habits of the Heart* (New York: Perennial Library, 1987).
9. She often read to me and others from that play. She loved its bold populism addressed to an America on the ropes, economically, in the first decades of the twentieth century.

Epilogue

1. I have described an aspect of that work in a "Point of View" essay on volunteerism, *Chronicle of Higher Education*, May 5, 1993.

· INDEX ·

DATE DUE

MR 2 3 '0			

DEMCO 38-296

Please remember that this is a library book,
and that it belongs only temporarily to each
person who uses it. Be considerate. Do
not write in this, or any, library book.